INSIDE NORTH KOREA'S THEOCRACY

INSIDE NORTH KOREA'S THEOCRACY

The Rise and Sudden Fall of
JANG SONG-THAEK

Ra Jong-yil

Translated by

Jinna Park

Cover images from Wikipedia.

Published by State University of New York Press, Albany

© 2019 State University of New York

This book (previously entitled *Path of Jang Sung-Taek*) was first pubished in Korea in 2016.

All rights reserved

Printed in the United States of America

No part of this book may be used or reproduced in any manner whatsoever without written permission. No part of this book may be stored in a retrieval system or transmitted in any form or by any means including electronic, electrostatic, magnetic tape, mechanical, photocopying, recording, or otherwise without the prior permission in writing of the publisher.

For information, contact State University of New York Press, Albany, NY
www.sunypress.edu

Library of Congress Cataloging-in-Publication Data

Names: Na, Chong-il.
Title: Inside North Korea's Theocracy : the rise and sudden fall of
 Jang Song-Thaek / Ra Jong-yil ; translated by Jinna Park.
Other titles: Chang Sŏng-t'aek ŭi kil. English
Description: Albany : State University of New York Press, 2019. | Includes
 bibliographical references and index.
Identifiers: LCCN 2018021848 | ISBN 9781438473734 (hardcover : alk. paper)
 | ISBN 9781438473727 (pbk. : alk. paper) | ISBN 9781438473741 (ebook)
Subjects: LCSH: Chang, Sŏng-t'aek, 1946–2013. | Kim, Chŏng-il , 1942–
 2011. | Kim, Kyŏng-hŭi, 1946– | Politicians—Korea (North)—Biography. |
 Korea (North)—Politics and government—1994–2011. | Korea (North)—
 Politics and government—2011– | Political persecution—Korea (North)—
 History—21st century.
Classification: LCC DS935.7773.C438 N3313 2019 | DDC 951.9305/1092 [B] —dc23
LC record available at https://lccn.loc.gov/2018021848

10 9 8 7 6 5 4 3 2 1

The art of biography is not unlike the creation of sculpture. Out of a raw material of artifact and anecdote must emerge the semblance of living form.

—James Panero

Contents

Preface	ix
Chapter 1. In the Shadow of Greatness	1
Chapter 2. A Shadow Cast Across Love	25
Chapter 3. Edgy Romance	41
Chapter 4. Kim Kyong-hui's Residence	59
Chapter 5. The Dark Side of Success	77
Chapter 6. Northern Snakehead and Rice	91
Chapter 7. Sunshine, Shade, and Shadows	117
Chapter 8. The Past Is Never Dead	145
Notes	171
English Bibliography	187
Korean Bibliography	189
Index	191

Preface

Back in late December 2011, inter-Korean relations were as icy as the fierce winter cold. In the northern half of the Korean peninsula, the Dear Leader, Kim Jong-il, who wielded absolute power for almost two decades, was finally dead. As a result, I was tied up for a considerable while answering countless phone calls from all corners of the globe. Many people even came to see me personally.[1]

As a matter of fact, this was not the first time. Whenever an incident takes place in North Korea, several non-Koreans will, almost without exception, seek my view. Most are acquaintances of many years' standing, and a good many visit me despite having to travel all the way to Korea to do so. Some actively contact me for professional reasons, while others call out of curiosity as they pass through.

That day was also one of those times. However, I was in the same position as the people who had come to see me, for I had no information of the real situation in North Korea. I did have a chance to discuss the inter-Korean situation with a handful of key personnel, though. Their main curiosity was the possibility of change in the North Korean system as a result of Kim's death. The country's new leader Kim Jong-un is a young man and his educational background is in Western Europe; therefore, many [North Korea watchers] had high expectations, and wondered aloud whether he might lead North Korea toward reform and opening, the same road chosen by other Socialist countries.

However, I was pessimistic about North Korea changing. Past cases of Socialist states adopting a broad range of reforms and opening their systems mostly required change at the very top. North Korea is different, with its unique hereditary power succession practiced over the last three generations. The North Koreans' main objective is to guarantee the future of their system and to justify the continuity of the existing power structure. Therefore, it seems hard to imagine a fundamental change. I offered my honest view.

Dictators who seize power after overcoming all sorts of obstacles are well aware of the nature of that power: the minute it passes to someone else, the achievements of the dictator disintegrate overnight, like a sandcastle before the onrushing waves. The policies initiated, all the official achievements, fame, mythos are put at stake, to say nothing of the dictator and his families' lives. This is not only the nightmare of all dictators; exaggerating only a little, it is the same for all holders of power.

One may have erected an impregnable fortress, but even so there is an ultimate limit. Dictators being mortal human beings, they cannot escape their physical limit: life. They ask themselves whether they have a trustworthy successor at hand, someone who will ably hold the power they built even after they are gone. The more unjustifiable the power, the more difficult the succession.

Of course, this leaves just one alternative. Even if it results in a long line of unjustifiable acts, one after another, the answer is to hand power down to one's own flesh and blood.

Another key point of interest that day was whether the new, young leader could peacefully and steadily build the foundations of his power and effectively rule the country. I forecast that he could, because there is no other alternative due to the characteristics of the North Korean system. It is often said that the new leader is young, but it is a historical fact that statesmanship cannot be evaluated on age alone. There are plenty of cases in history where leaders entrusted with somber duties have accomplished remarkable things despite being even younger than Kim Jong-un. One need look no further than his grandfather Kim Il-sung, who founded an entire state in a much harsher environment and maintained his power at an age only slightly older than that of the current leader.

Kim, the grandson, grew up in the center of state power from the moment of birth, and his father at least made an effort in his final years to build a succession system. Because of that, even though the young leader may have had to deal with some confusion in the early phase of assuming power, maintaining and guarding the power he inherited would not be overwhelmingly difficult. Then, my interlocutors and I exchanged views on the prospects for future inter-Korean relations, including the potential for improvement.

Jang Song-thaek came up toward the end of the conversation, almost as an afterthought. While discussing the various problems that could arise under the rule of a new leader, I asked aloud whether Jang wouldn't be the one who felt most threatened.

I wasn't basing my statement on any concrete circumstance or credible information. On the contrary, Jang's position seemed firm and secure as the guardian of the newly enthroned leader. Along with his wife, Kim Kyong-hui, Jang had recently received a military title and was appearing at official events dressed in uniform. He had not only become a member of the Party Central Military Commission, but the following year also became a member of the Politburo. In the year that followed, when he visited China at the head of a huge delegation as a special envoy, Jang was greeted by the Chinese government like a head of state. Many experts on North Korean politics commented that Jang had solidified his position as the number two in the new regime.

But this was the very point that made me feel uneasy. In the political world, there are constants. In any system of power, the number two's circumstances are subtly problematic. Particular difficulties arise when power is concentrated in one person, and the system is devoid of clear rules regarding power succession.[2] Jang Song-thaek was a textbook example.

News of his purge and execution were first reported in December 2013. Various explanations were suggested as to why Jang was purged and executed. Most cited a power struggle over the sharing of economic resources, or proposed that Jang opposed Kim Jong-un's parallel pursuit of nuclear weapons and economic development, preferring instead reform and opening.[3] All of these explanations could be true. However, quite irrespective of those details, Jang's general circumstances within the ruling structure suggested to me that he was the obvious candidate for execution under the new regime.

Some asked me if Jang Song-thaek was destined to be executed, and if so when the time would come and what form it would take; or, if Jang personally also felt that danger, what could he do?"[4]

I took an educated guess. "I suppose it would be in about two years?"

Naturally, I had no way of knowing the specific circumstances in any detail; my reply was based on a general inference; the simple assumption that during the first year, the new leader would focus on cementing his own system and then, once settled, it stood to reason that conflict would mount between the person called "number two" and the supreme leader, Kim Jong-un, who had succeeded to the "monolithic leadership system."

In that case, what would Jang Song-thaek's response be? Although it was all but pure speculation, I thought that if Jang were aware of his situation, he could possibly take a few steps to change it.

First, in whatever form, he could take over the regime himself through a coup d'état, like King Sejong the Great's second son Prince Suyang (later King Sejo), who removed his nephew King Danjong and appointed himself. As a matter of fact, articles making precisely this comparison appeared in the South Korean media. Those suggestions, of which the North Korean leadership would doubtless have been aware, may even have affected how the incident evolved.

Second, taking the opposite approach, Jang could sharply lower his status and offer to take a titular position or role. More importantly, he could refrain at all costs from seeing people close to him or increasing his degree of personal influence, and completely free himself from the center of politics. If possible, it would be desirable to leave Pyongyang for his hometown and live as a private individual.

Realistically, however, Jang wouldn't have been able to do either of these things. North Korea thoroughly controlled even the tiniest hint of threat to the regime, to such an extent that a coup was unthinkable. That did not leave much chance of Jang stepping down from power, either. First of all, he would need a good excuse, something like health reasons, in order to retire. But if it weren't actually the case, he would end up inviting suspicion. Moreover, Jang may not have been wise enough—or had enough time—to think of it.

The most realistic and thus best option that he had was to flee abroad. Not simply to save his life, but because it would have been possible to free himself from his political status that way. He could escape not to the United States or a European country, but he could go to another Socialist country where he could establish a North Korean government-in-exile. Not an "anti-DPRK" government, but a "real DPRK" government.

Unbefitting its name, the "Democratic People's Republic of Korea" has deviated from the socialist line by adopting a monolithic ideology and implementing a hereditary system of power succession.[5] But what if one were to put an end to such a regressive situation and establish a true Socialist republic? In the discussion, I expressed my thoughts: were Jang Song-thaek to set up a government-in-exile, regardless of its success or failure, wouldn't he be able to secure his status in history? That was the way to justify all of his prior actions, and achieve personal security.

It may be apochryphal, but it is said that upon hearing people dispute his appointment as emperor, Napoleon Bonaparte commented that he merely picked up the crown which was "just lying in the gutter." Were Jang Song-thaek to set up a government-in-exile, couldn't he simply claim to have picked up the Democratic People's Republic of Korea, which had fallen to the ground?

It was a fiction. I said that Jang wouldn't be able to choose that option, either.[6]

Two years after Kim Jong-un's power succession from his father, Jang Song-thaek was executed.[7] It was tenfold ghastlier a scene than I had imagined it would be. When the Dear Leader finally parted in the winter of 2011, with his death Jang Song-thaek's fate had also been sealed. However, Jang was the only one in the dark about that fact.

When I heard the news of Jang's execution, and the horrifying way he was purged, leaving no corpse or burial site, it crossed my mind to write a book on him. Jang Song-thaek was someone who lived a very unusual life in a particular circumstance, one that is inevitably deeply connected to South Korea and thus affects the lives of all South Koreans. Therefore, recollections and testimonies of and about such a person should not be forgotten. They ought not to disappear with his body.

Some readers may question where this work stands on the spectrum of history, biography, and fiction. It is not unique in that respect. For a biography is a procedure through which a person's inner self is reconstructed based on limited data. The facts quoted in this work, with just a few exceptions, are mostly those known to the public already. With the exception of a handful of unique segments, especially on Jang and his married life and the couple's inner thoughts, the author did not write based on his imagination alone. As far as possible, using documents whose provenance is difficult to make public, the writer made an effort to remain faithful to what actually occurred.

Based on hard-to-obtain, yet also inadequate and, by necessity, fractional materials, this book aims to reconstruct the situations that the main character faced, how he dealt with them, and most of all, his inner world.[8] That was the only way I thought I could tell the story of a man who lived in such an *unusual* world, with a *special* status, and ended his *uncommon* life in a most miserable manner, without even a grave for his remains. Someone had to do this job. Only in this way could a man who was killed and ripped from his corpse be recalled.

I believe that people's stories must be told, whether they be the man who died alone, all forgotten, after decades in prison in a foreign country,[9] or the man brutally executed after years in the international media spotlight. Only by telling stories can we remember that person and his or her related past, and realize the fact that they coexist with us. To revive a dead person's story is not a simple task. Particularly that of a man like Jang Song-thaek, whose personal or political life, as well as his death, were so colorful.

It is the writer's small hope that this humble work may stimulate further, related projects. Footnotes were included for all quotes with clear sources. However, the information and data that could not be publicly clarified are used without proper citation.

Some parts of this book are indeed fiction, derived from the author's imagination. For instance, the account of Jang Song-thaek and Kim Kyong-hui's life in Moscow, with their unique set of sentiments, consists mostly of the writer's imagination. Nevertheless, my retelling is not only fantasy and conjecture. The author refers to the thoughts and overheard comments of people who were within range of the couple.

The inner thoughts of Kim Jong-il are also fictional. Jang Song-thaek and Kim Kyong-hui's sojourn in Moscow was written with reference to the writer's own experience of a temporary stay in the former Soviet Union in the late 1970s. The description of the cause of the scene where Kim Jong-il and Jang Song-thaek get into serious conflict, so much so that Kim loses his temper and bursts out in rage, is also based on the author's imagination. It is known that that event occurred, but what the problem actually was remains unclear. And finally, the part describing Kim Kyong-hui's feelings when she confronts her nephew Kim Jong-un is again fictitious. The same goes for what Jang Song-thaek felt upon hearing news of the bombing of Korean Air Lines Flight 858 in 1987.

Other parts were written relying on old data, or information recovered with no small difficulty. People who provided the writer with rare data were reluctant to reveal their identities, and on occasion the writer initially did not insert footnotes, taking the informer's situation into consideration. Some even made special requests to the writer to avoid even mentioning any hint that could reveal the witnesses' identities, so not only the sources, but several interesting facts could not be made public. That is not to say the testimonies of these interviewees were accepted without verification. Almost all statements were cross-checked as thoroughly as possible and other methods were also used to check the facts. The biggest problems arose when credible testimonies from more than one source seemed to be in contradiction. In such cases, the writer had no choice but to make the final decision.

Once the draft was completed, it was circulated among the people who gave advice and, taking their comments into consideration, some parts were corrected. Though their names are not revealed, those who gave priceless help are mentioned in the endnotes as *advisor*s with an alphabetic letter code. The author takes this opportunity to convey his deepest gratitude for their generosity in sharing information resulting from the at times complicated and very time-consuming experiences. Without their assistance, this book could not have been published.

Finally, the author would like to explain why the subtitle of the Korean version of the book describes North Korea as a *Theocracy*.[10] Academia defines North Korea's unusual system along several conceptual lines, one of which is exactly that. The term is used because North Korea deifies its supreme leaders and their families.

However, the author used the term *Theocracy* in a slightly different way. Political power takes on religious characteristics depending on the intensity of its concentration. To the mortal man, who desires the eternal, power can at times be a secular confinement replacing a religious savior, and it becomes the glory that takes the place of God's glory. This phenomenon existed in pre-modern times, quite possibly since the birth of mankind.

The Old Testament contains the myth of the Tower of Babel, wherein men who have been banished from the Garden of Eden unite and strive to reach the territory of the Lord. What makes the challenge possible is man's political skill. That is, the ability to unite, stay in one location, and work together toward a shared goal. Another aspect of the political ability is specifically premised on power. The myth of the Tower of Babel, of course, ended in failure. However, similar trials have occurred repeatedly throughout the history of mankind. The powerful, who seize supreme power, soon dream of immortality. In other words, deification.

Both Kim Il-sung and Kim Jong-il defeated their competitors and seized supreme and unlimited power, at least domestically. They craved immortality. That very desire led to the handing of power to offspring, who could neither criticize nor deny the will of the Leader; the "sociopolitical living organism" pseudo-theory; and measures to preserve the corpses of past leaders. That is to say, power does not exist for certain specific purposes, or for the people over whom that power rules; most of all, it exists for power itself. Above all, the people who are persuaded by the new government are freed from the burden of criticism sessions. They merely express their thanks, praise, bow at all times, and follow the new god.

So, what must it have been like for a person at the core of this government? In particular, what would the situation have been for that person standing on the border between the inner core and the outsiders? There Jang stood. And there, Jang fell.

1

In the Shadow of Greatness

> Evil is committed by human beings who are only life-size when you see them up close.
>
> —Sheila Fitzpatrick[1]

When all is said and done, the life of North Korea's Kim Jong-il—the Dear Leader and the Great General, as so many called him—was a paradox: at once a supreme victory, and a deplorable failure.

From the earliest days of his childhood, he was nurtured at the very epicenter of state power, and yet the path to securing power of his own was by no means smooth or imple. As the oldest son and heir of North Korea's revered "Great" Leader, his whole life would be one long cycle of seeking and seizing power, then scrambling to hold on to and expand it.

From a young age, Kim Jong-il enjoyed extraordinary privilege, yet he lived in isolation from his surroundings. Immersed in the presence of absolute power, he acquired the vigilance that the powerful must always have, not least as it pertains to the people closest at hand. The nature of power, he learned, was constant readiness: being poised for struggle.

Kim Jong-il learned to think of the people around him as competitors first and foremost, all of them stealthily, hungrily looking for their right moment to take power. He heard rumors that his father Kim Il-sung was thinking of dividing his life-long built regime among his three sons: specifically, the military and administrative divisions would be given to his stepbrothers Pyong-il and Yong-il, respectively, and the Workers' Party apparatus to him. It sounded plausible as his father was getting old; his stepmother Kim Song-ae, then-much loved by his father, was fully active; and his uncle Kim Yong-ju allegedly in his own way also bore a different intention.

As a youth, Kim faced a very particular set of challenges. He was a defiant teenager, the cause of headaches even for his all-powerful "Great Leader" father. Kim Il-sung consulted his top education experts, "Since my wife (Kim Song-ae) isn't his biological mother, my son is deviating from both myself and my wife. He is going awry. My whole attention is given to playing mediator between my wife and my son, but he is going even further astray. . . . All conditions are more than sufficiently met, yet the kid vents anger for no reason, and he bursts in fury at his stepmother and even at me . . ." The elder Kim ended up issuing an order that a special school be built for children of stepfamilies.[2]

It is not clear exactly when and how younger Kim, a defiant adolescent with a "soft chubby complexion and two cheeks that would redden in shyness," grew up to become the very definition of power hungry. What is quite certain is that his puberty was like the metamorphosis of a caterpillar in a cocoon: Kim Jong-il emerged completely different in character and disposition.

He won his father's goodwill by putting the finishing touches on his father's nearly godlike ruling authority. At the same time, he also learned to weaken his elderly father by surrounding him with young women who could make him happy.

Hwang Jang-yop recalled that Kim Jong-il was seen as the heir to power as early as the late 1950s—upon a trip to the Soviet Union, to be exact, where he accompanied his father on a visit to the country to observe one of the regular congresses of the CPSU, or Communist Party of the Soviet Union. Hwang was among the delegation, as secretary. He wrote that Kim Jong-il meticulously took care of his father from official meetings to his daily itinerary, writing up reports of each day's events and preparing for the following day, even polishing his father's shoes and setting them neatly by the front door. Kim Il-sung was moved and is quoted as saying, "My son is truly the best! I can trust no one else but him." Not long after that, someone who had been a plausible candidate for the leadership, Kim Il-sung's younger brother Kim Yong-ju dropped out of the race, and was sent down from Pyongyang into the countryside. Kim Jong-il got rid of his keen competitors in this way, one-by-one, finally securing the kind of power that even his father couldn't ignore.

However, a critical moment arose when Pyongyang found itself in discord with Washington over the development of the North Korean nuclear program, and Kim Il-sung vowed to take the initiative and hold a summit with the then-South Korean president, Kim Young-sam. Rolling up his sleeves, the aging North Korean leader declared that he would personally overseee other administrative matters, too. The issue of food insecurity was increasingly a problem. Kim Il-sung had not been properly informed of the dire reality of impending famine many of his people were facing. Even if he may have heard rumors, he remained silent. But now he was deciding to take a hands-on approach to state affairs.

No one could tell what the outcome would be, but for Kim Jong-il, it was as if he had suddenly been halted by an enormous red light on the final stretch of the road to supreme power. He was in opposition to his father, but he couldn't directly dissuade the Great Leader from his decisions. Kim Jong-il could only sidestep this crisis when his father rather fortuitously passed away.[3]

Thus, Kim Jong-il finally rose to become Supreme Commander. That did not mean, however, that he was free of challenges. The succession of power was both his greatest new challenge and the most critical moment of his whole life: the country he had inherited was in a hopeless state.

The pressing reality was that the son was incapable of filling the gap of his father's absence, a void left by the man who governed for almost half a century with an indisputable power that resembled theocracy. Still, Kim Jong-il had successfully seized nearly all actual authority; virtually all key government organizations, such as those for national security and state economy, were in his hands. While Kim Il-sung was still alive one could hear political chatter that the father was but a leader in name only, if you were to take into account the realities of running an authoritative state. In fact, in his final years the "Great Leader" would go as far as to break a Korean traditional taboo, writing and distributing widely a poem that sang the praises of his son:[4]

> On the Paektu Mountain ridge Jong-il Peak rises,
> The crystal clear Sobaeksu rapidly curls along the valley.
> Already fifty years since the birth of the Bright Star of
>   Hope?
> Distinguished in both pen and sword, loyal and a good son,
> All look up to him, and in one voice, praise him,
> Their cheers so loud, the heavens and the earth shake.[5]

In spite of everything, Kim Jong-il would discover that aquiring power was a completely separate thing from living up to the image of a people's leader, with all the personal charisma that it commonly entails. The crown prince was completely incapable of filling the tremendous gap left by his father's death. After all the years that he had worked so hard, fought and prepared for this very moment to come, Kim Jong-il was at a loss. Seizing and exercising real power in his father's shadow was totally different from stepping into the spotlight that his father had occupied. How could he have failed to foresee this, and not made any preparations for it?

Kim Jong-il was strikingly different from his father. Compared to his well-built, handsome father whom women found attractive, the son fell short in height and looks.[6] Sometimes he would even remark to others about how short he was. In one private sitting, he showed particular interest in the traits of being short and having short legs.[7] He also once casually let it drop that he wore height-enhancing platform shoes, a popular trend among young people at the time, so that he might seem at least an inch taller.

This was not merely a matter of petty personal interest. In Korea, a pleasant physical appearance acts as an important barometer of one's thoughts about others. To sum up the mentality in a nutshell, Koreans look at a person's body and appearance first, then speaking, then writing, and then finally judgment, in that order. This propensity is apt to be especially prevalent under a dictatorship where the popular image of the leader is a matter of utmost importance.

An even more serious problem at the time was the fact that Kim Jong-il had no major achievements to his name in either the domestic or the international arenas. His father had led anti-Japan resistance, founded the nation, achieved the so-called "victory" of the Korean War (which the North Korean regime calls the "Glorious Fatherland Liberalization War") and led the ensuing post-war reconstruction. His father also enjoyed a fair amount of public support worldwide. Particularly after World War II, the majority of the world's political sentiment was tilted toward either communism or socialism. There were sympathizers even among the ruling class of imperial states, and it was common to see people turn against the land of their birth to help socialist causes. It wasn't rare to hear news of "traitors against the state" among intellectuals of the Western imperialist states and members of the ruling class.

Sentiment had evolved in quite a different direction by the time Kim Jong-il had succeeded to power. The myth of socialism was looking like a relic of the past. Arising in its place instead was the so-called neoliberalism of Margaret Thatcher and Ronald Reagan: an ideology of efficiency and productivity, free markets, consumption, and borderless capital.

The biggest obstacle of all was the reality that North Korea was in crisis. The Juche Kingdom that Kim Jong-il inherited was literally bankrupt. From the late 1980s to the early 1990s, Communist regimes in the former USSR and Eastern European countries collapsed like dominoes. Then these once strong and reliable supporters of North Korea lined up to establish diplomatic ties with the South, one after another.

Yet the greatest shock for the North Korean regime wasn't ideological or political, it was economic. Compared to the South Korean economy, which achieved remarkable, rapid progress from the 1970s onward, the North Korean economy lost its driving force for development, and descended into a swamp of stagnation. In straightened times, economic cooperation between socialist countries, particularly in terms of foreign aid, became a thing of the past.

The imminent problem was the food. When Kim Jong-il took the seat of the "Great Leader," the North Korean people were starving.

From the late 1980s until the mid 1990s, North Korea's grain production plunged by one third. The fundamental cause was the regime's terrible policy choices, but a series of climate misfortunes, including a series of floods, also played a role. Reduced grain production in turn sharply increased the risk of a political crisis.

With the collapse of the food distribution system, one of the key elements by which North Korean society was controlled from the center, citizens scattered throughout the country to find means of survival. The regime could no longer feasibly restrict them from travelling as it had in the past. Widespread starvation naturally impacted factories and collective farms, taking its toll on their production and management. The land of *juche* had to swallow its pride and request food aid from the international community.

Meanwhile, North Korea's arch rival, South Korea, steadily became more democratic and economically developed. Although it went through years of demonstrations and tear-gassed streets, South Korea was unmistakably reaching a stable political equilibrium.

Hwang Jang-yop said that in the mid 1980s he confided his fears about a possible crisis with one of his former university students, one Jang Song-thaek. "If things carry on this way, won't our economy collapse? What can we do?"

To which Jang replied placidly, "That will never happen."

Taken aback at the answer, Hwang described several pressing difficulties and asked once again, "Can we take measures against this?"

And once again, Jang replied in an unmoved manner, "Our economy has already collapsed, so how can it collapse again?"[8]

That may just be the most accurate comment ever made about North Korea's economic situation at the time. But more importantly, it reflects Jang's position and his view of the regime. He was part of the power structure, held a major position within that system; he was a member of the core group, a Kim family insider. But despite all that, ideologically he was unsteady, standing on the very edge of the North Korean system and ruling clique.

Some statistics on North Korea put the number of people killed by the famine somewhere between two and three million. One study based on more objective data estimates between 300,000 to 400,000 died between 1996 and 1998 during what came to be known as the "Arduous March."[9]

The North Korean regime couldn't provide its people with rice, but it had a rich surplus of propaganda and demagoguery, from political slogans to light entertainment. This was what the successor to the "Great Leader" did best. The resources of propaganda were the materials most familiar to the ruling class and people. The regime made use of the way Kim Il-sung led partisans on a 100-day march to avoid Japanese attack, a historical memory of extreme cold, hunger, and suffering that nonetheless stirs up a swell of pride linked to resistance against Japanese Imperial occupation in the winter of 1938 to 1939:

"Remember the Arduous March! Bear in mind the Glory that follows that Pain."

The North Korean people, who are used to hardships, dutifully obeyed those orders. Slogans instead of rice; glory instead of nutrition.

But amid all the problems facing the North Korean state, the biggest of them all was one nobody thought of, including Kim Jong-il himself.

Every now and then Kim Jong-il had his doubtful moments. Was he indeed the ruler of his regime, or a prisoner locked up in it?

Did he really have the power and capacity to move and control his State according to his will? Or was he merely managing and running a system built by his father, unable to change or alter things in his way? Was the power he inherited limited to that of a servant doorkeeper who must guard the system at all costs?

No one understood better than he the paradox and weakness of the system. Kim Jong-il also knew better than anyone in his country about what was going on outside the "Workers' Paradise," including all of the remarkable changes occurring on the global stage. Kim Jong-il himself had long since abandoned any inner faith in socialism. Socialist countries were not only impoverished, but also culturally unrefined and inferior. Kim himself felt attracted to the West. He once even tried to visit a country in Europe using a fake passport. But the passport was soon detected, and his special, secret excursion cancelled.

> Nevertheless, the Western bastards act as freely as they please . . . but look at the Socialist countries. In this video I saw, which was sent recently, really, starting from that guy called Gerasimov (the head of the USSR delegation) is it? They are all somehow rigid and give the air of country bumpkins.[10]

Even the ideologies of Marx and Lenin could no longer inspire people, to say nothing of Stalin. The former great names had disappeared; they were nonexistent in the minds and conversations of the North Korean people. The firmly held mythos of socialist revolution and the regime's socialist system collapsed in front of the immense power of the market. The socialist system collapsed early in its countries of origin, the USSR and China, with a whimper rather than a roar. North Korea's socialist allies raced each other to engage South Korea, while even the USSR, the birthplace of the revolution, came to Seoul for a loan. North Korea's rival from birth, a state with which it was thought "impossible to reconcile and coexist under the same sky," South Korea continued to develop remarkably despite being in the midst of a tumultuous era.[11]

What and where could one begin to reform?

Nothing was easy. One false move could jeopardize the power he had inherited. Though Kim Jong-il may have tried to assess his system's problems and make amendments in a logical fashion, these were highly likely to run into obstacles.

The problems overlapped in several layers. Were it not for South Korea, the North could by all means have conducted an open-door reform policy just like other socialist countries. Yet it had to be aware of the South if it wished to maintain regime legitimacy, which is to say its policy experiments could not be seen as following in the footsteps of the South. Doing so would be admitting that the South's line after liberalization in 1945 was correct, and the North's was incorrect. It couldn't admit defeat in the fifty-year competition for superiority.

Kim also had to consider his filial duty toward his father. As the son who had succeeded to power, he couldn't appear to downplay his father's achievements. As in other Socialist countries, such as the USSR or China, if a leader deviated from or criticized his predecessors' policies, all blame would instantly be focused on him.

Moreover, the regime, which had been firmly sustained with a firm grip for several decades, could be gravely affected if the leader pressed the wrong button. In the case of the USSR, when Gorbachev, under the slogans of Glasnost (meaning openness) and Perestroika (meaning restructuring), attempted reform, it was comparable to simply opening the window for a while to air out the house, Doing the same thing in North Korea could bring down the pillars and cause the rafters to buckle.

The father, Kim Il-sung, probably was well aware of these facts, and would have meticulously planned things, including his people's consideration of the time after his death. Among other preventative measures, the older Kim would have reminded his son of the danger of reform and opening.

Once the father, sensing a downturn in his health, secretly summoned ten of his most trusted men. He took out ten pistols with silver plated handgrips and gave them out. Then he addressed them in a serious tone, saying that when he's gone, if his son, the heir, Kim Jong-il were to dare deviates from the regime's policies or plays around with reform, "Any one of you, shoot him with this gun."

However, not a single person took his dying wish literally. And there was probably not one among them who would dare utter the words and convey the message directly to the new leader. If anyone dared to pass on the news, it would have been preceded by a whole lot of masking rhetoric and delivered with extreme caution.[12] At any rate, it was a cold and severe final wish the leader set forth for his son, the successor.

Throughout the history of both the East and the West, a curse follows dictators who monopolize massive power and authority: they cannot trust anyone.[13] Kim Jong-il was no exception.

Making matters worse, there were traitors among his relatives. Despite granting all sorts of privileges to the siblings of his wives and his nephews and nieces, they kept fleeing to enemy countries. His first wife, Song Hye-rim's older sister Song Hye-rang, as well as her children, Ri Il-nam (who took the name Yi Han-young in the South) and Ri Nam-ok, were considered to be close relatives, yet they sought asylum in the South. His third wife, Ko Yong-hui's[14] younger sister Ko Yong-suk, and her husband Pak Keon were of VIP status, too, yet along with their children they sought asylum in the United States.[15]

Although he had abducted them to the North in the first instance, Kim Jong-il gave enormous privileges to a famous couple, South Korean film director Shin Sang-ok and actress Choi Eun-hee, believing they would remain loyal to him, but in Vienna in 1986 they too seized an opportunity to flee the regime. Up to then, whenever his close acquaintances reported suspicions that the couple might escape, Kim Jong-il had said, "Why would they run away? Where would they be more appreciated than here? They can make all the films they want without having to worry about money."[16]

But in the end, flee they did.

With this series of events, Kim Jong-il's heart remained closed and cold toward the public who were passionately pledging oaths of loyalty to him. They looked up and cheered enthusiastically, but he viewed them with cynicism, doubting their sincerity. "Mr. Shin," he told the kidnapped movie director, "that is all fake. Their cheers are all feigned."[17]

From the very day that he was bequeathed absolute power akin to any monarchy, Kim Jong-il became skeptical. Did his title endow him with omnipotent power and authority, or a prison cell? He once suffered from such extreme depression that he considered suicide. According to one testimony, his wife (the current ruler's mother, Ko Yong-hui) found him in deep contemplation with a pistol placed before him. Ko exclaimed, "Darling, what are you thinking?" and took away the gun.[18]

Arguably the best-known aspect of Kim Jong-il's rule was hs famous "dinner parties," something his father had never done.

Stalin used to host similar events. Prominent high government officials in key positions attended vodka parties with Stalin in the middle of the night. Even in the moment when the Soviet Union faced the peril of collapse after Germany lauched a surprise attack during World War II, Stalin stopped key officials from leaving his side, which held them back from performing their duties.

Holding drinking parties frequently can be a manifestation of a ruler's anxiety about the people around him. That is, the events are also a scheme to keep major government personnel near him for as long as he could. They were therefore gatherings of artificial pleasure, emitting an atmosphere of disguised and thereby all the more exaggerated loyalty and trust.

In a way, Kim Jong-il's dinner parties had similar aspects with the so-called "room salon" parties popular among South Korean executives today.[19] At such gatherings, men build camaraderie and trust as they drink like fish, all the while making advances on and even harassing female staff. Kim Jong-il was no exception in using his parties to check on loyalty to his authority and confirm the reliability of key personnel.[20] This was how the powerful became bound by a secretive sense of brotherhood.

However, the invitees to Kim Jong-il's night drinking parties were nervous at the honor. The invited were the leader's most trusted, as well as maybe those whom he suspected and feared the most. Both host and guests would check their fears about one another and access their reliability through the gathering. Kim Jong-il would assemble the party invitees by his side, and for no particular reason assure them of his trust, and the guests would confirm their trust toward him. Even if only for a short while, both sides could ease their minds and be relieved.

Hwang Jang-yop, who could not handle his alcohol at all, had an extremely hard time among the heavy drinkers. On one occasion, the Dear Leader spoke to Hwang, "I would very much like to see Mr. Hwang drink for once."

Then people around Hwang all started to force drink on him. When Hwang continued to turn down their offers, finally the Dear Leader reacted and decided to offer a drink personally. He filled a glass with whisky and brought it over to Hwang, who therefore wouldn't be able to reject it. Hwang closed his eyes tight and drank it in one gulp, having steeled himself for the consequences. However, it turned out that what he drank was not whisky. Instead, it was tea.

The evening parties also had a work component. In a regime where all policy-related decisions are determined through top-down vertical channels, the drinking parties became a rare occasion where the officials from different departments could exchange views in an ostensibly comfortable manner and off the record. Kim Jong-il could also discuss matters that were not included in official reports. But this was merely incidental; the feast venue was not suited to earnest discussion.

The Dear Leader would lose his temper if anyone imitated his night drinking parties and would punish them severely. It was natural that Kim Jong-il would harbor suspicion and anger toward his brotherhood-affirming confidantes. People who do something they themselves believe is abominable tend to find it even more loathsome when their close acquaintances imitate them. Thus, Kim Jong-il would be overwhelmed with complex emotions when he saw his close personnel imitating his parties.

This complex feeling would eventually erupt into wild fury.

Amongst all the difficulties, during the seventeen long years that Kim Jong-il was Supreme Leader, at least he succeeded in protecting the system he had inherited and in passing on the power to his successor. This was no simple task. Yet, significantly, the North Korean system was in fact much more stable and consolidated than when he inherited it.

The greatest and most realistic success was completing the regime's nuclear weapons development program while inter-Korean relations were on relatively good terms. The temporary safety afforded by a reduced military threat was an economic boon for the South as well. Kim Jong-il made good use of the period on his own terms to revive declining regime authority.

Those who have met Kim Jong-il judged that rather than being a politician he was closer to a hot-tempered and emotional artist. "Sensitive and intuitive rather than reasonable and logical" was the evaluation of Lim Dong-won[21] after he visited Pyongyang to meet Kim as part of the South Korean government's preparations for the first inter-Korean summit of June 15, 2000.[22] Lim's character analysis comes with a negative connotation, but it is important to consider North Korea's special circumstances. In so-called "normal" cases, power is controlled and exercised following well-established precedents and institutions in an environment where the ruling system's legitimacy is commonly accepted by the people.

However, despots or tyrants must take power with their own strength, and create by themselves the environment to govern and to exert it.²³ They are akin to artists making masterpieces, realizing their will and determination with hostile materials in unfavorable circumstances. One could compare it to the Renaissance sculptors who took cold, lifeless marble and created upon it forms which seem alive with warm blood flowing beneath their flexible, curved lines. If not an artist, one could imagine a magician leading people away from reality to a world of fantasy by manipulating their senses.

Were Kim Jong-il a man of logical and reasonable thinking, North Korea's Kim family regime might not exist today. Had Kim Jong-il been a man of reason like Mikhael Gorbachev, and thereby had attempted to reasonably reform his crisis-ridden state, it would have been impossible for him to succeed his father and the North Korean regime would not be in the condition we find it today. Among those who met Kim Jong-il during his lifetime, some testified that he was unable to discuss a subject consistently and logically, and that he had such a short attention span that one could not follow his train of thought. However, this also could be an exceptional merit.

> The test of a first-rate intelligence is the ability to have two opposed ideas in mind at the same time and still retain the ability to function.²⁴ (F. Scott Fitzgerald)

Kim Jong-il was someone who had the capacity to simultaneously think of several matters that conflicted with one another. In that respect, he had a different talent from his father, who had a gift for riding the tides of an era of socialism. One of the South's most important personnel in charge of North Korean affairs over many years thought highly of Kim Jong-il's political abilities:

> North Korea managed to survive the crisis of the '90s largely thanks to Kim Jong-il's abilities. In a certain sense, he was more competent than his father Kim Il-sung. I was always nervous during the (second) inter-Korean Summit. Frankly speaking, President Roh Moo-hyun was no match for him.²⁵

Kim Jong-il was a sensitive person, forbidding his personal bodyguards from using impolite grammar forms regardless of rank or position.²⁶ This was a measure taken to forestall the possibility of emotional conflict rising from rough verbal expressions among men who were, after all, standing on guard near him with lethal arms in hand. One couldn't be too careful as no one knew how violent men might react when provoked.

Kim Il-sung once said, "The Party is about running people." Kim Jong-il once said, "Running people is about managing emotions." In short, Kim Jong-il paid a greater degree of attention to people's emotions than their thoughts.

Kim Jong-il mobilized intellectuals volunteering for the regime, and had them devise theories to justify his authority. Nevertheless, he himself did not think much of them. The reason he had these theories made was not to prevent people from "thinking" but to prohibit them from taking interest in "other thoughts."

In the few years prior to his death, Kim Jong-il was immersed in thought. In the end, what was this power that he had devoted so much effort to gaining? What did it mean to him personally, or for the North Korean people? Just as money itself is the goal for misers, is power itself the aim of power?

Whenever he'd ponder this he'd be upset for awhile, just like someone suffering from extreme depression. But he soon pulled himself together, and looked to the tasks before him.

Lying on his death bed, the tyrant of Florence in the medieval period, Lorenzo Il Magnifico of the Medici family reflected on his past sins and couldn't help fearing for the days to come. He called for Friar Girolamo Savonarola, confessed to him, and asked for forgiveness. Savonarola named three conditions.

First, that he must confess every single sin he had committed. The tyrant easily agreed. Second, that he should return all of his unlawfully accumulated property to the original owners. Lorenzo immediately agreed to this condition, too. And third, to return his illegally usurped power to the people. But to this, the Medici head gave no reply and turned his back. Even in his final moments, political power meant more to him than his own soul.[27]

Kim Jong-il skillfully governed his regime throughout the critical 1990s, which meant that he won at least a strategic victory at the level of authoritative power. He not only tackled the biggest crisis the Kim regime faced—the "ordeal" of the Sunshine Policy—but made it a brilliant success.

From the beginning, he had read the intentions of South Korean President Kim Daejung. The latter was no ordinary guy. Unlike other, ordinary South Korean politicians, he had studied North Korea and unification problems for decades. He would say that during his long imprisonment he imagined playing chess with the Great Leader and leading the game. In that sense, he saw himself as a huge threat to the North Korean regime.

The name "Sunshine Policy" came across as a serious threat, too. It claimed to consist of truthful reconciliation and exchange, and cooperation not only with President Kim but also between the two Koreas. But Kim Jong-il was well aware of the dark pitfall hidden within the warm sunlight. The warm, bright sun's rays would eventually make North Korea take off its protective overcoat. Its shaggy body would be exposed thanks to the sunlight. The sun's warmth and brightness to him meant death.[28]

But rather than rejecting this sunshine, he used it to his benefit: believing that he could reinforce his position, he set up an environment aimed at weakening the South Korean system from within the South itself. And this strategy turned out to be very effective.

First of all, he needed to earn time in order to gain power. Ideologically, he did not plan on emphasizing socialism which had already seen its glory days. Instead, he emphasized the weakness of the South, along with the phrases "the Korean people (*minjok*)," "between us Koreans (*uri minjokkkiri*)," and "sovereign autonomy (*jajuseong*)," which had an immediate effect on the North Korean public.

He sought to draw as much material aid as possible from the South. In the process, he believed he could chip away at the South's anti-North national security capabilities, and foster an anti-U.S., pro-North group inside. But while strengthening exchanges and cooperation with the South, he moved to prevent loose discipline and code violations in the North. His strategy over the ten years of the Kim Dae-jung and Roh Moo-hyun administrations can be seen as quite appropriate.

Once the Lee Myung-bak government took power in early 2008, there were alterations in inter-Korean relations, but Kim Jong-il did not worry too much, for North Korea was not the same country that it had been a decade earlier. Whatever people may argue, his North Korea had become a nuclear state, which neither the United States nor any other power could ignore.

Of course, the North Korean economy had endless problems. But the North Korean people just stayed put and remained faithful to the regime until they died, or at worst fled their country and sought survival (mainly to northeast China, South Korea, or a few other countries). They did not openly vent their dissatisfaction within North Korea; the system simply did not permit it.

Kim Jong-il spent most of his life planning to become state leader, and enjoyed only a short time (seventeen years) living his dream. Yet he managed some remarkable achievements during that period.

Nevertheless, no matter how great and secure a leader's power and authority, all leaders become powerless in the face of fundamental human limits. In history, it is common to see political leaders fight long and hard to win their titles, only to experience a pathetic setback known as the human condition. The grandest, most secure power becomes useless against a mortal fate no man can avoid.

Would it be a consolation for a living leader, who has exercised absolute power, to know that his descendants will all remember him and hold memorials for him? Would he find solace at the thought that his followers will tear up parts of his body to embalm him and preserve him forever?

The fundamental cause of the setback lies in the leader himself: his fantasy that power will solve everything for him, and his imagination that absolute power can enable him to overcome the impossible. Having bet all he had on the power of mortal men, the shock and setback of reality would have been indescribable.

Just like anyone else, there was not one single aspect to Kim Jong-il's character. On the contrary, he had a much more complicated personality than most ordinary people. He would be indifferent to sending even his closest personnel or relatives to the gallows, and could enjoy with his family an exquisite gourmet meal, which ordinary North Koreans could never dream of, straight after hearing a report of many citizens dying of hunger. Even when his people were in a dire state after floods and food shortage, "as if he weren't aware of the situation," he was absorbed only in jet skis.[29]

On the other hand, he would take pity on himself and weep, and could easily shed a tear upon hearing a "sentimental" song. He also cried "like a child" when his son left home to go and study overseas.[30] When a staff member walked away from his post then, upon being called came running straight out of the shower, Kim planned to "give him a good scolding" but then took pity after putting himself in the man's mother's shoes. Another time he shot a pregnant deer while hunting, but then felt tremendous remorse and had the beast sent to a maternity hospital. He sighed in relief after hearing a report that "the doe gave birth safely and is well along with her fawn."[31]

Kim Jong-il was a man of paradoxical qualities. His girlfriend Song Hye-rim described him as a "meticulous and humorous comedian,"[32] but he was nonetheless capable of ordering acts of terror and abductions of women and children. Possessed of a cowardly spirit, he would choose to travel for hours and even days by train instead of flying because of his morbid fears of airplanes. However, there was also a belligerent, even nihilistic character about him, which believed that if North Korea were to lose in a war, there would be no need for the world to exist thereafter.[33]

French writer Albert Camus once said that Heathcliff in Emily Brontë's *Wuthering Heights* could have destroyed the whole world for his Catherine, but he wouldn't have tried to justify his acts with reasonable words. How should one see Kim Jong-il's thinking that if North Korea were to lose in a war, the whole Earth would have to go down with it? Not to mention his father Kim Il-sung's mind, which praised those words and thoughts?

Actually, North Korea's rulers are not alone in thinking along these lines. Several dictators from past centuries would have wanted perhaps not the whole world but at least their own country to go down with them if their regimes collapsed.

Before turning 70, Kim Jong-il suffered a stroke. With some difficulty he did recover, but his future prospects were not bright. He was the party, the regime, and the state—a situation he had brought about of his own accord. But now he couldn't perform those roles properly. His aides called for doctors within the regime and also from afar. Invited under top secrecy, medics were compensated with the utmost caution. When traditional Chinese medicine doctors were invited from China, about a dozen patients of similar physique and similar illnesses to Kim Jong-il were laid down with their faces covered before the doctors for diagnosis. This was to prevent the leader's health information from being leaked to Chinese intelligence. The doctors from China examined several patients with the same illness, but none of them could tell which one was Kim Jong-il. Therefore, it goes without saying that the doctors couldn't gather any proper information about his health. Of course, a person's symptoms vary hugely depending on the severity of the illness.

Medics flown in from the West at enormous expense counseled that even if Kim Jong-il could be cured right then, he ought to continue taking extreme caution, otherwise he would once again find himself in a critical condition. Discreet measures of precaution were taken to keep information regarding the leader's health absolutely classified, but foreign intelligence agencies judged that Kim would suffer another health setback in about three years. Most noteworthy was U.S. intelligence, which was the most precise: estimating that Kim had only two or three more years to live. Even on his death bed, other sacrifices were called for. Once Kim Jong-il had fallen into critical condition, three doctors were summoned to take turns in eight-hour shifts to treat the Dear Leader. The doctor who was with Kim at his final moment attempted to perform the necessary emergency CPR, but Kim died on his lap. The poor doctor fainted. Yet that would turn out to be his good fortune. The other two doctors, who were off duty, were sent to labor camps for failing to take care of Kim Jong-il in his final moments.[34]

The last few years of Kim Jong-il were a succession of crises—both domestic and international. After the conservatives regained power in the South, Kim could no longer rely on inter-Korean economic aid as he had during the previous decade. In late 2008, the Six-Party Talks were suspended over the issue of onsite inspections. In the following year, North Korea openly declared its status as a nuclear weapons power after conducting its second nuclear test, worsening the regime's relationship with all of its neighbors as well as with the West. With the power transfer from Kim Jong-il to his second son Kim Jong-un only a matter of time, a reshuffle of the cabinet brought inevitable turbulence. Most noticeably, the currency reform measure of November 2009 caused an economic recession that severely impacted small and medium-sized traders as well as ordinary citizens.

Seen through a wide-angle lens, the seeds of Kim's failure lay in his success. His greatest success was that his power was absolute, and it was rendered entirely arbitrary. And for this, he mobilized the intellectuals. Even they, who are said to seek the truth and facts of life, along with beauty and reward, helped Kim abuse his infinite power to his heart's content. They coined new words and phrases: Juche, Marshal Theory, Sociopolitical Life Theory, the Arduous March, and so forth. For the sake of ideological persuasion, the state had to risk economic losses. However, the other side of all this phenomenal success was a runaway failure totally out of control. Of course, the failure was conceived within the success.

Arguably the biggest achievement of modern times is that rules—accepted by all participants—have taken root in highly competitive fields. This is true in all areas of human activity, from sporting competition to the acquisition of wealth. Whether it is a match or a catch, winners and losers in even the roughest and most confusing sports are determined by sophisticated rules rather than naked violence. Just as winner and loser not only accept the outcome but even congratulate the winner, losers too receive a certain recognition. There is a Western proverb: "The rules of fair play do not apply in love and war." Yet, even in the most irrational fields of love and war, certain rules have emerged.

Even in that fiercest arena of competition—the struggle for power known as politics—certain rules have emerged in the modern era. Generally, humans will risk life and limb for the sake of power. Relations with family and friends alike fade away in front of this struggle.

Plausible justifications are made, but fundamentally the question is to take control of and maintain power, and then to increase it to make it as mighty as one can. Henry Kissinger is quoted as saying, "Power is the ultimate aphrodisiac." People seek power and continue to do so despite all the obstacles they face during the process.[35] The sphere of power struggle is naturally anarchical; therefore, it becomes hard to follow the rules.

However, finally, even the tumult of a power struggle settles eventually back into the normalcy of day-to-day life. The unstable days when it is impossible to know what one's future holds and the brutal mercilessness filling the air with the scent of blood dissipate. The defeated willingly (or willfully suppressing their bitterness) acknowledge defeat and offer congratulations to the winner. These days, competitors who lose in the power struggle are generally guaranteed not only their personal safety, but also their social and political status.

Countries which emerge from revolutions or other external ruptures are apt to go through tough times for a while during the succession of power. The Kim Jong-il regime's irreconcilable foe, South Korea, was no exception. In the succession process of presidential governments, South Korean leaders too ignored some of the rules. Then, some four decades after the birth of the republic, the country managed—barely—to enact a stable, revised constitution which eased the struggle for power, and gave everyone rules they could abide. As a result, competitors today face their struggles with a smile, and the defeated candidates send flowers and convey their congratulations to the winners. Even though in heart they may feel bitter, the losers have not lost everything.

In contrast, Kim Il-sung focused only on the task of aggregating all power to himself, while totally neglecting the matter of enacting a reasonable and stable legal process that could succeed him. He avoided this most important matter by simply bestowing power upon his son. The commonsense fact that no government can be stabilized without rational legislation on the succession of power had no meaning to the late founder of North Korea.

What is more, Kim Il-sung had not even thought about a hereditary dictatorship, where, after his son, his grandson would inherit the regime. Had he conceived that "the Kim family will succeed to power," he surely would have paid more attention to his grandchildren while alive. But there is no indication that he took the slightest interest in the third generation of his dynasty. Were there at least one photograph remaining in which he appeared with his grandchildren, it would have been very useful for the current third-generation leader.

With abject failure in the matter of placing competition for and succession to power into the frame of rational legislation, so North Korea ended up painting itself into a corner. That is because alternative options can be effective only when it is possible to change the government.

But when the supreme leader continues to rule after his death, remaining as an embalmed autocrat, there is only the past, and then some more of the past.

Kim Jong-il was not unaware of this fact. Simply put, because the situation had no easy solution, he just kept procrastinating. He knew it would be a reckless risk to hand power down to his children. And he went so far as to leak his thoughts now and again to people around him. Faced with the reality of his physical limits, his increasing age and fatigue became urgent matters requiring his attention.

He thought and thought again. But there was no easy way out. Part of the deadlock was because he had been so successful in expanding and reinforcing his power, running counter perhaps to the expectations of a number of South Korean personnel.[36]

One day, Kim Jong-il suddenly summoned ten of his most trusted, closest men. They were personnel who played key roles in the regime.

Kim ordered them in a serious tone: "There won't be another succession of power through inheritance. The Kim family is the symbol guaranteeing the authenticity and identity of the state from now on, and will remain a subject of popular loyalty."

The style of power he spoke was in a way similar to that of the Japanese Imperial family. "The management of the State is left to you who came here today. In whatever way, devise solutions to run the country together."[37]

Already under the Great Leader Kim Il-sung, there was the principle that the successor will be chosen regardless of blood relation, and that he would be the one who most perfectly reproduced *Kimilsungism* and had to be a man of exceptional leadership. Kim Jong-il himself also said that his own case had been exceptional, but that there wouldn't be a repeat of the father-to-son inheritance custom. He made the statement personally at a welcome dinner for officials of Chongryon, the (pro-Pyongyang) General Association of Korean Residents in Japan, upon their visit to the North, and it is said that there is also a videotape of Kim making the statement. Chongryon, thereby, concluded for a while that there would not be a third-generation succession, so when the news of Kim Jong-il doing exactly that came out in early 2009, the association strongly criticized the South Korean intelligence for its "propaganda scheme."

Considering the nature of power and power struggle, Kim's thoughts were right in principle. What people dispute most fiercely is political power. Not only between siblings, but between man and wife, father and son; it is a zone where there can be no yielding. Power is fundamentally different from other values—material values, daily comfort or love, and physical pleasures between a man and a woman.

The most important basis for a society to maintain itself normally is to settle the issue of the struggle for power within a stable legislative system. How can a government have people abide by certain rules and norms in the process of struggling for power? Without a solution to this matter, the long-term stabilization of a society or even its minimum sustainment becomes impossible.

Nevertheless, from Kim Jong-il's point of view, some countries appeared to have succeeded in that difficult task. Nearby, North Korea's foe South Korea seemed to have succeeded in adapting new laws to keep struggles for power and power succession bound by certain rules and norms. But Kim Jong-il could not do likewise. Ought he to continue to take risks against his people's innate nature?

In South Korea, power is struggled over in corporations, schools, and even some churches, and the public accepts that reality without much resistance. Many South Koreans are not particularly critical of the near-idolization of the head of a family or a corporation; on the contrary, they praise such acts as filial behavior toward an esteemed ancestor. To that extent, the bigger the achievements of a company founder, the more easily idolization is accepted. If there is a difference in North Korea's case, it would be that the idolization and the inheritance of power is realized on the government level, and that power is the one and only ground for all authority within the country.

If one is to hand over power in a manner which lacks legitimacy, one must do so after sharply decreasing its authority. Such was the wisdom of successful hereditary monarchs, especially under illegitimate regimes. The reason why royal families in many countries in Europe, or in Japan, or in Thailand could retain their status for centuries and survive is because power was succeeded to descendants devoid of the majority of its authoritative power and attendant benefits.

The problem was that from the era of Kim Jong-il's father, Kim Il-sung, one single man had been far too successful in monopolizing power.

Where power is concerned, ultimate success lies in reaching the status of god. Whatever name that god has, the final point of man's pursuit for power is to become God, or on whatever pretext to become a being close to God. Kim Jong-il and his father Kim Il-sung were both gods, or at least demi-gods. In fact, the Kim Jong-il regime spread folktales with supernatural content about the leaders of the Kim family, who succeeded in obtaining absolute power.[38]

- When the Dear Leader Kim Jong-il was born at the birthplace beneath Jong-il Peak at the foot of Mt. Paektu, a rainbow appeared over Jong-il Peak.
- Upon Kim Jong-il's visit to a military site, a thick fog that had blanketed the De-militarized Zone lifted as his cars approached Mt. Osong.
- When Kim Il-sung died in 1994, a vast number of white cranes flew around the Kim Il-sung Statue on Mansudae

hill in Pyongyang and by a similar statue in Hamhung, and they cried sorrowfully.

- The hour that Kim Il-sung passed away on Mt. Myohyang, torrential rain fell with fierce lightning and thunder.

- When Kim Il-sung died, mystical birds and rarely seen animals were spotted at a number of places in the provinces, and they all cried grievously.

- During Kim Il-sung's anti-Japanese partisan struggle years, once he was being chased by the enemy (the Japanese imperial military). Suddenly a bridge appeared over the Amnok (Yalu) River and magically helped him outrun the Japanese.

Members of Kim Il-sung's family were like living gods, just as members of the Japanese Imperial family were considered so until the end of World War II. The Kim family did not carry identification cards, nor were they bound to respect any legal procedure. That fact is true of the Japanese Imperial family today.[39] If there is one difference, however, it is that unlike the Japanese Emperor, the Kims have complete control of all actual power, right down to the most trivial detail. Therefore, at least in North Korea's official political discourse, the Supreme Leader has to be a "highly respectful" and omnipotent presence close to God. Actually, the person in charge of producing and distributing such myths was none other than Kim Jong-il himself. But this deification was bound to become the very reason for the power inheritance system's failure.

When the author informed then-former President Kim Dae-jung that North Korea's Kim Jong-il was considering setting up a succession system similar to the old Japanese Emperor System in preparation for his death, President Kim sighed in disbelief. "Does that make sense? Is it even possible?"[40]

President Kim was right. The idea would have been born of much thought, but it had no outcome. That day when Kim Jong-il summoned his men was the dramatic climax of fifty-plus years of regime history, but it was at once a comical non-event.

The men summoned that day trembled in mortal fear. They could not contact one another, not to mention bring up that day's event, ever again. Rather, they all apprehensively conjectured the impact the event might have on their personal safety. They were afraid to even wonder what the real intentions of the Great Leader could have been that drove him to make such a comment.[41]

Finally, when his lifetime was almost over, Kim Jong-il started to have his son take lessons in becoming his successor. And with that, he prepared to safely hand over power. The result was a political failure. That is to say, the North Korean system has no other choice but to continue hereditary power succession, with all the risks that it entails.

In an ordinary political succession, a new leader would be born among the senior statesmen after a keen competition and finally gain power, while the defeated contestants would offer words of congratulations. However, in a state where that system does not exist, the fruits of tragedy came into bud. This was apt to arouse the need for unexpected scapegoats, especially among the previous generation of senior officials.[42] And one of them was the new state leader's uncle Jang Song-thaek, who was also called the regime's number two.

2

A Shadow Cast Across Love

From deep in my heart, I enjoy laughing and joking.
This helps me each day to live my daily life.

—Konstantinos Petrou Kavafis

If Kim Jong-il was an artist or magician, then Jang Song-thaek was an entrepreneur, and a very passionate one at that. One could compare him to that handful of businessmen in the South who used their exceptional insight and abilities to miraculously build business empires, and attracted attention from around the world in the 1960s and 1970s, during the early period of South Korea's economic development.

In this sense, Kim Jong-il and Jang Song-thaek made a good pair. They were counterparts, facing in different directions yet walking the same road. The paradox between them was not immediately obvious, but only because of the bluntness of the armed authoritarianism that ruled over real life in North Korea.

Jang Song-thaek ought to have been content. A fantastic fortune, along with love, had rolled into his life. The kind of luck that one wouldn't dare to dream of was showered upon him. For a while, his life was one long series of fortunate incidents.

It was his great fortune to enter that school so envied by all North Korean youths: Kim Il-sung University, and its still-more elite Political Science and Economics department at that. And the daughter of none other than Great Leader, well on his way to demigod status, not only showered him with affection, but persistently demanded his hand in marriage.

Kim Kyong-hui was by no means unattractive. Her face suggested prosperity, and she could have passed for a traditional beauty of the

Joseon era. Was she hiding great passion and obstinacy beneath that appearance of hers? The contours of her broad, bright eyes expressed at once humility but also hinted at a volcanic passion. Her fair skin and complexion were especially striking.

Her active and stubborn character, uncaring as to what those around her might think, was that innate, or was it the influence of growing up in the country's most powerful household, and being able to have everything she desired? Or was it because she had inherited the character of the woman known to have always been cheerful and positive: the Lady of the West (the western half of North Korea), and the Beauty of Pyongyang? Kim Kyong-hui did not hesitate to court Jang passionately.

That is not to say that Kim forced an unwilling counterpart to accept her affections. Along with her good looks, Kim Kyong-hui had a good character. Always cheerful, she was good with people and relatively open. She never showed arrogance, nor did she take advantage of her father's absolute power. On the contrary, she had excellent relations with her university classmates. She had little trouble starting a relationship with Jang Song-thaek.

Kim Kyong-hui and Jang Song-thaek drew closer together through a shared passion for entertainment. Like Jang, Kim enjoyed singing and dancing. Peers heartily applauded Jang as he played the accordion and sang, but Kim would be simply overwhelmed from head to toe with rapture.

It's been said that there are two things in this world that you cannot hide: love and sneezes. Well, Kim could not hide the way she flushed in Jang's presence; those around her were mesmerized by her passion.

Later there was an instance where Kim Il-sung issued an order through his younger brother Kim Yong-ju for then-Kim Il-sung University President Hwang Jang-yop to separate the two. Hwang Jang-yop had to try and obey. However, there was in fact little he could do; he could only play a kind of make believe: keep the two in separate classrooms, or hide Jang Song-thaek in places unnoticeable to Kim Kyong-hui during non-class hours. Jang was of course cooperative; he obeyed the order. But Kim was a different matter. Restless, she personally went to see Hwang at his office, whereupon she criticized the school's attempt to interfere in students' private affairs. At such moments, even Hwang couldn't help being moved by the earnest feelings of the woman, regardless of her background.[1]

When she couldn't find Jang Song-thaek at school, Kim Kyong-hui even went to see his sister to ask whether he had returned home. If the answer was negative, she'd return wearing a long face, inciting wistful feelings in those around her. Some people even associated the two with Psyche and Orpheus, who went as far as the underworld in pursuit of lost loves.

No one dared to treat the two as mere subjects of gossip, or to make up scandalous rumors about them. Even to the people around them, this relationship was a touching sight, rare in the average lifetime.

For Jang Song-thaek, the matter wasn't so simple. Were North Korea a normal country open to the outside world, this couple may well have drawn wider public interest, possibly becoming the romance of the century. For Jang, it was a love that guaranteed both a beautiful bride and a brilliant career.

But he was not in a state of mind to simply enjoy the situation. Instead, he was anxious. He had mixed feelings and they confused him; he was beyond worry, yet trembled with fear. First, he was afraid of the attention of people around him. Were one slip of the tongue to reach the ears of the Great Leader, no one could know what fate would await him. It could be his end. For a romance, it was terribly frightening.

Kim Il-sung's daughter actively approached him from the beginning. Sometimes as if teasing, at others like a reckless daredevil. Even during class, sitting at the back, she would tickle his ear with a grass leaf to distract him.[2] Jang would first and foremost be conscious of whether others around him had noticed and were taking an interest.

The main female character in Gustave Flaubert's novel first reads the pages where the characters fall in love, and then takes actions to pursue those experiences for herself. People prepare themselves for how they will react when in different situations. This is the case when a man and a woman date. Even before one falls in love, people are already somewhat prepared by the stories of other people's experiences, whether from a movie or novel, and act accordingly. Even if subconsciously, people rely on a template, a so-called "role model."

But even the exceptionally bold and calm Jang Song-thaek was anything but prepared for this situation: that he should fall in love with the daughter of the country's demigod Great Leader!

He was perplexed and confused, unable to firmly collect his thoughts and handle the situation. The two were born in 1946, with Kim Kyong-hui on May 30, about four months after Jang. Yet while

Jang was older, so to speak, in terms of age, it was always Kim who played the leading role.

On Kim Il-sung University campus at the time, dating among male and female students was not that unusual. In principle it was forbidden, and personal freedom was not guaranteed as it was elsewhere. But with the exception of situations like pregnancy, the university authorities did not pay any great degree of attention to or interfere with student dating.

The student body was an equal mix of discharged soldiers, admitted after almost ten years of military service, and so-called "direct students," who entered right after high school. Then there were the so-called "present-post students," who had gone out into society and worked, then returned to school. A fair number were married.

Thus, it wasn't that unusual that Kim Kyong-hui had fallen in love with Jang Song-thaek. But Kim's immense background was extraordinary. "If only there weren't any one following behind her back . . ."—The Kim Il-sung statues erected throughout North Korea, the Great Leader's teachings posted anywhere, and all kinds of notices and banners. No one could be free from those shadows. Not from any of them.

"To date *the* demi-god's daughter!"

Even when Jang, led by Kim, walked in the nearby woods, or along the grass hills connecting the campus with the Taedong, the Great Leader was omnipresent. The Great Leader's shadow always followed them, just as it did for all North Koreans. But the dense shadow cast over Jang wasn't dark for Kim.

Dating etiquette at the time was that a man would earnestly seek the hand of a woman. Even if the woman found it difficult to make up her mind, or did not show interest, generally the man would lead the way and draw a positive response. Though not so extreme as to be called macho, it was commonly accepted that male chauvinism prevailed.

But in this case, things were different. If the Supreme Leader were a demigod, then his daughter was a demigoddess. No one could think lightly or badly of her. And that very goddess had aggressively approached him.

Jang was not prepared, nor did he know what measures to take. There was another female student who was interested in him. Jang was that popular. But once people learned of Kim Kyong-hui's reckless courting, no one dared think of coming between the two.

Jang Song-thaek had always been confident and calm that he could proficiently deal with any situation. In fact, his was a typical leader personality acknowledged by himself and everyone who knew him. Wherever he went, in whatever situation, he would draw people's attention, and people gathered around him. Firmly built, taller than 5'7", his facial features might not be that of a "flower boy,"[3] but they were manly. He scored well in Korean chess and North Korean card games, without becoming addicted to them.

He was able in the arts also. He was good with musical instruments, as well as singing and dancing. In particular, he was far beyond an amateur level on the accordion; on school outings or special performances he was the first to be sought out to play. Years later, even actress Choi Eun-hee,[4] who was at an outdoor party of Kim Jong-il, named Jang Song-thaek as the best singer among the people present.[5]

That wasn't all. Jang Song-thaek's distinctive quality was his humanity. He wasn't the academic type, or a scientist focused on intellectual stimulation. His grades were average. But he had the ability to control every element of any situation, and to take the lead. In short, he was a natural-born leader. An easy-going character, he associated well with everyone. Even when there was a problem among his class friends, or between students and the university authorities, Jang would handle the matter well and find a solution. He did not simply enjoy drinking; he was a heavy drinker who could easily drink a half-bottle of whisky at one sitting. Whenever there were student events, he was a celebrity who couldn't be left out.

Jang Song-thaek was well aware of his ability and of his popularity, and gradually he grew ambitious. Lots of young people are, but in Jang's case, he was equipped with the confidence and leisurely ability to make his dreams a reality.

A quick skim through the positions he held during his school years offers insights into his qualities as a person. While at Kim Il-sung University, Jang was class leader, chairman of the League of Socialist Working Youth, student chairman, and cell chairman of the Worker's Party.[6] One Worker's Party official commented that Jang has "a warm, lively, and cheerful character" and "is active and optimistic," as well as possesses "a strong determination at all times." In addition, he was quoted as being "direct and positive" in tackling matters, and in his personal relations, "easy going, modest, well-mannered, and popular." Moreover, rare in North Korea, he is said to have been an avid reader in a wide range of fields, including politics, economics, science, world literature, and the Chinese classics.[7] He wasn't outstandingly brilliant in his studies, but he was smart.

Jang Song-thaek wasn't merely an all-embracing, amicable man. When injected into a certain task, he was praised for exceptional performance. In the late 1980s he even received the honorary title "Hero of Effort" for his work on Gwangbok Street and the May Day (5.1) Stadium. Especially when he was in charge of the construction project for Pyongyang prior to the 13th World Festival of Youth and Students in 1989, or when he supervised the evacuation of Pyongyang residents' in 1976, he demonstrated accomplishment in work performance, which was assessed as being almost excessive.

When military tensions escalated on the Peninsula during what came to be known as the Panmunjom axe murder incident,[8] North Korea issued a mobilization order nationwide, and evacuated citizens en masse to mountain regions in case of bomb attack. Jang was responsible for carrying this out in Pyongyang, but he was so competent at executing the command that he was later blamed for going too far. In the process of evacuating 40,000 households in a matter of three months, there were apt to be coercive measures taken, and the director-general of section four of the State Security Department and his men were criticized and removed from their positions as a consequence. However, Jang was recognized for his deeds and received a level-2 state medal.[9] Jang also logged remarkable achievements in 1973 during a 70-day battle to execute the people's economic plan. Wherever he went, production increased. And for that, he was awarded the level-1 state medal.[10]

Years later, even after Jang Song-thaek rose to very senior positions, he never dealt [oorly with people of lower position. A diplomat who once acted as Jang's guide on an overseas trip recalled that once he returned to Pyongyang after serving abroad, Jang remembered the man's assistance and invited him to dinner. Jang sent his chauffeur to pick up the diplomat and then treated him at the Koryo Hotel. That memory remained an unforgettable, touching experience for the diplomat.

Another man who had assisted Jang in Italy remembered how, upon returning to Pyongyang at the end of the year, Jang asked whether he needed anything. The man wanted to ask for his family to be sent so that they could be reunited, and he thought Jang might even grant that wish. But he cleared his thoughts and did not ask for anything, saying, "I do not need anything, sir." However, on New Year's Day he received a telegram in Kim Jong-il's name which said, "Well done!" No doubt, it was Jang Song-thaek's doing.[11]

A former bodyguard of Kim Jong-il, remembered that Jang Song-thaek was extremely considerate to those of lower social standing. There were many fruit trees in the garden of the headquarters' building where Kim Jong-il and Jang worked together, and if Jang saw guards resting while he was taking a walk during his break time, he'd pick cherries and hand them to the guards. Moreover, unlike Kim Jong-il, Jang Song-thaek never addressed bodyguards in impolite grammatical forms.[12] People close to Jang commented that despite his rank and power, Jang threw himself into humane tasks, and had a very strong sense of justice.[13]

Gamesome, Jang also had the talent to entertain those around him with unanticipated mischief. Kim Jong-il's former chef Kenji Fujimoto recalled an episode at the swimming pool of a Wonsan resort in the summer of 1992. A group of about forty high ranking officials and members of the Pleasure Troupe was present and having a good time when Jang Song-thaek stealthily approached from behind and pulled down their swimming trunks.[14] In addition, during a banquet, the minute other officials were about to sit down, Jang would pull out their chairs and make the men fall on their behinds, creating a burst of laughter.[15]

During the first seven years of the 2000s, there were frequent inter-Korean exchanges. At this time, the South Korean officials who met Jang Song-thaek were impressed by his masculinity. However, understanding and affable as Jang Song-thaek may have been, Kim Kyong-hui's passionate courting often left him at his wit's end.

Prior to 1967, there was an air of freedom at Kim Il-sung University. It was not until later that military and ideological culture would overwhelm the place. Many of the professors in the early era had studied in the USSR or East European countries, and so Kim Il-sung University felt close to the college culture of those countries. If you set aside ideology, to a certain extent a free, collegial, and intellectual atmosphere prevailed. "Back then," some people even recalled, "it was the South Korean universities that still had remnants of the imperial Japanese era."

One pleasure the male students used to seek out was to occasionally go to a nearby dog meat restaurant for a filling feast.[16]

The students were organized in military formation: each year a platoon; each college a battalion; and the whole university a regiment. (In the South, middle- and high-school students were also organized in military formation.) However, this did not mean that the students' lives were conducted in military style; that came later. Students got to enjoy a little romance and leisure in their spare time.[17]

The natural environment surrounding the school was exceptional. Mt. Ryongnam, on which the university campus sat, connected to Moran Hill and looked out over the Taedong River. As it was the highest hill in Pyongyang, the view was simply breathtaking. This was before Natural Science Building 1 and Social Science Building 2 were built, so there was only the Main Building. Likewise, various other buildings around the university had not been built yet, so the 30-minute walk downhill from the university to the river had a romantic ambience of grass and pine trees. Those who have not seen Kim Il-sung University in this period might imagine the view of the Potomac from former U.S. President George Washington's house. Behind the Main Building there used to be the university president's residence. No longer there, in the environs of the former president's residence site there are now faculty housing and grand trees, including old willows.

But later, after 1967, Kim Il-sung University went through massive change. First, following special instructions from Kim Il-sung, discharged soldiers began to make up more and more of the student body, with only a small number of female students and officials' sons and daughters continuing to gain admission. Military culture soon became the university mainstream, especially as the dormitories collectivized and students had to follow strict rules. Student life became indistinguishable from life in the barracks. This was a huge change.

One person who attended Kim Il-sung University in the 1970s recalled that among the majors there was a "Kim Il-sung (Literary) Works Department" and some twenty full-time professors were experts in this field. The game changer had been the 15th Plenary Session of the 4th Central Committee of the Worker's Party in May 1967, which coincided with Kim Il-sung's warning about the infiltration of capitalist ideas.

However, during the courtship of Jang Song-thaek and Kim Kyong-hui, Kim Il-sung University was still in its golden age.

Kim Il-sung University was the fast track to success in North Korea. It was a destination beyond the wildest dreams of anyone not from a good "class" background. Had Jang gone to university two or three years later, he might not have been permitted to enter, because it is possible that his class background might have been recategorized, and his life inevitably would then have been very different.

It's important to understand how the Kim family regime developed. First and foremost, one must look at the so-called "class" structure, which acts as a decisive element in determining the public fate of a person in North Korea.

There is a famous maxim by French journalist Jacques Mallet du Pan: "A l'exemple de Saturne, la révolution dévore ses enfants," or, "Like Saturn, the Revolution devours its children." It seems that this paradoxical wisdom has been true of almost all revolutions. Some politicians, though there is a fair degree of difference among them, also claim that this is a general phenomenon that applies to all authoritative power. Once power is seized, a new leader abandons his supporters, especially those with the potential to challenge his seat. The resulting vacuum is filled with new supporters.[18]

The best case of this secular wisdom appeared in the late 20th century, in particular in North Korea after the Korean War. The Kim Il-sung regime arrested key figures who might compete for the mantel of revolutionary leadership and executed each and every one under various criminal pretexts, leaving only Kim Il-sung's activities as nominally legitimate. It was as if one page of North Korean history, the one about Kim Il-sung, was sufficient to render meaningless all other pages in the history of the struggle against imperial Japan and the socialist revolution. That single page denied all other activities by anti-revolutionary dissenters.

First it was the former South Joseon Worker's Party politicians who had to go, led by former leader Pak Hon-yong. They were accused of spying for the United States and executed. Then came the so-called Yanan and Soviet factions of Choe Chang-ik, Pak Chang-ok and Yun Kong-hum, who were criticized as "anti-party anti-revolution factional elements, revisionists, right wing surrenderists, doctrinists," and made to disappear forever.

The final grand event in the process of securing the "monolithic" system of rule was the so-called "Gapsan faction purge," which was waged at the 15th Plenary Session of the 4th Central Committee of the Worker's Party in May 1967. There, a great number of party officials who had failed to adequately back Kim Il-sung as the uniquely legitimate core of the revolutionary movement were purged and executed. The person who led the purge is said to have been Kim Jong-il, making his violent bow as Kim Il-sung's successor.

The executed men included leading figures such as the fourth-ranking member of the KWP Central Committee Political Committee, Pak Kum-chol; its fifth-ranking member and the official in charge of liaison with South Korea, Ri Hyo-sun; head of the propaganda section of the Central Committee, Kim Do-man; international director, Pak Yong-kuk; and science, education director, Ho Sok-son. The crimes imposed on them were factionalism, familism, and regionalism. In the South, they were called the "Gapsan faction" after their involvement in the "Gapsan Anti-Japanese Activity Planning Committee," a socialist anti-Japanese movement organization formed on the peninsula in North Hamgyong Province in the 1930s. With the execution of the Gapsan faction, the sole remaining force capable of opposing Kim Il-sung and his family as the sole center of the state was dissolved.

From then on, only Kim Il-sung's activities during the Japanese occupation era were mythologized and exaggerated, and they became the only meaningful version of the anti-Japanese struggle. All other movements were deemed not only meaningless but even reactionary.

Military personnel were also executed. The military had to belong to Kim Il-sung and the party alone. The director of the military's General Political Department Kim Ul-kyu was criticized for arguing that the North Korean military should succeed the Kilju and Myeongcheon areas farmers' movement.[19] But Jang Song-thaek's father was involved with this very socialist farmers' movement during the Japanese occupation era. This may have been the reason Kim Il-sung hesitated to accept Jang when talk of marriage to his daughter surfaced.

In principle, Jang Song-thaek had to belong to the central class. Politically, however, he was considered something of a sect even within the same religion; a heathen that could be more dangerous than a heretic. Jang was in a position to diminish the legitimacy at the basic foundation of Kim authority, and could one day even challenge its power.

It's a good thing for Jang he entered Kim Il-sung University in 1965. He would likely have fared differently if he had sought to matriculate in 1967 or thereafter.[20]

Hardly anything is known of Jang Song-thaek's biography before he entered university. It is really his relationship with Kim Kyong-hui that brought him into the spotlight, and it is thanks to that relationship he advanced into key public positions. But Jang Song-thaek also hardly ever mentioned his earlier life. In nearly any other country, anyone reaching such elevated positions would have left some kind of paper trail in the form of records, a biography, or some similar medium. In North Korea, however, whereas Kim Il-sung and his immediate family are storified and memorialized to the extreme, the stories of other people are hardly known, except to the extent that they may be useful in glorifying the central family even further.

In the early 1960s, the memoirs of Gapsan faction personnel were published. Pak Dal's memoir was published as an independent volume in 1963, and in an album introducing the North Korean revolution museum, which came out in the following year, photos of Pak Kum-chol and Pak Dal were printed along with that of Kim Il-sung. In *the Life and Acts of the Revolution Ancestors*, printed in the same year, the story of the Gapsan faction's Ri Je-sun (the younger brother of Ri Hyo-sun, executed years later) is introduced in detail.

When Pak Kum-chol's wife, Choe Chae-ryon died, a funeral committee was convened and a film was made about how, despite suffering in extremely harsh circumstances herself, she supported her husband while he was imprisoned in Seoul. The film was called "Sincere Devotion" (*Ilpyondansim*), and was screened several times. In later years, however, Kim Il-sung criticized the film for its feudalistic ideas, as if to say that devotion for one's husband, and not solely for the revolution, was reactionary.

The underlying truth was that there was no room for state myths except for those centered around Kim Il-sung himself and his family.

A few things are known about Jang Song-thaek's family. His paternal uncles belonged to the intellectual class during the Japanese occupation era, and, as noted, took part in the Socialist farmers' movement in the Kilju and Myeongcheon regions. Years later, his father Jang Yong-hwan served as a deputy chairman of the Provisional People's Committee of North Hamgyong Province, and his uncle Jang Jong-hwan served as a deputy director in the Korean People's Army.

Jang's younger brother Jang Song-kil served as a brigadier general of the North Korean military, then became a political commission member of the 5th Corps of the KPA and commander of the Ryu Kyong-su 105th Tank Division. He died in July of 2006.[21] Jang's older brother Jang Song-u was a military unit leader, then a director of the

Workers' Party of Korea (WPK), received a promotion to vice marshal, and died in August of 2009.

It is also said that Jang's father fought in the Korean War. Considering that both of Jang's older brothers were soldiers, and Jang himself attained admission to the Mangyongdae Revolutionary School, the rumors about his father may well be true.

In any event, Jang Song-thaek principally belonged per classification to the core class. However, after the aforementioned 15th Plenary Session of the 4th Central Committee in 1967, Jang's class changed to one that had to be hushed up rather than discussed officially out in the open.[22] Nevertheless, his family and brothers in their own way were categorized as a good class, received a good education, and can be said to have smoothly entered public service.

Fortunately, Jang Song-thaek's brothers all died before Jang was eventually executed. Jang's older sister Jang Kye-sun was married to Jon Yong-jin, the North Korean ambassador to Cuba. They have not been heard of since being summoned to Pyongyang after Jang Song-thaek's execution. Jang's nephew Jang Yong-chol was ambassador to Malaysia, but word is that he was also recalled and executed along with his two sons, Tae-ryong and Tae-ung.

Jang Song-thaek was born in Chongjin on January 22, 1946. He went to Mangyongdae Revolutionary School at the age of thirteen. This school was established by Kim Il-sung after Korea's independence to accept the children of anti-Japanese partisans and later the surviving children of those fallen in the Korean War. The reason this school was built at Mangyongdae—Kim Il-sung's mythologized birthplace—was to raise future talents to inherit the tradition and tasks of the revolution from age ten. The school uniform itself takes after that of the Korean People's Army, and student life inside and outside the classroom is entirely militarized.

Graduating from the seven-year program is the equivalent of graduating from high school, so students may directly enter Kim Il-sung University, Kang Kon Military Academy, or Kim Il-sung University of Politics, embarking on a path to becoming a key official or military officer. The reason Jang was able to enter this school was most likely because back then the anti-Japanese farmers' struggle, the key event in his family's background, would have been recognized as part of the revolutionary tradition.

Kim Kyong-hui was born on May 30, 1946. She is the only daughter of Kim Il-sung and his former wife Kim Jong-suk, and sister of Kim Jong-il. Kim Kyong-hui graduated from Namsan Upper Middle School in Pyongyang and entered Kim Il-sung University in the same year as Jang.

North Korea's classification system was a principle reason Jang Song-thaek had to tread carefully in his relationship with Kim Kyong-hui. North Korea's class divisions can lead to very different treatment in society. The North Korean regime divides the residents into approximately 28 percent core class, 45 percent ordinary class, and 27 percent antagonistic class. State Security and Public Safety, the main North Korean security forces, manage the classes accordingly, suitably handling or dealing with each on its own terms.[23]

To enter Kim Il-sung University, one of course had to be of the core class. But even within the core class, not everyone received the same treatment. Within the core, some 200,000 enjoyed elite status. The core of the core, equivalent to one percent of the population, are the former anti-Japanese partisans' families and families awarded merits during the founding of the nation or the Korean War. On top of this elite layer is a micro-thin super-elite made up of Kim Il-sung's family members, surpassing even partisan and veteran families. Commonly they are referred to as the Changbaeksan or Nakdong-gang range, using the terminology of the ancient Kingdom of Silla: Seonggol (pure noble) and Jingol (half noble).

Non-Koreans have pointed out that such a blatantly outdated class system ideologically contradicts North Korea's labeling of itself as a "Democratic Republic." And yet, despite all its shortcomings, this class discrimination system seems to have played a huge role in the regime maintaining its stability and rallying power. That is because at least within the core group that is responsible of running the country, loyalty to the regime and the ideology is equivalent to loyalty to family, and betrayal is likewise betrayal to family. North Korea's regime has made good use of the so-called blood kinship of ideology,[24] a typically Korean phenomenon seen in left-right conflicts and struggles.

As a result, Jang Song-thaek belonged to the core class. However, he was not a perfect seonggol. Indeed, after the 15th Plenary Session of the 4th Central Committee, he became someone to guard against, or at least keep an eye on. The reason Kim Il-sung fumed with anger upon hearing the news that his own daughter was having a relationship with Jang and was even considering marriage (the idea which the elder Kim initially rejected) was not because Jang's background was pitiful or antagonistic. It also wasn't a common scene where father opposes his daughter's fiancée just because he doesn't seem suitable for her. Rather, it was because Jang's family itself posed a question to Kim Il-sung's singular legitimacy.

Whatever the circumstances, the relationship of the two developed over the years and nearly everyone in the whole school knew about them, as did those outside the campus via the inevitable rumors.

Kim Il-sung might have been the last person in Pyongyang to hear the rumor about his one and only daughter's boyfriend. In any case, the Great Leader received reports and upon reviewing Jang Song-thaek's family background became enraged. This was something unacceptable. It felt like an impure substance had permeated the family that must always be divine. Kim Il-sung had to be the only "tradition of the revolution."[25] In a country where one family was directly connected to the state's destiny, this was a serious matter.

Even at such a moment, it was politics and power that mattered to Kim Il-sung. The personal circumstances of his daughter as an individual, and as a woman had no importance. It was a matter that could taint the foundation of the state and the regime if not handled carefully, and of such utmost importance that it transcended the very British scandals of the Duke of Windsor and Mrs. Simpson, or Princess Margaret and Group Captain Peter Townsend.

But Kim couldn't punish a young man simply for being close with his daughter. Whatever the situation might have been before, first he had to separate the two. He immediately had his younger brother Kim Yong-ju order the school, via Hwang Jang-yop, to forbid Jang from coming close to his daughter, and eventually he had Jang transferred far away to Wonsan University of Economics.

The Great Marshal and father Kim Il-sung's orders came to the third-year junior couple, deeply in love, as a moment of truth. For Jang Song-thaek this measure was not at all surprising. As a matter of fact, it was a much lighter treatment than what he had feared. For Jang, this was an end to the connection with Kim Kyong-hui. Maybe with this he could be free from a sweet yet terribly burdensome fortune.

He wasn't without wistful regrets, but the greatest weight that remained in his heart was that he had to leave Kim Il-sung University, his ticket to success. From the minute he was given his transfer order to an unfamiliar place without much of an explanation, he started to think about his future and calculate the new choices lying ahead of him. First Wonsan University of Economics. And then?

But that wasn't the case for Kim Kyong-hui. What mattered to her wasn't a career or a future job. The most pressing matter for her was her memories with the man she loved with her whole mind and body, and she could by no means erase those memories with fruitless dreams. She made up her mind to withstand any obstacle.

The day Jang Song-thaek packed his things and was leaving the university, his class friends bid him farewell without a word. They could not dare question or utter a sound against an order given directly by the Great Leader. It was certain, however, that one person would disobey the order: his daughter.

Upon their last date, the woman clearly conveyed her determination in a strong tone to the man who was saying goodbye. She would never follow her father's decision, and she would never give up her man. Of the 23 million people living in North Korea, she was the only one who could conceive of defying Kim Il-sung, and she was barely twenty.

Kim Il-sung sat down with his one and only (official) daughter to seek the truth; what he got was defiance. The father's anger, long lectures, persuasion, admonition, and conciliation was all to no avail and could not change the woman's mind. The Great Marshal, who was invincible, omnipotent at least in North Korea, failed to fathom the stereotypical worldly truth that the stronger the opposition, the more powerful a stimulant it becomes for a couple in love. Until the end, Kim Kyong-hui told her father that she could not live separated from Jang Song-thaek, and she made it clear that she would never give up Jang and date or marry someone of an eminent family suggested by her father.

Kim Kyong-hui was not given to words alone. She acted on her determination without delay. The distance between Pyongyang and Wonsan was only 124 miles, but the rough unpaved nature of the 1960s roads could easily extend that trip to seven or eight hours. Travelers making the journey also had to overcome the infamously steep Masikryong Pass, so named because even horses could not traverse it without taking a rest. The winding unpaved roads were prone to road accidents if not carefully navigated. Yet still, on weekends, Kim Kyong-hui drove the family's black Soviet-made Volga all the way out to Wonsan to visit Jang. She carried in the car all sorts of presents, such as food and clothes, which one could not easily find even in Pyongyang.

At Wonsan University of Economics, the arrival of a luxurious car with a license plate denoting the Great Leader's family was to some extent a source of panic. Kim Kyong-hui was indifferent to everyone else but the person she came to see: Jang Song-thaek. They were in a remote world of their own. Kim Kyong-hui spent one weekend night with him, and returned to Pyongyang the following day. The princess of the republic, daughter of the Marshal who owned the country like a possession, washed Jang's piled clothes, made his dinner, and tidied up happily for the man she loved. As a woman in love, she viewed the service as a rewarding pleasure.

Even at this time Jang Song-thaek couldn't help being passive. He was secretly happy to see Kim Kyong-hui, and he was surely touched by her determination and kindness. However, he couldn't openly rejoice at her behavior which directly opposed the orders of the beloved Great Marshal; he couldn't encourage Kim Kyong-hui or let her know that he was grateful. The only thing he could do was be hesitant and embarrassed, and simply abide by this laudable young woman's brave acts.

Once again, the winds of fortune would blow in Jang Song-thaek's favor, and he would soon benefit from incredibly rapid change. North Korea was about to shift to a new system under new leadership.

3

Edgy Romance

> All sorrows can be borne if you put them in a story or tell a story about them.
> Perhaps robbing someone of his or her story is the greatest betrayal of all.
>
> —Anna Fels

Kim Jong-il was quietly strengthening his struggle for power.

Things were moving in his direction. He had signalled his readiness for power to his father and now, finally, he was in a position to try and seize it. However, he was well aware that the game he was playing was both dangerous and profoundly uncertain. One minute all could be going to plan, and the next something might go gravely wrong. One unforeseen incident could turn fate against him in a single morning. That was the nature of the power game: one false move could mean a permanent fall.

Jockeying for supreme power was a lonely and relentless struggle. It is a game played alone, always unsure of who is on your side. The people around you are all variables in flux, their decisions wholly dependent on unpredictable circumstances.

As a father, Great Leader Kim Il-sung was kind and generous to his children. It was the mother, Kim Jong-suk, who was strict.

Once, when Kim Jong-il was in elementary school, somebody gave him a gold watch. Back then it would have been a luxury item the like of which few could possess. Kim Jong-suk saw Kim wearing his gold watch and immediately scolded him, warning that he could be tainted by luxury goods from a young age. However, Kim Il-sung just laughed, remarking that a leader's son ought to be able to enjoy that degree of privilege.[1]

But even Kim Il-sung was not always benevolent when it came to questions of power. Power was an unpredictable variable in the political realm; but it was also the single most important entanglement of the family business. The father was still demonstrating immense vigor. It could be dangerous to rush into the successor's seat too early, or indeed to start playing too large a role too hastily. On the other hand, it could also be dangerous to let it drag for too long, for he could end up facing restrictions when he finally got into position.

The big picture wasn't bad. Kim's uncle, Kim Yong-ju, who had once been thought of as the successor, made some mistakes. What is more, he had very serious flaws. For one thing, he was not a former partisan and had not fought against the Japanese. But in addition, his health had deteriorated quite badly, and he was no longer a threat to the nephew. On the contrary, the uncle could be of help.

The biggest threat was Kim's stepmother, Kim Song-ae, and her children. His father still loved his stepmother, and his step-siblings were a non-trivial threat. The oldest, Pyong-il, was a good deal more handsome than Kim, and he was distinctly unlike Kim Jong-il in that he was strikingly tall and had a soldier's air about him. People often remarked that Pyong-il took after his father in many respects. There was also the younger stepbrother, Yong-il, and younger stepsister, Kyong-jin. His only full sibling was the thoughtless younger sister, who defied their father and was making a fuss over some man.

In his heart, Kim Jong-il bore a deep wound that few were aware of. It involved the death of his younger brother, Shura, who had been two years younger than Kim Jong-il and very fond of the older boy. The year Kim Jong-il turned five, the two were playing together at a house that had been provided by Pak Jong-sik, a businessman during the Japanese occupation, upon the family's return from the USSR. There was a small pond in the yard—which is where little Shura drowned.

It was only two years since the family had returned to North Korea. The two brothers were still called by their Russian nicknames, Yura (Kim Jong-il) and Shura. Yura got distracted by something while the two were by the pond; Shura fell in the water and did not reappear. The accident was over before anyone realized it had happened. There was the sound of splashing, but Kim Jong-il just thought his brother was playing and ignored it.

Nobody blamed Kim Jong-il for the accident. Members of staff were reprimanded for leaving the two children by themselves, and Kim Il-sung ordered the pond to be filled in. But Kim Jong-il felt a huge burden of guilt. When others were being scolded or his parents' glances were directed at him, young Kim Jong-il shrank back in both mind and body.

Afterwards he never mentioned the accident again. But the deeper he pushed that memory down into his heart, in one corner there remained a vivid image of his younger brother's ice-cold body, swollen from all the water he had swallowed. Maybe the wounds left then made Kim Jong-il more determined to seize power later.

Not long after that, Kim Jong-il lost his mother, Kim Jong-suk, and he acquired the habit of connecting his brother's accidental death to the death of his mother. Meanwhile, their father brought his former secretary, Kim Song-ae, into the house as stepmother. Kim Jong-il and his one and only sibling, two-year-old Kyong-hui, were raised under the care of the stepmother. His father was always busy, so it was stepmother Kim Song-ae's duty to look after the two children. In particular, he rarely saw his father after the Korean War broke out a year later.

Naturally, the stepmother looked after the two young ones with all of her ability. In terms of childcare, she may have been kinder and more generous than the children's biological mother. However, the distance between a stepmother and her stepchildren cannot be narrowed through care alone. What is more, the stepmother was the father's former secretary. Kim Jong-il found it hard to call her mother.

It got worse once the stepmother started having babies of her own. The year Kim Jong-il turned nine, she gave birth for the first time. It was a daughter. Within a few years, she had given birth to two sons and one more daughter. This was an indescribable shock to young Kim Jong-il, and would be a vital turning point in his life.

From then on, his relationship with not only his stepmother but also his father would never be the same again. Children often feel almost instinctively threatened and even repulsed by one of their biological parents' newborn children. As ordinary people would say, "The boy is angry." Young Kim Jong-il's feelings toward the children born to his stepmother aren't all that difficult to imagine. Moreover, while he did not suffer any hardships, he did have to live in an unfamiliar part of Jilin Province, China, for two years. He returned to Pyongyang the year he turned nine, and from that point on attended Mangyongdae Revolutionary School, but his living conditions were unstable.

Parents cannot avoid making their newborn infants the family's first priority. Kim Jong-il's endless philandering once he reached manhood may have been a result of the continuous pursuit for motherly love that he felt he had lost as a child. Besides the other women he spent time with, he lived as husband and wife with Song Hye-rim and Ko Yong-hui, both of whom showed remarkable motherly qualities. However, he could not be satisfied; he continued to see one woman after another. And it was power that enabled him to do so.

In later years, the younger Kim would establish his position as the so-called "main branch" of the family, whereas other members, particularly his stepmother and her children, would be relegated to "side branches." Treatment of the two different "branches" would be distinct. A political motive can surely be read into the separation, but it also seems as if Kim felt deprived of motherly love as a child, an unmet need of which antagonism toward his step-siblings may well have been a subconscious by-product.

His behavior toward the "side branches" could even be described as pathological. At one point his own daughter, Sol-song, was to go into the elite class at Namsan Senior Middle School, but he cancelled her entry after hearing that his stepmother Kim Song-ae's nephew would be entering the same year. Years later, he had the school torn down without a trace, and put the Central Party Organization and Guidance Department building on the site.[2]

Throughout their childhood, Kim Jong-il and Kim Kyong-hui lived as brother and sister, depending on each other in the midst of their dark loneliness.

But that same sister was on a deadly path. His father's denial and his sister's stubbornness might collide any day, resulting in a huge crisis for him. If he did not do something, his father's anger could turn toward him: "What were you doing when you should have been taking care of your little sister?"

Besides, Kim Jong-il's father had several other successor candidates he could choose from. They were all ready to dedicate their love and loyalty to him. Therefore, he had to bet his all on earning his father's goodwill.

He calculated the unthinkable in his mind. His opponents had the advantage of numbers. Besides the stepmother and her relatives, there were her healthy and energetic children, the two sons and two daughters. To Kim Jong-il, there was only the immature younger sister who was recklessly embarking upon a dangerous road.

Jang Song-thaek's family background could scar the Kim family's singular legitimacy, something that he was trying hard to establish. But that matter could always be thought of differently. Jang Song-thaek was a talented person who could plausibly wait on Kim Jong-il hand and foot. The sooner the better, he thought. He made up his mind to solve the matter by standing by his little sister's side.

To his surprise, Kim Jong-il did not find it difficult to persuade his father. Saying that he needed to tell Kim Il-sung something in private, he met his father alone, and there brought up the matter of his younger sister.

First, he said that the point had been reached where it would be hard to split Kyong-hui from the man in question. Then he explained that unnecessary rumors could spread if they weren't careful, and that "the man in question's background is not satisfactory; however, he is an able man and is regarded as genuine," so "wouldn't it be better just to recognize the relationship?"

The father remained taciturn for quite a while. Then, with an unsatisfied air, he declared, "I will leave this matter to you; do as you please." Kim Jong-il cried silently in joy.

That was a good thing. It was good that things were to be decided according to his will, not his father's, but also that he could help his younger sister to pull through a difficult moment. She no longer had to go on her risky weekend car journeys to Wonsan, and not only his sister but also the young man Jang Song-thaek would remember his generosity from now on. Most important of all was the fact that his father had left him in charge of a task that as leader he had felt uncomfortable dealing with. This was a sign of trust, and another good sign that credibility was building between the two: not only as father and son but also as supreme leader and hopeful successor.

Kim Jong-il did not assure his little sister right away that all problems had been solved. Instead, he thought he had better first meet with the young man who had caused all these problems for his family. He summoned Jang Song-thaek to Pyongyang.

Kim Jong-il met his future brother-in-law at his own office. The reason he chose his office for the first time meeting was the outcome of meticulous consideration. He wanted to convey the message that even if he and Jang did become the closest of relatives, their relationship would not be that of the older brother with his younger sister's husband, but rather an official one of master and subordinate, and Jang's future would be assessed according to his loyalty to Kim Jong-il. The future Dear Leader's affection for his little sister did not automatically extend to her husband, as well.

Upon their first meeting, Kim Jong-il made a positive assessment of Jang Song-thaek. Jang was capable, so Kim judged that he could be a great asset. Jang was a useful talent in terms of Kim Jong-il's struggle to succeed his father, as well as to establish a new ruling order, different in his own way from his father's. However, he also thought the guy was a little too talented, and would need to be checked from time in order that he not become a problem.

For Jang Song-thaek, the road to meet the person who could become his brother-in-law was one half of hope and the other half of fear. His future prospects were bleak, but as he was summoned back to Pyongyang, he also hoped that the reason wasn't something bad.

"If it were bad news, wouldn't I have been dealt with right away there in Wonsan? Calling me all the way to Pyongyang, and that the Republic's crown prince wishes to meet me, isn't that good news?"

Yet still in one corner of his mind, there was suspicion of a different nature.

"What if the order is given to break off the relationship with Kim Kyong-hui and go to a place further away from Pyongyang, perhaps to a foreign country? They wouldn't frame me with a crime and execute me, would they?"

Meeting with Kim Jong-il suggested a turning point in his life. Already his relationship with Kim Kyong-hui was no longer the most important thing. Through their brief meeting, he could see what the regime crown prince, inured to the struggle for power, wanted from him.

"The relationship with the man's younger sister is but a superficial decoration. What matters from now on is the brother-in-law; no, the relationship with this ambitious man aiming toward supreme power. I must dedicate my loyalty to this man, and play the role that can win his heart."

That was the conclusion of the meeting.

Jang Song-thaek thought hard about his future.

"First, I will be reinstated at Kim Il-sung University. And at a suitable time, I will be able to marry Kim Kyong-hui. After graduation, I will work in a suitable position in the Party."

With the end of his exile in Wonsan, a new road opened for him. It wasn't bad. But he didn't feel light-hearted. On the contrary, he felt a heavy weight remaining.

As he came out of his meeting with Kim Jong-il, Jang couldn't get rid of the unpleasant feeling in his heart. It would not disappear. He wasn't so much marrying a woman as being forced into marriage with her. This marriage, strictly speaking, was not a voluntary one. He couldn't do anything the way he wanted to regarding this wedding; he simply wasn't in the position to do anything. He saw the freedom to both act and not to act as equally important, yet here he had lost both.

However, he didn't have the leisure to think deeply about such things. Everything depended on decisions made above. In even the most private matter of dating and marrying, the Republic, or rather the shadow of the Great Leader, who is the Republic itself, was cast over him just as it was over all North Korean residents, albeit perhaps a couple of shades darker over him.

That wasn't all. Just as with his marriage, Jang had no power whatsoever to decide for himself the terms of his entry into public life, including his position in public service. Everything had to be decided under the watch of the Great Leader. His career and public duties could be performed only under the General; only through his wife Kim Kyong-hui could he overcome the limits of his social standing and be recognized as a member of the core class. In short, he was being positioned and played, like a knight on a giant chess board.

The harder he tried to erase the thought from his heart, the louder he heard the internal whisper of a proverb known to all Koreans: "If a man had three bags of unhulled barley, he wouldn't live with his in-laws."

That is to say, he was married into an incredible household and lived depending on the whims of his wife's parents. Jang knew well that his life was lived on the tightrope between North Korean social classes, and he could not help but feel unstable and in flux. Whether he was promoted or demoted, became stronger or weaker, inevitably the sands beneath his feet would always be shifting. The system that he served with all his might brought him power and many benefits, but he also became more sensitive and aware of the system's deficiencies and inconsistencies than almost anybody else.

Foreign personnel saw Jang as someone with a different perspective from other typical North Korean officials. He was known to pay an unusual degree of attention to the reform and opening of the motionless North Korean regime.

Jang Song-thaek returned to Kim Il-sung University, and in due course he graduated. Shortly thereafter he left the country with Kim Kyong-hui to study at Moscow State University.

Kim Jong-il decided that the circumstances were not right for him to keep the two by his side. His father was in his own way still dissatisfied with his son-in-law, and he still lacked the status or power to demand that the new family member stay in Pyongyang to be utilized as Kim wished. He thought it would be better to keep his future good horse out of the picture temporarily. Thus, the couple left for the USSR.

Looking back, those days of student exile in the Soviet Union would turn out to be the happiest time of the couple's lives. They lived on the third floor of an apartment building on 85 Vavilova Street. The apartment belonged to the DPRK Embassy in the USSR and was only a ten-minute walk from the university.[3] The shadows of the Great Marshal and the Dear General were cast here also, but much more lightly than at home.

DPRK–USSR relations were sharply improving thanks to a summit meeting between Kim Il-sung and Leonid Brezhnev in Vladivostok in May, 1966. There had been a period of friction following Nikita Khrushchev's "secret speech" criticizing Stalin, which had surprised not only the Communist bloc but the whole world. However, after the appearance of Brezhnev in 1964, the two countries' relations gradually recovered. Oppression was building again as a counter to the somewhat freer, mildly thawed atmosphere of the Khrushchev era.

Despite the clampdown, Russian dissident intellectuals struggled more fiercely, and underground press materials circulated. In the late 1960s, Aleksandr Solzhenitsyn's *One Day in the Life of Ivan Denisovich*, *Cancer Ward*, and *In the First Circle* were all published overseas. Solzhenitsyn received the Nobel Prize for Literature in 1970. The Soviet Union government oppressed free-thinking intellectuals in many different ways, and had a policy of permitting them to leave the country and then cancelling their citizenship. As a result, authors Solzhenitsyn, Vladimir Voinovich, Vassily Aksyonov, Andrei Sinyavsky, cellist Mstislav Rostropovich, and biologist Zhores Medvedev were all either deported or banished. In 1966, when Yuli Daniel and Andrei Sinyavsky were found guilty of publishing works abroad, many people opposed the sentence and petitioned for it to be commuted. Five citizens arrested for protesting in Red Square over the invasion of Czechoslovakia in 1968 received four- to five-year sentences.

Although it was a reactionary time, the USSR was a much more plural, free society than the DPRK, and living there affected the couple immensely. The gap between the North Korean regime that they had internalized became a dichotomy deep in their consciousnesses, especially for Jang, albeit that there was no real change in their basic belief in Socialism. And besides, all of this was secondary on the road to power.

Even in Moscow, daily necessities were always in short supply. Food, alcoholic beverages, cigarettes, and clothes: the couple could not easily afford any of them. Particularly, imported goods preferred by Russians were hard to procure. However, the two received good care from the North Korean embassy and lived without feeling any serious material shortages. Thanks also to the embassy, the couple both had diplomatic status, so they could go to Beriozka, a chain of stores that sold goods for hard currency, and other special stores used only by the Communist Party officials and privileged others.

Yet that did not mean they could always buy what they wanted, because the standard of living in the USSR was far behind that of Western countries. But the young couple, liberated from the North Korean authorities, actually lived happily despite the shortages. In later years, Kim Kyong-hui would remember this period fondly, saying how thrilled she was when she managed to get hold of things that were hard to obtain. Consumer goods were overflowing when the couple returned to Pyongyang, and Kim Kyong-hui said that the thrill disappeared.

Although the couple was in the USSR to study, the academic course was actually superficial. They did study the Russian language seriously, even hiring a private tutor. The person who helped Kim Kyong-hui at this time with both her Russian and in various ways with ordinary daily life was Pak Sung-ok, a student of Moscow State Medical University. Pak was the fiancee of Hwang Jang-yop, who was also in Moscow to study. Thanks to her friendship with Kim Kyong-hui, Pak received many favors after her return to Pyongyang, especially after she was selected to be the private tutor of Kim Jong-il's daughter, Sol-song.[4]

Kim Kyong-hui and Jang Song-thaek enjoyed some free time of their own without being noticed by the public. Around this period,

Kim Kyong-hui was like a good housewife. She took the utmost care to go shopping and prepare meals for the man she loved, with whom she was finally together after all sorts of difficulties.

Jang Song-thaek especially liked steamed beaten eggs and cheese. The couple both appreciated good wine. They both drank heavily, from Georgian wine to vodka and brandy to champagne. These were also not easily procurable items for the ordinary public.

The couple also enjoyed a wide range of cultural events, in which Moscow took great pride. One of the good things about the Soviet Union was that high culture was open to the general public. Opera, ballet, classical music concerts, the like of which only a small portion of the upper class could enjoy in Capitalist countries, was offered inexpensively so the majority of the public could also benefit from the performances. Moscow took pride in the high standard of these cultural events, which did not fall short of any other country in the West.

Whenever they had the opportunity, the couple went to see ballets and operas, as well as circus shows and ice skating. The couple both had an eye for song and dance, and so the high cultural life of Moscow was an unforgettable memory.

Compared to the cultural standards of Moscow, the entertainment of Pyongyang is third or fourth rate, and drenched in political propaganda. Kim Kyong-hui would often say so out loud, exhibiting no fear but leaving Jang Song-thaek in a panic by her side.

* * *

In later years Kim Kyong-hui would cause scandalous rumors due to her extramarital affairs. There was an aspect to the scandal that couldn't be brushed off as a married woman's fling, or as a simple act of revenge for a husband's affairs. One of her extramarital companions was a winner of the Tchaikovsky International Music Competition, her private music tutor, Kim Song-ho. Music first played a huge part in shared understanding and feelings between the two. It could be compared to young Kim Kyong-hui falling for Jang Song-thaek, himself a talented accordion player and a good singer and danger.

The couple enjoyed a free and easy life far from the frustrations of Pyongyang, but Jang's position was inevitably different to that of Kim Kyong-hui. Wherever Jang went, he was the Great Leader's son-in-law and the husband of the Great Marshal's daughter, rather than himself.

Koreans, especially Korean men, have a tendency to look at men married into wealthy families with complex feelings of envy and mockery in equal measure. The North Koreans the couple met in Moscow avoided showing any such attitude in front of Jang or Kim. However, among close friends, one can imagine what stories might have been shared. But what mattered in the end was not what other people thought, but what was on Jang's own mind. Jang couldn't help greeting people differently than his wife. At times, he had to pay the utmost attention even to small matters.

Once the couple was returning home from a performance of the Bolshoi's longest running ballet, *Swan Lake*. They were familiar with the production as they had seen the ballet on several previous occasions, but that day's staging was particularly moving. The interpretation of the work, the stage art, choreography, and everything else seemed outstanding. Most of all, the star dancer of the evening, the prima donna was a sensation. After the curtain call, the audience cheered and applauded for a long time. On their way home, the two talked hurriedly about the performance, unable to calm their emotions.

In the midst of it, Jang Song-thaek blurted out that North Korea's cultural performances still do not reach an international standard, and at least for that one reason more active international exchanges were required. It was a trivial comment made without much thought, but Kim Kyong-hui passionately agreed with it and, taking it one step further, she even said that North Korea's performances were too unsophisticated and obsessed only with the collective.

Afterwards, whenever she'd meet an embassy employee, or someone from Pyongyang, she'd repeat this. And each time, Jang Song-thaek felt as though he was having a heart attack. "How would these words be conveyed? Wouldn't words circulate in connection with the *Sea of Blood*, the North Korean opera Kim Jong-il was then painstakingly producing?" He tried to close down the situation by adding, "Each country has its own tastes and methods, yes?"

Back at home, Jang Song-thaek firmly advised Kim Kyong-hui that her words were likely to be misunderstood. Still, Kim Kyong-hui kept on making similar remarks. Whenever he was alone, or when he awoke in the middle of the night, Jang would ponder "Who am I? What am I doing right now? What will be my fate?"

Around this time, Jang Song-thaek by chance came to borrow a copy of French writer Stendhal's *Le Rouge et Le Noir* from a South Korean expatriate. The main character of the novel is Julien Sorel, highly able yet of an impoverished family background, who is hired as a private tutor by an affluent upper-class household. He tries hard to climb the ladder by marrying his employer's daughter, but in the end, he is ruined and is sentenced to death. It was only a novel, but Jang Song-thaek couldn't help thinking of his own situation. "Aren't my circumstances similar to those of this novel's protagonist?" "Is the fate that awaits me the same one that befell Julien Sorel?" The answer was always the same.

There was one more vulnerability, too. Jang always knew that his family background could be lethal to him. So he never spoke of it to anyone, not even to his wife. But when he was alone, he'd recollect the memories of his childhood, his parents, and his brothers. And he determined that he ought to become successful, look after his peers, and gain more power.

While Jang Song-thaek and Kim Kyong-hui were living a non-newly-wed-like life, and a non-student-like life in Moscow, Kim Jong-il was waging a brilliant struggle in Pyongyang.

Inspired by Vietnam, Kim Il-sung thought he could stir a revolutionary movement in the South. However, the idea that North Korea could be the base of revolution that would help revolutionary forces in the South to achieve a great uprising was only the source of sacrifice, and failure. The series of Special Forces operations to infiltrate the South in particular, which began in early 1968, all vanished into thin air and achieved practically nothing. The Revolution Project targeting the South was a failure.

Other Socialist countries made clearer assessments than North Korea itself. "There is not a single organized revolutionary group that can properly influence the South Korean public." Vietnam's revolutionary tactics did not work on the Korean peninsula.[5]

The result was the sacrifice of innocent young lives, as well as helping to reinforce the anti-Communist government system in the South and buttress the authoritarian South Korean government's legitimacy by encouraging anti-North sentiment. Within the North Korean regime, this failure was closed with the criticism and firing of a few high-ranking military officers.

However, the actual crisis of the North Korean system lay in its economy, which had boasted of active growth for some time but began to gradually reveal its limits from the 1960s. The seven-year plan launched in 1961 and the six-year plan that began in 1971 both ran into setbacks. From the 1970s, the North Korean economy was hamstrung by the fundamental limits of its state-mobilization system, around which the walls gradually began to thicken. Externalities like the oil crisis and the fall in prices of North Korea's main exports impoverished the regime to the extent where it could not clear trade transactions due to shortages of foreign currency.

It was under those conditions that Kim Jong-il surpassed his competitors and solidified his position as successor. He went one step further, taking control of all power of the party and the government, finally rising to de-facto president, a person who even Kim Il-sung could not disregard.

The fact that Kim Jong-il was the Great Leader's son obviously played a huge part in his surge to power. Ironically, however, his father also turned out to be his ultimate competitor in obtaining power as well.

In the world of power, an unconcealed conflict inevitably exists between the current man in power and his successor. During his last year in office, Prime Minister Winston Churchill faced a fierce conflict under the surface with Anthony Eden, whom Churchill had groomed as his successor. This was the same when the power succession was between father and son. It was merely that the facts were hidden behind other phenomena.

In Kim Jong-il's case, he did not hastily rush out to the front until he reached the last stage of the power struggle to stand before his father. He dedicated his full loyalty to his father, and insisted the latter be absolutely worshipped to a standard that could rightly be called deification. He personally waited on his father hand and foot and saw to his every need. When Kim Il-sung started to feel it a burden to read reports due to his deteriorating eye sight, Kim Jong-il verbally read out all the important reports to his father. At each evening meal, he called his father's duty officer and had the latter report to him daily whether Kim Il-sung had eaten his meal, and what his health and mood were like.[6]

Kim Jong-il dedicated his filial duty and loyalty to his father, and at the same time seized all the levers of practical power. One by one, the key positions were filled with his own people. At least for the time being, he chose not to risk the opposition of his father (or his father's people) by making a loud entrance at official events. He had to praise his father by standing behind him, not in front, and only conduct activities that deified the national founder. A living god could not interfere in every single detail of daily life. Such things were naturally left to Kim Jong-il to take care of.

It was only in 1980 that Kim began to officially reveal himself. Then, upon the occasion of the 6th Congress of the Workers' Party, he was elected to the Standing Committee of the Politburo, secretary of the secretariat, and member of the central military commission.[7] He was the only man besides Kim Il-sung to hold seats at all the three tables: Politburo, Secretariat, and Central Military Commission. It was not historically common, but he had reached his goal of obtaining power in the present, not only in the future. A considerable portion of regime administration had fallen under Kim Jong-il's governance.

Not long afterwards his official title changed from "the Party Center" to "Dear Leader," and Kim Jong-il initiated his personality cult: to have the regime worship him as it had his father. Kim Il-sung's ability to rule gradually ebbed, and the father watched with pleasure and satisfaction—even sometimes with pride—at the trustworthy activities of his son, who managed everything from his personal safety to official matters. When the elderly founder finally realized the severity of the situation and attempted to make a move against Kim Jong-il, it was already too late.

The fate of Jang Song-thaek and Kim Kyong-hui, Kim Kyong-hui's passion and her love story with Jang, Jang's personal dilemma and political ambitions were all concluded within this frame of power relations.

Even as the North Korean regime failed to revolutionize the South or to develop economically, Kim Jong-il increasingly distinguished himself. Working first under his uncle Kim Yong-ju at the Organization and Guidance Department, he accompanied his father on visits to Indonesia. After his promotion to the central guidance department within the Organization and Guidance Department, he was in charge of maintaining a historic battle site, that of the Battle of Pochonbo.

The fields in which Kim Jong-il particularly stood out were cultural and ideological. North Korea's best known movies, *Sea of Blood* and *The Flower Girl*, were both produced on Kim Jong-il's orders. Upon the celebration of his father Kim Il-sung's 60th birthday, Kim Jong-il was put in charge of the construction of a new museum as well as erecting gigantic Kim Il-sung statues.

In terms of ideology, he developed the juche ideology into a new guidance philosophy for the whole republic: "Kimilsungism." The juche ideology, which originally derived from the need to stand against so-called "toadyism," or unconditional worship of the powerful, was part of North Korea's response to domestic and international criticism of Kim Il-sung after Stalin's death in the 1950s. However, this ideology of reliance on the self in national affairs was newly transformed under the orders of Kim Jong-il, becoming a monolithic ideology centered on the leader. The fulcrum of all historical development shifted from the people to the leader. Kimilsungism, a theory of succession, and the theory of the sociopolitical living body, all of which started to take shape in later years, were posited in the shape of theories, but in fact they were the discourse of the new government.[8]

At a time when the political prospects for a South Korean revolution and for economic development were looking bleak, culture and ideology were new sources of systemic vitality, and Kim Jong-il used them in a timely and formidable way. In the cultural sector, he took on the role of theorist and propaganda instigator in project planning, creation, production, and direction.

Academics describe this aspect of North Korean statecraft as the Theater State, borrowing a term coined by Clifford Geertz.[9] It can be seen as an attempt to realize political planning through psychological or cultural persuasion. However, even power decorated as persuasion through symbol and ceremony is futile without surveillance on a massive scale, to say nothing of political violence. As one security officer from the former-East Germany put it: "If there were no Siberia, there would be neither Marxism nor Leninism."

As Kim Jong-il started to receive praise for his active duties, his reputation evolved into that of someone who could be trusted in high positions. Before the 5th Party Congress in November 1970, there were discussions about recommending him as a candidate member of the Party Central Committee. The following year, Kim Yong-ju, citing reasons of personal health, recommended his nephew Kim Jong-il take his place as secretary in charge of organization. However, Kim Il-sung opposed these two suggestions, claiming it was too early.

When Kim Yong-ju retired in 1973 amid deteriorating health, Kim Jong-il became both organization secretary and propaganda secretary, simultaneousy holding the positions of director of the Organization and Guidance Department and the Propaganda and Agitation Department. The following year he was elected to the Party Political Commission at a meetng of the Party Central Committee, and from that time on came to be called "Party Center." He had solidified his seat as the successor.

The struggle with his stepmother, Kim Song-ae, wasn't easy. She had the heart of his father. And carrying that support on her back, she became chair of the central Women's League, and naturally became keenly interested in her own son Pyong-il's future. What is more, she was in a position to influence the succession. As for Kim Jong-il, the mere thought of having to share power with his half-brothers, much less having them stand in the way of his power, was unacceptable.

Still, Kim Song-ae had risen to the status of "Mother of Joseon." Before that time only two women had been called by that title. Kim Il-sung's mother, Kang Ban-sok, and his former wife (and Kim Jong-il's mother), Kim Jong-suk. Soon, Kim Song-ae's stature and influence in the North Korean media were on an almost identical footing to Kim Il-sung. With the rise of Kim Song-ae, her two sons and two daughters also became subjects of public interest. There were even rumors that father, Kim Il-sung, was thinking of handing down some of his power to them, as well.

First and foremost, Kim Jong-il had to separate his father from his stepmother. That led to the introduction of the peculiar organization hardly seen in the 20th century: the Pleasure Troupe.[10]

Kim Jong-il selected young, beautiful women from all around North Korea who could please men with their singing, musical talents, performances, massages, and even comedy monologues or magic shows, and had the women deployed to entertain his aging father. The department in charge of this task was Section 5 of the Organization and Guidance Department of the Central Party, or simply called Section 5. It was a pleasing thing for Kim Il-sung, but he couldn't personally see to the matter, so he was touched at the thoughtful filial piety of Kim Jong-il.

However, another aspect of this "filial piety" was Kim Song-ae. That wasn't all. While he placed beautiful women by his father and had him enjoy a little rest and rejuvenation in the winter of his life, Kim Jong-il continued to expand his practical governance. To his father, who felt all the more burdened to read documents, Kim Jong-il reported verbally and monopolized the direct reporting line. Then he seized actual power in the matter of checking his father's safety, health, personal security, censorship, party life instructions, and the authority to appoint (and lay off) government officials.

One particular episode illustrates the dynamics of power between father and son. In the late 1980s, Kim Il-sung and Kim Jong-il's orders on a co-education matter at one point contradicted each other. Kim Il-sung ordered co-ed schools to be prohibited and even ordered the punishment of professors who proposed the idea. However, Kim Jong-il gave the opposite order: that co-ed schools be permitted. Education Ministry officials and professors were at a loss. Finally, after much thought, they chose the rising power over the falling power. That is, they followed Kim Jong-il's orders.[11]

For scholastic assessment of students, Kim Il-sung ordered a ten-point grading system, whereas Kim Jong-il ordered a five-point grading system. Again, after much deliberation, the professors chose to follow Kim Jong-il's orders.[12] In the late 1980s, Kim Il-sung was already losing touch with reality and would give orders detached from the practicalities of ordinary lives. For instance, without considering the reality of malnutrition he would order exercises to help children grow, or that sweets and confectionery that were pie-in-the-sky fantasy to most ordinary North Koreans be promoted as part of daily life.[13]

Kim Jong-il investigated the corrupt acts power-intoxicated Kim Song-ae and her aides had committed, and reported the findings to his father. The most infamous was Kim Song-ae's brother Kim Song-gap, who had built a luxury home. Upon hearing that Kim Song-gap, the then-second secretary of the party committee of Pyongyang, was building a luxurious house for himself at a key real estate area in downtown Pyongyang, Kim Il-sung raged with fury.

After this incident, Kim Song-ae and her children became "side branches" of the ruling family. There was no force left to challenge Kim Jong-il as successor. His position now rock solid, Kim Jong-il called his younger sister and brother-in-law in Russia back to Pyongyang.

4

Kim Kyong-hui's Residence

A friend is someone who knows all about you and still loves you.

—Elbert Hubbard

In 1972, Jang Song-thaek and Kim Kyong-hui became officially husband and wife. The marriage did not receive universal blessing; in fact, plenty of people saw it as scandalous. It caused trouble right to the very end, and it demanded sacrifices. The fact that the family of Jang's brother-in-law was of the landlord class was one obstacle to the couple's union. The matter had to be solved by Jang himself: his elder sister and brother-in-law listened intently and made the necessary arrangements for their divorce.

Prior to the wedding, Jang Song-thaek pleaded with all his relatives to live extremely cautiously from then on, reminding them that joining the ruling family would be as risky as it was beneficial. "You must avoid doing anything that will stand out in the eyes of others," he said. "And if you run into any difficulty, please consult me first."

If he caused any trouble himself, there was no knowing what might befall his whole family.

A huge mansion was given to the newlywed couple. It was Villa No. 7, almost half an acre at the foot of Mt. Changgwang. The 2nd Guards Department was in charge of security. Of course, the house was the official residence of Kim Kyong-hui, not of Jang. Kim Jong-il also lived in a villa on the same mountain, as he started to live with Ko Yong-hui in 1979. The current North Korean leader, First Chairman Kim Jong-un and his siblings also spent their childhoods there.

These facts are not widely known, as the private lives of the Kim family were not (and to a large degree still are not) in the public domain. That may have been because of the thought that revealing their private life could harm the authority of the god-like leader. But that is insufficient by itself. The Japanese Imperial family was worshipped as living gods until the end of World War II, but the weddings or births of the imperial family were not kept a secret. The imperial family married and bore children and continued to be worshipped. The additional reason why the North Korean regime kept the Supreme Leader and his family's private life a taboo subject could be because the regime was a makeshift authority, which, unlike Japan, lacked traditional legitimacy. Or it could have been because the Kim family's private life did not quite comport with the (in name only) "Democratic People's Republic." Either way, ordinary people received severe punishment, and could even be taken away to forced labor camps, for even the briefest mention of the private life of the Kim family.

Anyway, after seven years of ups and downs, Kim and Jang finally became an official couple and settled in Pyongyang. However, Kim Il-sung had only barely given his blessing to the two, and against his will at that. He felt neither particular affection for, nor interest in, this son-in-law. The Jang couple existed thanks to Kim Jong-il, who was emerging as the new center of power. This was not a bad thing for Kim Jong-il. He had acquired a capable close aide who was completely unrelated to his father. The marriage also meant his sister Kyong-hui had to keep a certain distance from their father. Both Kim Jong-il's baby sister and this new fellow had left Kim Il-sung's side and were now beneath his wings.

As Kim Jong-il firmed up his status as the Party's Central Committee's Organizing Secretary, as well as the most likely successor to the current leader, Jang Song-thaek also got on to the fast track of a successful career. The very year that he got married, Jang was appointed to the Party Central Committee's 6th International Projects Division. Kim Kyong-hui also went to work at the 1st International Projects Division. It was to be expected.

But at the same time, the chapter in the love story of Kim Kyong-hui and Jang Song-thaek entitled "the good ol' days" was closing; their relationship was heading down an arduous road. Their romance passed from its pure and innocent stage and transformed to something much more complicated and worldly. If Kim Jong-il had truly hoped for his younger sister's happiness, he would have excluded either Jang or both Jang and Kim Kyong-hui from official posts. However, to Kim, Jang was mostly a close aide: a tool for his own power rather than the man his sister loved.

For his part, if Jang himself had wanted a happy married life, he should have stayed as far away as he could from power, even the shadow of power, just as he had in Moscow. The nature of the world of power is that once you set foot inside, you are bound to live strictly according to its logic and reason. It is no longer life for the sake of living but a constant cycle of fighting and killing and dying.

That was especially true in the case of the North Korean regime. You can enter the circle of power, but there is no exit. The way to exit is to die, or to be banished and put in a political prison camp, or maybe just maybe to take the dangerous road of asylum in a foreign country. Strictly speaking, there is no private life. There is not even the hope of retiring honorably and becoming a private citizen.

In the era of the ancient kingdoms, a man who married the daughter of a king or an emperor was on principle excluded from all official positions. The husband of a princess would on occasion receive level one or level two senior government status, but officially he wasn't permitted any political participation, except that, due to his high social standing, he could visit foreign countries as an envoy. Even in the Joseon era, a princess's spouse could lead delegations to ancient Chinese dynasties; however, he mostly played a symbolic role related to the reputation of the delegation, and did not interfere in the practical tasks at hand. Even in exceptional cases where the princess's husband played a genuine role behind the scenes, he could not formally present himself as having an official title. The reason for this was not only to prevent private relations from interfering with the order of official posts, but also out of a deeply thought-out principle aimed at bestowing a smooth married life on the couple. Similarly, in the case of the sons-in-law of wealthy families, unless the man's family was of comparably powerful status to the woman's, the relationship tended to be sensitive and insecure. Needless to say, it would have been more so for the husband of a princess.

Jang Song-thaek's in-laws were not to be compared to a super rich or royal family. They were far mightier: a de facto theocracy. Tragically, Jang could not treat his private life and the theocratic power system as two separate things. That was impossible. Just like Kim Jong-il, Jang also could not separate his marriage from the power system. Marrying the theocrat's daughter and the one and only sister of its successor meant he would always feel uneasy.

According to the peculiar circumstances of the North Korean theocracy, Kim Kyong-hui's stature could not be overlooked, except of course by Kim Il-sung and Kim Jong-il. People considered Jang Song-thaek to be the number two in the Kim Jong-il regime, but in truth it was Kim Kyong-hui more than Jang who occupied the second rung on the power ladder.

In late 2010, the penultimate year of Kim Jong-il's rule, Kim Kyong-hui was elected to the Politburo, while the military title of general was given to Choe Ryong-hae and First Deputy Director Kim Kyong-ok. Jang Song-thaek, however, was excluded. Even Ri Yong-ho, top commander of the Korean People's Army (KPA) became a permanent member of the Politiburo and first deputy chairman of the Party's Central Military Commission, but Jang remained only a candidate member of the Politiburo and a member of the Party Central Military Commission. Questions were raised over his stature as "the number two." At the time, one North Korean source remarked rhetorically, "Historically, has a princess' husband ever reached the number two seat?"[1]

Politics and power were not that important to Kim Kyong-hui. Only her happiness mattered. She could not understand why the happy married life that had been possible in Moscow could not continue in Pyongyang. Kim had little desire for power. She didn't even have the will to struggle to obtain greater power. Fortunately, as long as her older brother Kim Jong-il, the person closest to her, controlled all authority, she didn't need to be obsessed with power for the sake of her own security or influence.

Kim Kyong-hui was interested in two things: making money and interfering in personnel affairs. Again, for as long as her powerful and reliable older brother Kim Jong-il was in charge, she had nothing to worry about on either of those two scores. But upon the death of Kim Jong-il, everything changed. She realized what had kept her going was not her ability, but the power that her father and brother had maintained over the years. And that if this situation were to change, she would be incapacitated.

A few episodes illustrate the nature of Kim Kyong-hui's power. In the late 1990s, she was appointed to the Department of Light Industry, which is responsible for supplying ordinary daily necessities to the Korean People's Army. However, it wasn't Kim Kyong-hui who went to the department, but vice versa; the department office was moved to Kim Kyong-hui's office, a building with a separate garage, stairs, and elevator for her exclusive use. Ordinary employees could only see the car in which she came to work. They could not see how she entered her office.

In 2003, Kim Kyong-hui and Jang Song-thaek spent time in France. At the time, a problem occurred at the department. In theory, she, as director, would be subject to Organization and Guidance Department audit as a result, but departmental staff dispatched to the scene did not dare do it. Learning of the situation, Kim Kyong-hui immediately picked up the phone and demanded to speak to then-Organization and Guidance Department deputy director Ri Je-kang. When he picked up the phone at the other end, she just said, "Don't play petty games," and hung up on him. That was the end of the matter. When a relatively high official visited a provincial area on business, unless he was above the rank of first deputy director, the provincial party responsible secretary hardly ever hosted a dinner. A provincial party responsible secretary was that senior in rank. However, the exception to this rule was the first deputy director of the Department of Light Industry. Of course, this too was because of Kim Kyong-hui's existence.

At her department, Kim Kyong-hui only took care of the personnel and finance affairs, and left all the rest to the employees, hardly ever interfering in their work. Once, she set a limit on funds that the department could spend while she was away on business. However, first deputy director Kim Hui-thaek obtained permission from Kim Jong-il to spend about 200USD more, then replenished the amount prior to Kim Kyong-hui's return. Upon hearing the report after her return, she demoted Kim Hui-thaek with immediate effect.

All ministries and departments had a "handwritten order execution chart" confirming that Kim Jong-il's personal instructions were being executed. But after Kim Jong-il one day uttered, "Kim Kyong-hui is the same as me," a Kim Kyong-hui order execution chart appeared in the Department of Light Industry. At least within the department, Kim Kyong-hui's stature was the same as Kim Jong-il's. When Kim Jong-il made a special request to China and had a North Korean consulate opened in Hong Kong, the State Security and anti-South departments all wished to dispatch delegates there. However, only the Department of Light Industry was successful.[2]

The greatest difficulty for Jang Song-thaek in his relationship with his wife, Kim Kyong-hui, was that he could not differentiate her from the incredible power behind her. Kim Kyong-hui, before she was Jang's wife, was an axis of the great power that he was compelled to serve. Simple pleasures that could exist between a man and a woman were all linked to that power. When he might give her a small present or make an attempt to please her in other ways, he did so in the shadow of a lingering power. The same was true when they argued.

Kim Kyong-hui also faced difficulties. It isn't easy for a couple from different backgrounds to get married in the first place, but it is even harder for the two to harmonize their lives once married. Perhaps that is why most fairytales about a beautiful princess and a brave prince getting married end with the somewhat vague "they lived happily ever after." One of the biggest obstacles to a happy marriage is the external force that can intervene between the two. Fundamentally, a marriage is the successful outcome of a couple's close and continuous effort. If an outside force, such as an in-law, acts as a serious hindrance to the couple's union, the marriage often ends in separation.

As long as Jang actively sought power, right from the beginning it was impossible for his marriage to last happily in power's shadow. It is actually a wonder that the relationship of the two did not end in a complete rupture. It means that despite all kinds of tribulations from the outside world, there remained a protected realm known only to Jang and Kim.

What mattered most to Jang was not the romance of his private life. There is one paradox in a society where politics stands before everything else, and where the State's power is firmly fixed in all areas of human life: the only way to be free from power, even in the slightest, is to stay as close to it and as aware of it as possible. And so, Jang strove down the road of power, willingly devoting all his might and passion to the journey.

Jang's rise paralleled that of Kim Jong-il. He was appointed to the 6th Division, which was officially the Foreign Ministry department entrusted with policy instruction. In North Korea's socialist system, government organizations are directed by divisions of the party, which means that the head of the 6th Division actually has the power to inspect and censor the Foreign Ministry. The foreign minister at the time was Ho Dam, who was the husband of Kim Jong-suk, a Kim Il-sung's cousin. Minister Ho was an elite diplomat, a Moscow graduate who first became foreign minister in 1970. On many levels, Jang was no match for him. Nevertheless, it was common knowledge at the foreign ministry that Jang wielded far more influence than Minister Ho. The source of that power, of course, was Jang's relationship to the "rising sun" who controlled everything.

Jang Song-thaek read Kim Jong-il's intentions well, without needing direct verbal explanations. Jang understood why Kim Jong-il helped him with his marriage, and that he had been appointed to a successful career path for reasons that transcended simple brotherly love for the leader's younger sister. Jang's future already depended on how he served the rising power.

Jang had to take care of the things that the authoritative power wanted done, yet could not speak of. Together with Ho Dam, Jang enlarged and revised the "Pleasure Troupe," which was managed by the Organization and Instruction Department 5th Division, and had been limited to serving only Kim Il-sung, but now had been expanded to serve Kim Jong-il as well. Furthermore, he had "special pavilions" made for Kim Jong-il at all famous sightseeing spots throughout North Korea. Terminology such as "Mt. Ami materials"[3] came into being thanks to Jang.

After the mid-1970s, Jang became more ruthless in his actions. He mobilized the resources to build a luxurious facility known as the "aquarium" for Kim Jong-il's relaxation. The plan was to build a huge aquarium exhibiting all types of rare fish on the first floor, physiotherapy rooms, a gymnasium, massage equipment on the second the third floors, and a bedroom and a party hall on the fourth floor.

Under Jang's supervision, construction of this huge project was carried out in complete secrecy—a feat which would be next to impossible in any other country but North Korea. The people mobilized for the construction were party officials and diplomats. In particular, foreign ministry employees working at headquarters and diplomats returning from overseas to wait for new assignments were called to the construction. Jang Song-thaek directly ordered the diplomats and officials overseas to supply the required materials. Occasionally he would go abroad personally and micromanage the purchases. Italian marble, high-end Northern European furniture, and luxury chandeliers were brought into Pyongyang one after another. The nature of the project was not easy to justify to outsiders.

However, from the logic of those inside North Korea, it was more than a matter of individual extravagance. It was a tool to engrave the absolute demi-god authority of the supreme leader to the general public, as well as to the people in the core class of the regime. If the small tools to maintain this authoritative power were Rolex watches, and Mercedes-Benz cars, the extravagant buildings or statues were its stage, decoration, and mechanism.

While the writer was serving in London, there was a period when North Korean personnel were invited to participate in projects and exchanges with the United Kingdom. One British government representative who had guided the North Korean visitors confessed a shocking experience. During a tour of Buckingham Palace, members of the North Korean delegation sneered, saying, "This (small place) is where the Queen of the Great British Empire lives?" "(Come to North Korea and) take a look at our Marshal's palace." The British guide was bewildered, thinking "How can people from a country that asks other nations for food aid say such things?" He obviously did not understand the meaning of stage mechanisms for the maintainance of theocratic power. The author explained, but he did not seem to get it.

Once, the writer provided an opportunity for some young North Koreans to study abroad. Upon asking them which major they would most prefer to read, it was interesting to hear them answer, "Architecture." Considering the outdated North Korean economy, you might imagine their reply to be Agriculture, or Business Management, or Finance, or Science and Engineering. In North Korea, however, power and majestic architecture were historically inseparable. For an analogy, consider the ancient relics of Luxor, or the Forbidden City in Beijing. "Architecture is a physical manifestation of politics. It is literally power made of bricks and mortar."[4]

Moreover, theocracy requires not only a doctrine, but a shrine that is visible to the naked eye. As secular as the North Korean theocracy was, there needed to be a shrine that could inspire awe among ordinary secular citizens. When people see structures that they are incapable of imagining, they sense the stature of the powerful. The duty of Jang Song-thaek was to prepare those structures for the rising power.

The "aquarium" project hints at a deeper political meaning. The project consumed phenomenal resources and the manual labor of hundreds of over-qualified individuals working day and night, yet it ended in a major disaster.

In the spring of 1978, only minor tasks for the project remained. But then one day at dawn, a great fire broke out on the first floor, burning the whole structure down and taking the lives of Party officials and diplomats who were inside either sleeping or doing odd jobs. Someone had tried to light a cigarette near highly flammable paint and paint thinners, the fumes of which were thick in the air. The diplomats who were sleeping on the ground floor all died. Those who had fallen sleep after working all night on the upper floors ran from the blaze, but many fell from the windows and lost their lives as well. Each floor of the building was much higher than those of an ordinary building, so even the third or fourth floor was the equivalent height of the seventh or eighth floor of a standard building.

As many as 130 people died in the accident. It was obviously a problem that a building that had absorbed so much material investment and human effort had burned down, but the far more serious issue was that the victims were Party officials and foreign ministry employees. In the case of the Foreign Ministry, as much as ten percent of the workforce was killed overnight

To make matters worse, the project itself had been a secret and nobody was allowed to discuss it. The surviving families of deceased diplomats and Party officials heard the news, and tried to learn what had happened, but were stonewalled. In the end, Kim Jong-il and Jang Song-thaek vaguely explained to the families that the deceased died in an accident while working on a project of great importance for the fatherland. They closed the case by conferring posthumous medals upon them. The families naturally could not demand government responsibility, nor get any explanation of the project or what had caused the accident. They simply had no other choice but to take their socialist honors and let the incident go.

Jang Song-thaek was not questioned over his responsibility, nor was he punished. He did say that he would take responsibility, but Kim Jong-il closed everything, saying, "Accidents can happen, and there is nothing we can do about them, so don't mention it again."[5]

However, this accident was not an unfortunate random case that "can happen." From the very start it was a dubious idea to mobilize diplomats, who are far from expert in construction or manual labor, to undertake a secretive building project. Making matters worse, the process of the work was rushed through at reckless speed, so it is more accurate to say that the accident was entirely foreseeable rather than purely incidental. But just as the project itself was a matter of *politics* and *power*, the post settlement was also finalized in political terms according to the logic of the *powerful*.

At the launch of a new authority, whether intended or not, there has to be a sacrifice placed on the altar. The more magnificent the beginning of a new power, the greater the number of its victims. North Korea suffered an immense loss of the country's elite.

The KPA engineering battalion was dispatched to the site and all that remained was blown up and cleared away. On the plot of land, Pyongyang First Middle- and High-School was built. The victims were forgotten along with the mammoth project. Only the small number of people who knew the truth of the disaster recall the brutally sacrificed victims whenever they pass in front of the school building, and they have to console their aching hearts.

The incident cemented Jang Song-thaek's role at Kim Jong-il's right hand. His job was to read Kim Jong-il's mind and to complete tasks in advance at his own judgment, which the latter would find difficult to ask for by giving actual orders. In other words, his role was to bridge the official power structure with the leader's private realm.

As if to make up for the fire disaster, Jang Song-thaek ordered the North Korean embassies and consulates abroad to prepare "a thoughtful present." The items were foreign currency, or each country's indigenous products. Danish dairy products and smoked meats, Black Sea caviar; French wine, cognac, lobsters, foiegras, and so forth.

This was an extremely troublesome task for the diplomatic outposts, which were struggling to even meet maintenance costs due to the unfunded mandates handed down, to say nothing of conducting their core diplomatic activities. Still, no complaints were made, for Kim Jong-il's health was tantamount to the Republic's security, and Kim Jong-il's pleasure was the people's pleasure. This was an absolute proposition which no one could question or dream of opposing.

Around this time, the international media started to report on the alleged involvement of North Korean diplomats in illegal activities. In 1976, North Korean ambassador to Sweden Kil Jae-gyong was targeted in a police crackdown on narcotics smuggling and consequently kicked out of the country.[6] However, once back in the fatherland, he did not receive any punishment. For what one does for Kim Jong-il is a deed for the nation, and for the revolution.

With all his active initiatives of the period, Jang Song-thaek won the favor of Kim Jong-il. In the early 1980s, he was promoted to the deputy director of the youth projects department of the Party Central Committee. Back then, the youth projects department was in charge of the Socialist Workers Youth League, and it was like a pool of talented personnel, raising the future state, military, and party officials. Kim Jong-il called the place "the party officials' reservoir." It was at this time that Jang Song-thaek came to first meet Choe Ryong-hae, the Party's secretary in charge of the work groups, and grew close to him.

While Jang Song-thaek was busy climbing up the ladder, his family life was heading in the opposite direction. The straightforward cause of the first crisis was Kim Jong-il's Pleasure Troupe parties. These parties are frequently cited as a symbol of Kim Jong-il's descent into depravity as he consolidated power. So, in the South and other foreign countries, the "Pleasure Troupe" is mentioned as a mere grotesque curiosity.

Certainly, the evening parties were in dubious taste, but enjoyment wasn't their only purpose. They were an important tool for managing power. Spending a good time with officials responsible for key roles within the regime in a carefree manner (at least superficially), laying down one's shield and personal control, was an inexpensive way for the new face in power, Kim Jong-il, to build a sense of solidarity and trust with them, as well as a good opportunity to observe their true natures.

Stalin also enjoyed similar events. Former South Korean President Park Chung-hee is also known to have entertained himself with private, secret parties. In Kim Jong-il's case, the only difference was the grandeur of the events.

Kim Jong-il first created the Pleasure Troupe as he started to consolidate his position as successor. His excuse at the time was the wish to provide pleasure to his father, who had earned the right to enjoy the "Pleasure Troupe." Kim Il-sung thought his son's decision was commendable, and praised Kim Jong-il publicly for it. "Indeed, it's only the Organizing Secretary (Kim Jong-il) who truly thinks of me."

At first the Pleasure Troupe was limited to entertainment performances and services like massages, comic monologues, singing Korean traditional chang while plucking the strings of the gayageum, magicians, choir groups and so forth. However, from the late 1970s when Kim Jong-il's power took root, the size of the organization and its output greatly increased. A party organization was officially mobilized and prepared these peculiar events throughout the whole country.

The instructors of the 5th Division and of its subordinate departments in each provincial party committee selected and managed classical-looking teenage girls from middle school age. A few years later, when about to enter university, they would be admitted to professional education institutes according to the functions they were assigned, which included cooking, medical care, massage, dance, music, acting, and other services for men. There, the young women were once again strictly trained and went through another selection process to finally earn the honor to serve at Kim Jong-il's evening parties.

This enlarged Pleasure Troupe was organized to serve mainly Kim Jong-il. And here lay the very role of his close right-hand man, Jang. Even as the supreme leader exerts his mighty power, there are things he cannot order directly or take care of with his own hands. It was Kim Jong-il who actually organized the Pleasure Troupe that Kim Il-sung secretly wished for, and had the women serve the old founder. And likewise, it was the successor's confidant, who led the way to organize and run a new Pleasure Troupe that Kim Jong-il secretly wanted. And it was then-vice premier and foreign minister Ho Dam, along with Jang Song-thaek, who played that role.[7] The officials who were frequently invited to these parties were in key positions within the new power system, playing important roles for Kim Jong-il.

From the KPA, O Jin-u, Jo Myong-rok, Kim Yong-chun, O Kuk-ryol, and Hyon Chol-hae were all regular attendees. Among Party and governing officials, Foreign Minister Ho Dam and Secretary Kim Yong-sun, Vice Premier Kang Sok-ju, Kwon Hui-kyong, Kim Kuk-tae, Kim Ki-nam, Kye Ung-tae, Choe Tae-bok, and Yon Hyong-muk always participated. And as for others, there were the Party's Organization and Guidance Department's First Deputy Director Ri Je-kang, and Kim Yang-gon, Ri Yong-mu, Chon Byong-ho, and Chu Sang-song, who showed their faces from time to time.

Kim Jong-il usually ended his work on Friday mornings. On weekends, he enjoyed fishing and hunting with his close personnel, and at night he luxuriated in sumptuous banquets—the famous dinners of drinking and dancing.

The invitees arrived to the all-night parties at Kim Jong-il's villa in Mercedes-Benz luxury cars with the special plate numbers bestowed by the Dear Leader: numbers like 216-9999, 216-7777, and 216-5555. The first three digits, 216, derived from Kim Jong-il's birthday, which is February 16, and the odd numbers 5, 7, 9 were simply his favorite numbers.

In the late 1970s and early 1980s, the parties became settled as the new power Kim Jong-il's events. The dinner parties overflowed with alcohol, money, and beautiful women. Participants could not avoid getting drunk.

"Placed in front of Kim Jong-il, seated at the dinner table, there were always four or five bundles of ten thousand US dollars in cash. . . . Kim Jong-il used to push us. 'Any who has the courage come up to me and drink! I'll give a hundred dollars to anyone who'll drink bottoms up.' Until the second or third glass, the officials from the top in turn come up to Kim Jong-il and drink, but after more drinks than that their legs become wobbly and they find it difficult to remain sober. Then this time Kim Jong-il designates people. "Fujimoto! Aren't *you* drinking?" If one's name is called out in the manner, one cannot help standing up."[8]

> At these parties, Jang Song-thaek's role is organization and party planner, projector and master of ceremony. Could he be the equivalent of South Korean corporations' so-called director of drinking[9]? Jang boosted the party atmosphere, and offering drinks to people, he'd swear loyalty to the "Dear General." He himself would drink before the party even began, and he couldn't sit at the dinner table unless he had a drink. Before the start of the dinner party, Jang Song-thaek would ask the waiter to pour wine at the entrance, and he would first drink down a glass. Then, he made others drink before entering the banquet.[10]

After half an hour or forty minutes into the dinner party, Jang Song-thaek stood up and gave an order out loud: "Fall in in front of the Dear General!"

Then about ten officials would come out to the front at a time. Jang cried out once again. "Salute!"

The salute would be followed by a toast and long life.

"To the Dear General!"

"Long live the Dear General!"

And this would go on seven or eight times. And each time, Kim's men had to pour down a shot of 100 ml if it was cognac, and of 220 ml if it was wine.[11]

For Kim Kyong-hui, this was impossible to ignore. It wasn't simply a question of jealousy at her spouse's affairs with other women. Kim Kyong-hui could not stand the fact that the man she loved was so denigrated to the level of servant at such a depraved event.[12]

Any authoritarian power can seem majestic and rapturous from the outside, with its various decorations and its superficial image. What's more, when it overlaps with dignity and moral authority, it can also emit a sense of coercion and, on occasions, even pious respect. However, the closer one approaches into the inner circle of any power, especially one so closed and authoritarian, one discovers its nonsensical, foul aspect.

Ever since she was a young child, Kim Kyong-hui grew up seeing the absurdity of all of nature living at the center of the regime's power. Unlike the ordinary public, who were innocent (or forced to be innocent), she could not be compelled to feel awe for the authoritative power, or be unilaterally persuaded of its value. She had once stood strongly against the orders of her father, the Great Leader, for trying to separate her from the man she loved, and she had held to her beliefs. Behind the scenes lay an awareness of the vain reality inside the power of the state.

As these dinner party events became a routine, the couple's relationship started to break apart. At first Kim Kyong-hui complained to her husband, and tried to gently persuade him not to attend the events. She said that even if he were helping her own brother, he should not participate in those parties. However, the answer she got was exactly what she had expected to hear. Absolute power was the absolute ground and alibi for everything he did.

Whatever he may be doing, wherever he was, in a situation where he could not leave the power circle, the only thing Jang could do was to follow the orders given from above. These words were not mere excuses. There is no real knowing to what degree the party invitees enjoyed the events: whether they pretended to enjoy themselves, or were filled with complicated feelings that they themselves could not define well. Not only Jang, but Kim Jong-il's party guests would have attended each with their own complicated feelings, such as motive, reward, pleasure, or fear. There was nothing to hate, but even if they might secretly not wish to attend, to turn down the invitation was not even thinkable.

Kim Jong-il sometimes excluded some members from the invitees list. Upon such an instance, those uninvited would tremble with fear of whether they had lost the trust of the Dear Leader, or whether they had done anything that might have upset him. The Central Party's Organization and Instruction Department's Deputy Director Kim Chang-son was someone who could not miss Kim Jong-il's dinner parties, yet he did not receive a single invitation for several months in early 2001. During that time, he and his whole family were perturbed, imagining all possibilities. Then one day he was summoned. Both Kim Chang-son and his wife burst into tears from relief, and they told the news to all their neighbors in the nearby apartments for officials.[13] Fujimoto Kenji, well-known as Kim Jong-il's chef confessed that he also did not receive Kim Jong-il's call, and the time between 1999 and 2000 that he stayed locked inside his apartment was like a living hell.

If there was somebody he liked at his dinner parties, Kim Jong-il would lift them off their feet and win their hearts by lavishing outrageous gifts on them, such as an imported luxury car. He was the playwright of this performance, and at the same time, the director and the only main actor. He would sit on a high chair, and watch the acting of the assisting actors and the background actors (the so-called extras), the Pleasure Troupe women. Reality to him, at least a part of it, was his own play.

The Pleasure Troupe parties were sometimes held outside Pyongyang at famous sightseeing places. During the day there were outdoor activities, such as hunting, fishing, foreign film screening, jet skiing, and boat parties. This at night would be drinking and dance parties accompanied by the Pleasure Troupe beauties and movie actresses.[14]

As the rising power's number one servant, Jang Song-thaek inevitably ceased to be Kim Kyong-hui's passion and love. First of all, it was difficult for the two to get time of their own. During the week, they were both busy at work. And on weekends, Jang Song-thaek was even busier due to Kim Jong-il's dinner parties; when he returned home at dawn, he'd be drunk as a lord and fall asleep immediately.

In despair, Kim Kyong-hui finally went to seek her brother and pleaded her situation. She strongly complained and also begged him to exclude her husband from the drinking.[15] Kim Jong-il's reaction strikingly differed from the last time Kyong-hui had asked for his help. He replied casually to his sister's earnest request. "It's not as if I'm doing it because I want to. If he doesn't like it, he can quit any time. I'll tell him to stop coming right from the very next event."

The Jang Song-thaek couple were not the only ones facing a marital crisis because of the Pleasure Troupe parties or the "Technical Secretaries" (the Pleasure Troupe women performing services such as "massages" allotted to Kim Jong-il's close officials).[16] One official's wife wrote of her dissatisfaction due to her husband attending the Pleasure Troupe parties and sent it to Kim Il-sung. The contents were of her regret and concerns regarding the lewd parties thrown by the Great Leader's would-be successor. What the poor woman was unaware of, however, was that by this time almost all documents addressed to Kim Il-sung went through Kim Jong-il's hands first. Kim Jong-il showed the letter to the official, and told him to take care of it himself. It is said that the man went home and shot his wife with a pistol.

Afterwards, the man was appointed to a key position as one of Kim Jong-il's confidants. He had two children: a boy and a girl, and the boy is said to be currently working at the Foreign Ministry. What memories those children might have about their parents, and what feelings they have about them after going through such a trauma, can only be left to the imagination.[17]

When Kim Jong-il told his sister that he wasn't holding the frequent dinner parties because he wanted to, it wasn't just an excuse. The Pleasure Troupe parties were not entirely for entertainment, nor just for human relations. The parties were surely a means that solidified Kim Jong-il's power and maintained it, but it also had a certain functional role.

In North Korea, where all reports and decisions are made only through the vertical channel, these parties became an opportunity for each department's decision-making personnel to exchange and adjust their views. It was a comfortable and soft atmosphere in which to coordinate policy. Separately, for Kim Jong-il it was also an opportunity to hear and understand the circumstances or background stories, which cannot be included in the official reports.[18] Of course, this was an excuse for the dinner parties, and was but a small circumstantial aspect.

In fact, Kim Jong-il did tell Jang Song-thaek that it would be all right even if he did not attend the Pleasure Troupe parties since Kyong-hui doesn't like it. However, Jang already knew far too well that this was not possible. He himself did not want to fall for these parties, but even if he earnestly wanted to abstain, he wouldn't be able to. Just as his relationship with Kyong-hui had started under the shadow of authoritative power, so it was also declining under that same shadow.

When it came to relations with women, Kim Jong-il was a typical Don Juan type. He couldn't overcome his constant desire to seek a new woman. Such a person was surely not equipped to understand how desperate his sister was. He may have enjoyed the problems rising between his sister and Jang Song-thaek with a peculiar sense of curiosity. Kim Jong-il maintained a fairly stable family life with Ko Yong-hui over a long period, but even he did not officially acknowledge her or formalize her as his wife.[19]

5

The Dark Side of Success

> What is the use of improving military morale and political reform when the ordinary people have starved.
>
> —Hong Sok-jung, *Hwang Jin-i*

In the 1980s, the South saw clashes between demonstrators, who filled the streets of major cities almost every day, and the police, who tried to stop them. At the same time, the economy was beginning to boom.

North Korea could not happily stand by and watch the South traverse the painful struggles of democratization. Inversely proportional to its spectacular pronouncements, the North Korean economy was in a downturn. The second 7-year plan, launched with the aim of taking "the Socialist economic foundation one step further by urging Self-reliance, Modernization and Science in the people's economy," ended in failure. The economic development plan announced at the 6th Party Congress came with astonishing numbers, but the reality was different. Miscalculations were cruelly exposed, especially in foreign trade, which remained at a standstill, then began to decrease.

What most affected people's lives was the food crisis. Actual crop yields reached only about half the plan. The situation was such that already in the early 1980s, the regime's vice president, Rim Chun-chu, sighed, "The people are starving right now," in front of visiting scholars from Yanbian in China. It was a statement that foretold the tragedy of the great famine that would occur a decade later.[1]

On the other hand, for Kim Jong-il this period lifted his power one step higher. He moved beyond being simply the "successor" to entering the era of co-leadership with Kim Il-sung. Under that shadow, Jang Song-thaek continued his successful career.

That is not to say that Jang was on a straight road to success. Like most people, Jang faced a number of difficult moments.

First, his marriage was cooling. The main reason was Kim Kyong-hui's disappointment and disgust toward her husband. But for Jang it was an inevitable situation. He just thought "que sera, sera." At some point, he couldn't recall when, the couple started using separate bedrooms. They hardly ate or spoke together. They were effectively separated.

Naturally, rumors about the couple began to spread. As the tales went from mouth to ear, over and over, they would diversify and become darker to suit the tastes of the whisperer. The stories were like living organisms; they grew and multiplied depending on how widely they spread. In North Korea, where there is no free or independent press, rumors are guaranteed to flourish in the darkness.

Certainly, rumors about the two spiced up the leisure time of some Pyongyang residents for a while. But what was noteworthy was how, even in difficult times, the couple's relationship did not end, but instead retained a sense of affection which could be revived given the opportunity. Exterior conditions would have played a role here.

Ultimately, there was a zone of greater understanding and mutual feelings between the two that others were unaware of. In assessing the success of a relationship, rather than when all is smooth and fine, it is important to look for the consistent will to revive it when faced with difficulties, conflicts, and deviations. The marriage of Kim Kyong-hui and Jang Song-thaek was made difficult by the colossal power lurking in the background, but it nonetheless endured. That fact in particular, along with Jang's ultimate fate, made the couple's love story all the more tragic.

Jang Song-thaek was becoming successful, entering the golden age of his life. That was true in both the official and private sense. Jang's duty as the deputy director of the Central Party department dealing with youth projects suited his aptitude and abilities, and thus he engaged in the work with passion. It felt rewarding.

Yet, in another regard, this was also when he started to feel conflicted and doubtful of the regime he was serving. And for the first time, he personally experienced the threat the regime could bring to bear on him.

The Youth Project Department was the policy and instruction section in charge of implementing the Party's instructions for the Youth League. Today it is an independent work group department within the Party in charge of four mass organizations (the Democratic Youth League of North Korea, the North Korean General Federation of Workers Unions, the North Korean Federation of Farmers' Associations, and the Democratic Women's Union of North Korea), but at that time it was affiliated with the Organization and Guidance Department as part of its youth projects division. Youths from age 14 to 30 signed up, totaling about five million at any one time. If you include rear preparation units made up of junior members aged 7 to 13, it amounts to one-third of the North Korean population. It was a political structure that came next to the Party, and played the role of a conveyer belt moving people of each class toward the Party and the Marshal through indoctrination.

Jang Song-thaek was promoted from the Central Party's assistant director to the deputy director of the Organization and Guidance Department's Youth Projects Division. Afterwards he continued to climb the ladder: in 1985, he became the first vice minister of the youth project division, and in 1987 vice minister of the newly formed Three Great Revolutions Team Movement. Finally, in the late 1980s he even became the minister of the merged Youth and Three Great Revolutions Team Movement Project Department. In short, ten or so years of the golden period of his life were spent on the youth project.

To outside observers, the North Korean regime of this period was already starting to show signs of stagnation, or at least regression. However, the actual crisis had not yet started. Within the regime, the authorities were about to try and overcome their various difficulties using mass mobilization.

In particular, the role of the youth movement was much anticipated. Jang Song-thaek, with his inate talent for organization and leadership, and more significantly as a member of the sacred ruling family, performed brilliantly. He made a good number of achievements mobilizing the youth league's to full capacity and placing the work force into policy projects such as the pipe water construction project, which was the state's main interest at the time. Placed at the front the Speed Battle Youth Raiders, a new permanent organization of 100,000, Jang played the leading role in the State's major constructions, namely the numerous construction projects of the capital, Pyongyang, and the construction of the northern inner-line railway.

The various construction projects for the 1989 13th World Festival of Youth and Students was of the utmost importance. One could say the regime had put its destiny on the line. Certainly, the fate and legitimacy of the whole regime was on the table. The background for the construction was the Seoul Olympic Games, which had been hosted the previous year by South Korea.

The two Koreas had been linked together by an invisible bond since the division. If an important event occurred on one side, the other side had to show an equivalent response.[2] The great work of one side became the failure of the other. Likewise, the failure of one side automatically became the success of the other.

Because of this unique binary relationship, the news that a summer Olympiad was going to be held in South Korea would have been received by the Kim Il-sung regime as a threat to its legitimacy. What's more, the games were to be attended by North Korea's closest allies: the USSR and the People's Republic of China, and all Socialist countries with the exception of Cuba.

Seeing how the North Korean regime even committed acts of terror by trying to interrupt preparations for the Games, one can fathom how great a problem the Kim Il-sung regime thought it was. Two terrorists sent by the North successfully bombed a South Korean passenger jet, but one of the two terrorists was caught alive and the whole plot was exposed. And as a result, far from leading to the suspension of the Games, the North only came to be stigmatized as a state sponsor of terrorism by the international community. Inter-Korean efforts aimed at a possible co-hosting of the games also vanished into thin air.

The North Korean regime had to quickly tackle the matter. That is how it came to host the World Festival of Youth and Students despite all the difficulties it already faced. And Jang Song-thaek—remarkably—completed his demanding tasks.

North Korea was unprepared to host such a major international event. First of all, it didn't have enough money, so they had to take financial risks. Moreover, it lacked both the experience and capacity to hold a multi-national event on a huge scale. In particular, they were self-conscious that the images of Pyongyang reaching the eyes of foreigners would inevitably be compared to those of Seoul, from the hotels to the restaurants to all the other facilities. The following is a recollection from Song Hye-rang, the older sister of Song Hye-rim, who enjoyed a life of extreme privilege as a member of Kim Jong-il's household at the time.

A huge port city like Wonsan was a complete black-out from there being no electricity. . . . So how on earth can one hold the 13th World Festival? Unless it's the 1988 Olympic Games! I felt wistful at the Party's intentions to compete with the latter. . . . How would they open doors to this city which doesn't have a single tea shop, not to mention even a single store. . . . In a trifling effort to try and hide our poverty to the people coming to this festival, (the citizens) took out their fanciest clothes in their wardrobe, and strolled around in front of the accommodations of the guests. Watching women dressed in bright colored hanbok, holding parasols of colors matching their traditional dresses, walk across the Ongnyu Bridge all day for several hours, hot tears of sorrow streamed down my face.[3]

Jang Song-thaek conducted his work as a "speed battle," in the literal meaning of the word, encouraging the youths to "charge" and "charge" again. Naturally, various special considerations and support followed. His unique status as the Great Leader's son-in-law, and the successor's brother-in-law, also helped enormously.

However, Jang's innately humane character and his leadership are also said to have played a big part. Pressure alone is not enough to get young people to work hard. Jang Song-thaek took the initiative to lead them, and gave them a sense of achievement through encouragement and compensation. He sympathized with the construction site workers over their difficulties, and sometimes made them laugh with his playful jokes. The young workers quickly fell for his down-to-earth nature. His ability to draw people around him worked even on that occasion.

In the early 1980s, commanders of the Speed Battle Youth Chargers (mobilized for the northern inner railway construction between Kanggye and Manpo) got stuck on their way back from a Pyongyang meeting and were pinned back by flooded roads. Jang Song-thaek sent a helicopter to rescue them, something possible only for the most senior government officials. It was possible to do that because Jang sometimes made good use of his special status. Of course, from Jang's point of view, he couldn't have made such a decision without a decent heart that wanted to help people in dire straits. When they achieved something, he would throw a party, hand out gifts, and boost overall morale.

Rumors spread that the Jang-Kim marriage was in crisis, and that they were both having extramarital affairs, yet Kim Kyong-hui helped her husband with his work both openly and behind the scenes. Sometimes she would visit the site and encourage the workers. Thanks to these considerate gestures, she helped the young workers forget their hard work and feel rewarded for their tasks. For the youths who participated in these projects, these kindnesses remained an unforgettable memory.

As a reward for his exemplary work, Jang was appreciated by his father-in-law, who had hitherto not been satisfied with him, and that same year he received the title "Hard Working Hero" at the personal recommendation of Kim Jong-il on his birthday. Furthermore, upon his 70th birthday on April 15, 1992, Kim Il-sung awarded the republic's top medal, the Kim Il-sung Medal to both his daughter and his son-in-law.

This period was the most rewarding for Jang Song-thaek, but it was also the time when he first doubted the regime he was serving.

The 1989 World Festival of Youth and Students was somewhat successful insofar as it saved face for domestic purposes. However, Jang Song-thaek couldn't help doubting even that. All the while that he worked hard on it, in one corner of his mind he carried the question, "Must these kinds of projects be done despite all the sacrifices and risks that they bring?"

Jang Song-thaek frequently traveled overseas to order materials for the construction projects, or to buy the items that Kim Jong-il liked. For a time, he was called "Kim Jong-il on the road (overseas)" by North Koreans working abroad. Naturally he became well aware of what was happening outside of North Korea, more so than others. There was no need for anyone to say anything. The world was changing quickly, and vastly. Already China was changing to a totally different dimension from North Korea. The USSR and Eastern Europe was also feeling the historical winds of change.

The ideals of socialism no longer delivered inspiration to the public. Doubts about the command economy could be felt throughout the Socialist bloc. Moreover, the control of communist parties started to show signs of collapse from within. Even the people were different from the past. Struggles against party and ruler became fiercer.

More than a superficially visible struggle, passive negligence and the problems of labor strikes grew serious. Witty jokes and parodies played their part in a form of passive dissent. A single joke could lampoon the political art and all its theories.

Only North Korea remained the same as ever, and the reckless regime fell deeper into difficulties. Already, Jang was curious about the South. "How could a land I have only had negative images of all my life achieve such phenomenal development?"

That wasn't all. For someone who was well aware of the North Korean economic situation, he couldn't help but doubt whether the projects he was conducting were indeed the correct things to do. "At a time when the people's lives are becoming more destitute each day, should the State host an event such as the World Festival of Youth and Students?" and "Should burdensome construction projects go on for the festival only in order to save face in front of foreigners?"

In later years, the problems were revealed in stark detail, but because of his particular status, Jang Song-thaek had a unique prospect about the future of North Korea, which was different from even that of an ordinary senior government official. In short, Jang started to look at North Korean affairs not only from the Kim regime's view, but also from that of the people. To describe it in mildly exaggerated terms, he overcame the royals' view that only the safety of the king mattered and the peasants exist merely for the sake of their monarch. He started to look at reality from the public's view, and he was the one and only man who could say what he was thinking, though he borrowed the crutch of alcohol to be able to do so, and even those utterances were made during overseas trips, rather than within the republic.

After the 1988 Seoul Olympic Games, the South's status soared in the international arena. China, the USSR, and Eastern European Socialist states scrambled one after another to improve relations the South. Jang Song-thaek already foresaw what was coming.

"If things carry on this way, North Korea will become isolated from the international community and be all alone!"

Around that time, Jang was on friendly terms with a senior Chinese government official, a former police official, who was on a long-term training session in the North commissioned by the Chinese government. This Chinese national was fluent in Korean and therefore knew many high-ranking North Koreans, but it is said that he became close with Jang in particular because of his unique, genuine personality. He was drawn to Jang's understanding nature and generosity. Even before his counterpart would say anything, Jang would guess that person's needs, and provide help so that the other person would not have to ask personally and thus feel embarrassed. During his stay in the North, the Chinese official received much help from Jang both officially and unofficially. He recalled the generous and innocent face put forward, one that never hinted at active assistance.

When he was to return to China, Jang Song-thaek came out to the airport to see the man. Accompanying him right to the doorstep of the airplane, he showed sadness to bid farewell. But the minute they were to part, Jang whispered into his ear. In a very low voice inaudible to others around them, Jang said: "Even if our two countries grow apart, let's try hard to at least not become enemies."

That was before China had officially suggested normalizing diplomatic relations with the South, and it was hardly imaginable for people in the North to predict that such a thing would happen. Needless to say, it wasn't something that could be said aloud. Jang Song-thaek already foresaw that China would normalize relations with the South, and possibly he even thought that the incident could lead China to break off ties with the North.

Some two decades later, upon hearing the news of Jang Song-thaek's execution, the Chinese official sighed in dismay that North Korea had lost one greatly talented man. And he forecast that the situation of key personnel being expelled and executed would continue under the Kim Jong-un regime.[4]

Being at the center of the power system, Jang Song-thaek perceived more sensitively than anyone else the paradox of that system. In particular, he could not tackle the rebellious impulse deep down in his heart against the absolute deification of the supreme leader.

Upon his final moment, in the ruling statement of his execution it is stated that Jang was guilty of undermining idolization events at Taedonggang Tiles and within the Korean People's Internal Security Forces, both of which were under his supervision. It is possible that he could have put into action, to whatever small degree possible, the thought that he bore for so long deep down in his heart while he still had the ability to do so.

In the late 1970s, Jang Song-thaek once went through the so-called *revolutionization* program. Most non-North Koreans would laugh at the word, but in North Korea under Kim Jong-il it was an extremely heavy penalty that could become a most critical moment in one's career regardless of rank.

There are two types of punishment imposed on high government officials in North Korea. First is the punishment of execution, or sending the individual with their entire family to a political prison camp if the fault is of a political nature. But if the mistake is an administrative error made in the course of one's duties, or if it is an act of disrespect toward the Marshal, the Leader, or the Kim family, one was sent for revolutionization. The fault of Jang Song-thaek in the late 1970s was a common error that most successful government officials commit; so-called "wielding political influence." As more and more people gathered around Jang Song-thaek and he started to earn a reputation as a leader, Kim Jong-il was not able to let the situation continue.

More specifically, Jang Song-thaek had gathered foreign ministry officials who followed him and threw parties just like Kim Jong-il's dinner parties. And on every weekend, he held gatherings at the Foreign Ministry's guesthouse in east Pyongyang. Even the Pleasure Troupe women participated in these events. As these occasions recurred, Kim Jong-il learned about them through State Security Department reports.

The reports about Jang Song-thaek's parties enraged Kim Jong-il, as was likely any time the leader saw someone imitating his style of rule. To think that none other than Jang Song-thaek, who was like his personal servant, was secretly holding his own gatherings was intolerable!

In the end, Jang Song-thaek his punishment involved construction site labor for almost two years at the Chollima Kangson Steel Mill in Kangson, South Pyongan Province, two hours from Pyongyang. Kim Jong-il did not forget to pass down some strict instructions: During Jang's revolutionization, the site supervisor had to report daily on Jang's whereabouts. No visits were allowed. All living conditions, including meals, were to be exactly the same as those of ordinary workers. His work consisted of moving melted iron and brushing the sand off the lumps of metal after the casting, which could sometimes be dangerous work. Jang Song-thaek fell while working and was badly injured. He suffered burns on his legs several times, which left scars.

But more arduous for the refined gourmet, accustomed to eating the best of all foods, was a diet poor in both quality and quantity. The staple food was corn, and the allotted meat was one chicken leg per week. Spirits he could buy in exchange for items like the watch he wore, but they were cheap chemical distillations. Still, he depended often on the help of alcohol to alleviate his plight. As a consequence, he sharply damaged his gastric functions. Indeed, he required surgery when his stomach burst after he one fall at work. An eight-inch wound on his abdomen was the result of that incident.

When he returned to Pyongyang after finally being pardoned, Jang Song-thaek would boast to other officials about his surgery and the burn marks on his legs, as if they were medals. Afterwards, Jang was sent for revolutionization on two more occasions, but he found the first time had been so strenuous that he would say the other two felt like vacations.[5]

That was how Kim Jong-il managed his close aides. No matter how senior a government official might be, if he displeased Kim Jong-il, he could lose all his positions and authority overnight and be left no different from any other worker. It was a measure that reminding everyone that the posts and rights of even high government officials originated from Kim Jong-il, not from themselves or their abilities.

However, if Kim Jong-il felt that the men he sent for re-education fully regretted their wrongdoings and had learned their lesson, he called them back and returned them to their former positions. To name this punishment process revolutionization is a prodigious idea, reminding one of the "newspeak" in George Orwell's *1984*. Could one say that revolutionization meant the course that straightens officials' wrong thoughts to a revolutionary mind? Even if one were an official, he would properly realize his status through revolutionization.

Anyway, Jang Song-thaek's first experience was to be repeated a couple more times in his life until, in the end, he received a penalty from which it was impossible to recover. He would have been fully aware of the dangers that always follow anyone enjoying high status and power in the Kim regime, but for some reason he failed to foretell or prevent the most critical moment of all from falling upon him.

The first punishment Jang Song-thaek went through was somehow connected to his married life. It happened around the time he and his wife started to use separate bedrooms. Upon receiving a report on Jang Song-thaek's parties, Kim Jong-il recalled how his sister had complained and pleaded about his dinner parties, which brought a wry grin to his face. By ordering Jang to revolutionization and punishing him for his presumptuous audacity, Kim Jong-il replied to his sister's complaints. Under his breath, he mumbled to his sister, "Now what more do you have to say?"

Kim Jong-il had literally killed two birds with one stone. From then onward his sister Kim Kyong-hui would not be able to make any complaint about his dinner parties. Kim Kyong-hui herself wasn't quite at leisure to express dissatisfaction or complain about her husband's punishment, let alone beg to her older brother for forgiveness on her partner's behalf. She was at her wits' end, occupied with her endless thoughts. On the one hand she couldn't care less for him.

"After all this while, serves you right, you conceited scoundrel!"

"Will this wake you up now?"

But on the other hand, she felt alone. Though they used separate bedrooms and had their own lovers, it wasn't easy to fill the emptiness Jang Song-thaek had left in her life. It was ironic, but now with Jang gone, she no longer desired someone else. It was more than merely not wanting to. She couldn't stand the sight of anyone near her, cautiously guessing which way the wind was blowing.

By no means, however, did she want to run to her brother and ask him to forgive her husband. She knew far too well Kim Jong-il's character. If there was someone he disliked, he would bully them to the end. It was clear that he wouldn't listen to her requests for a good while, and he would make her life extremely difficult. Therefore, after much hesitation, she went to see Song Hye-rim. Song was then Kim Jong-il's de-facto wife, and she was the second most influential person in the regime as she was much loved after the birth of the first son, Kim Jong-nam.

Song Hye-rim was a shrewd woman. Upon welcoming Kim Kyong-hui and exchanging a few words, as a woman herself she sensed her in-law's desperation. Kim Kyong-hui did not verbally convey any requests about her husband, but Song read the true intentions of the visit.

That very evening, Song Hye-rim first suggested to Kim Jong-il that they forgive Jang Song-thaek and bring him back to Pyongyang. More than anything else, Song added, Jong-nam's aunt seemed to be suffering too much.[6] Kim Jong-il was cried out for joy under his breath. Kim Kyong-hui will now be unable to complain about his dinner parties. He made a seemingly gentle facial gesture, but drew a stern line vocally, "There is no sign yet that he has fully repented. He has to receive some more training."

However, quick-witted Song Hye-rim could tell his real intentions. She knew that if people were around him when she took the initiative to resolve family matters, Kim Jong-il would pretend to follow against his will. The very next day Song Hye-rim had the residence's aide and assistant director of transportation go to Kangson Steel Mill and bring Jang Song-thaek back with them.

Song Hye-rim took Jang Song-thaek to where Kim Jong-il was having dinner and had the former bow to the latter. Kim Jong-il forgave Jang upon seeing how physically worn out he had become, and rehired him on a key duty. Receiving the Dear Leader's forgiveness and holding the glass of wine offered to him, Jang Song-thaek shed [hot] tears [of gratitude].[7] Seeing her husband return like that, Kim Kyong-hui also fought back tears and welcomed him home.

This, of course, wasn't the end to Jang's ordeals. Jang had to keep on going through the revolutionization. And this revolutionization was bound to be enforced whenever he reached his prime. This was something he had to keep in mind. His last revolutionization arrived in very different form from the previous two instances. Jang should have been aware of the danger which was apt to charge toward him once he was in the most powerful position of his whole life. Jang did not know that threats to personal safety arise when one is at his most successful moment, not when one is in difficulty or powerless.

Meanwhile, revolutionization was blissful for his family. Even stemming from something sorrowful, a bliss is a bliss. Whenever Jang was in deep waters, even for a short while, the couple forgot about everything and embraced each other.

Another incident that gave Jang Song-thaek doubts about Kim Jong-il and the road North Korea was on was the Korean Air bombing of 1987.

Workwise, Jang Song-thaek was not involved with this terror incident. The operation had been conducted by another department of the Party. Nevertheless, Jang had suspected Kim Jong-il was very concerned by the Seoul Olympic Games, and was devising several plans to try and stop the international sports event. Jang was aware that one of those plans was a secretive terror operation.

Being quite globally aware, Jang Song-thaek knew all too well that such operations were hard and, more than the dangerous nature of the plot itself, he feared that in case of failure, the consequences could be devastating for North Korea. The outside world was already full of anticipation for the Seoul Olympic Games—communist and capitalist countries alike—as a long-awaited chance to compete.[8] The games were not about to be cancelled because of one or two acts of terror.

Kim Jong-il, even Kim Il-sung, would have wanted to block the sports event using direct military action if that were possible. But not only were they not capable of that, they were also afraid of retaliation. The only remaining card was terror. Jang knew that there must have been opposing voices on this matter, even within the secretive special organization that carried it out. The reason was because the operation itself was tricky, and could far too easily be revealed as North Korea's doing. Jang Song-thaek knew in his heart and mind that such an act was not right, but he did not interfere because it was nothing to do with him. From the beginning, he pretended not to know anything about the operation.

But he was well aware that people who obtain power have the propensity to boast of their abilities. That wasn't limited to Kim Jong-il. People who hold power tend to display symptoms of megalomania. Even in the most advanced democracies, the people who hold power often start projects which are beyond their capacities, and then regret the outcome. It is only a difference in degree and situation.

We might compare and contrast President George W. Bush, who believed his country's armed forces so powerful they would let him set up an America-friendly, democratic government in Iraq by invasion, and North Korea's Kim Jong-il, who was not blamed domestically even after committing such an atrocious act while maintaining internationally that he was in no way involved.[9]

In the end, what Jang Song-thaek feared most came to pass. The operation to blow up a South Korean commercial plane succeeded, but the two agents were traced and highly trained agent Kim Sung-il took his own life right before his arrest, while the other, Kim Hyon-hui was arrested and later gave a full statement on the North Korean operation.

The fact that it was Kim Hyon-hui who confessed after she was taken into custody and taken to the South was also a shock to Jang Song-thaek. For he knew well her father, Kim Won-sok, who worked in the overseas economic project department. Kim Won-sok had served as trade secretary at the North Korean embassy in Cuba, and at the time of the incident he was working on overseas trade activities as the deputy of North Korea's Fisheries Representative in Angola. His job was to catch fish with a boat supplied by Angola, to divide the earnings in half, and to wire the proceeds to the fatherland.

It was a top-secret operation, but in a small society like Pyongyang, rumors spread all the faster the more secret they are supposed to be. Jang knew that Kim's daughter had been selected as an agent of the Party's overseas information research department when she was a sophomore in Japanese at Pyongyang University of Foreign Studies, and was undergoing training. As soon as she got arrested by South Korean intelligence, North Korea's State Security Department summoned Kim Won-sok back to the headquarters via Moscow. Necessary measures were taken so that the father would not escape and disappear. Afterwards, Kim Won-sok and his remaining family were all sent to Yodok political prison camp.[10]

All these incidents were heartbreaking for Jang Song-thaek. Right from the start, terror expert Kim Sung-il had firmly opposed the operation on several occasions from its planning stage. His reasons were not only that the operation was difficult to pull off, but that if they failed, the damage would be too severe for the Republic.[11]

In the end, the veteran spy Kim Sung-il had predicted correctly: this incident accomplished nothing besides depriving hundreds of innocent victims of their one, precious life, and stigmatizing North Korea in the international community as a state sponsor of terrorism.

"The supreme leader who gave such a risky order has no responsibility whatsoever, while the agent who goes through all kinds of hardship and gets caught has her family punished because she confessed to the enemy. Is this just?" Jang Song-thaek could not erase it from his mind. The backstreets of power and success were pitch black. At the bend toward success, he enjoyed all kinds of privileges during the golden period of his life, but he couldn't brush off ominous thoughts about the future. A dark cloud was cast over him, then a bigger one over his and Kim Kyong-hui's marriage, and then a massive one over the republic for the years to come. But there was no way to share these conflicting thoughts with anyone.

So, instead, he reached for a bottle. And for women.

6

Northern Snakehead [Mullet] and Rice

> Within the red gates (of government officials' houses), the stink of sour wine and rotting meat, while on the streets outside, lie the bones of the frozen and the starved.
>
> —Du Fu

In his later years, Jang Song-thaek told his closest acquaintances that the most fruitful time of his life was the period spent in charge of the youth project. "I felt it most rewarding when I busily ran about staying up all night with young officials."

Kim Il-sung, who was by then almost seventy, also said that were he a little younger he would like to "personally see to the youth activities." It is easy to understand how it would be a moving experience to work with idealistic, dynamic youths untainted by worldly concerns.

However, seen another way, a country's youth ought to be an asset for the future; except in the most pressing of emergencies, they should be preparing for what is to come rather than being consumed by the present day. They are the reserve manpower in waiting; they should reflect on the learning and culture of the present mainly for the purpose of drawing up tomorrow's plans. They must be given space to observe the achievements and failures of the older generation, and from there to design a critical new outlook. The fact that the regime urgently mobilized its youth indicates that the country was in no state to think about the future.

Previously, the fundamental reason for North Korea's failure as a country had been in its overly successful stabilization. A successful society is one that is forever realizing the problems it faces and preparing new countermeasures to overcome them. That driving force derives from new generations. The North Korean regime's failure was that it turned a blind eye to the basic truth that no success lasts forever.

Whereas the leaders of the South did not pass their problems on to the next generation, the leaders of the North did so to excess. In the South, the story of generations moving from liberation through to the Korean War and nonetheless achieving remarkable development despite immense difficulties was first and foremost a story of survival. However, successive generations of South Korean growing up in the affluence built by their parents were not in the least inclined to struggle against the communist threat. In North Korea, by contrast, the ruling class kept the next generation frozen in the struggles of the past, thus depriving their young people of a future.

In the 1990s, North Korea entered a critical stage. Its closest ally, the USSR, collapsed. The country which emerged as the Russian Federation essentially annulled its alliance with the North and warmed up to the South. Russia sought rebirth via radical reforms, and North Korea was like one big case study of everything that had been done wrong in the past. Russia conveyed news of the annulment of the Friendly Cooperation and Mutual Aid Treaty signed between the USSR and the DPRK; following some formalities, the treaty was consigned to history.

More bad news came from China. President Yang Shangkun, who visited the North with a delegation upon the celebration of Kim Il-sung's 80th birthday in April 1992, notified Pyongyang of China's plan to normalize diplomatic ties with the South. North Korea fiercely protested, calling the decision an "act of treason." Nevertheless, it had no choice but to depend on China's help amidst the diplomatic isolation and economic difficulties it faced. For the first time, China abolished the barter system in bilateral trade with the North and began to demand cash payments. After a while, however, barter trade was revived and economic aid resumed; this time around, however, it was purely a strategic decision in China's national interest, with the old policies shaped by a shared socialist ideology already a relic of the past.

The gravest problem was indeed the economy. North Korea's economy had long since lost its impetus for growth. But only in the 1990s did it tip over into a definitive downturn and begin to record consecutive periods of negative growth. Particularly in the civilian sector, everything stagnated. The key reason was energy, which was in short supply, but that was not the only explanation. Almost every sector faced problems, from the need for raw materials to outdated infrastructure.

When these shortages fatally undermined the food distribution system, it no longer remained simply an economic crisis. An increasing number of factories and mines suspended operations. There was a surge in instances of factory workers, suffering from starvation, dismantling factory equipment and exchanging it for food. As famished citizens roamed in search of food, it became difficult for the regime to control the people. Black markets sprouted, and ordinary North Koreans sought their own ways to make ends meet.

During all this, the Great Leader finally passed away. "His Highness has passed away. Long live the King!" For Kim Jong-il, who finally rose to supreme leader in both title and reality, his father's death was yet another incident of sorrow and crisis.

Nevertheless, the timing was not overly adverse. Right before his death, Kim's father had actively resumed state affairs, tending to matters he had not seen to for a considerable time. Facing a crisis caused by the DPRK nuclear program, and brushing off his son's implacable opposition, Kim went ahead and announced that he would have a summit with the South's president. Moreover, he promised to personally see to the collapsed food distribution system and the famine situation. Kim Jong-il was nervous as to how the situation would play out for him.

With domestic and international crises, the death of the Great Leader provided one more nationwide theatrical event.

> A nationwide funeral will provide an opportunity for the hungry people to express all their sorrow. In addition, they will reminisce about the good old days, and swear their loyalty to the next generation. . . .

At this moment, which should have been a critical milestone in national history, Kim Jong-il could have presented a brave, new outlook on the future of the country, taking into consideration both the flow of the outside world and the domestic situation. Instead, he chose continuity with the past. Perhaps that was his only choice, but what is clear is that while the world changed rapidly, North Korea tried to stand still.

The Constitution, newly revised four years after Kim Il-sung's death, was renamed the "Kim Il-sung Constitution." In the full text, it was made clear that Kim Il-sung would be regarded as Eternal Leader: "The Great Leader Comrade Kim Il-sung is with us forever." The Marshal's corpse was embalmed for eternal preservation.

Meanwhile, Jang Song-thaek continued to advance his career. After being made minister of the Party's youth and Three Great Revolutions team department in 1989, he became a full member of the 9th Session of the Supreme People's Assembly the following year. Upon receiving the greatest honor of all, the Kim Il-sung Medal in 1992, he became a member of the Party Central Committee. At Kim Il-sung's funeral in 1994, he was a member of the State Funeral Committee. A year later, he became first vice director of the Party Organization and Guidance Department, which was the most powerful state organization under Kim Jong-il. And three years later, he was appointed a full member of the 10th Session of the Supreme People's Assembly. All things considered, Jang Song-thaek was clearly the number two of the Kim Jong-il era.

However, the status or authority of a number two naturally differs according to circumstance. In certain situations, the number two continues to possess the basis of his authority. The number two in some cases assists the number one, but is also in a competitive relationship with him. Sometimes, this competitive relationship can develop into a feud. In such case, the number one and two each possess a different base of support, and that can manifest as both cooperation and competition.

In the case of North Korea, being number two is only possible with the tolerance of the supreme leader, as there is no such thing as a separate, independent power base. In a three-generation hereditary system, what was achieved after a lot of complications and dangers was to make it impossible in principle for a number two with independent authority to arise.

The regime devises all sorts of ingenuous rhetoric with which to support the legitimacy of this single power base: the monolithic ideology; the monolithic system; side branches; and revolutionization. No other form of independent legitimacy or official merit can be claimed, and anti-Japanese resistance and revolutionary merit are limited to Kim Il-sung and his family. No deviation can possibly exist on the matter, and if any independent narrative sprouts up, it is eradicated through the severest of punishments.

Despite all this, Jang Song-thaek could by all means be considered the number two. Among Kim Jong-il's numerous close aides, he enjoyed a special position; he existed in a special status shared by no other and with a quite unique role. Sometimes he would suggest a view in opposition to Kim's orders. Very rarely, he would voice a contradiction. Now and then, ignoring one of Kim Jong-il's spontaneous orders, he would maintain the pace and direction of his daily work. Kim Jong-il himself thought it a relief and for the best that Jang ignore his demands to work harder and faster.[1]

In that regard, reasonable and patient Jang Song-thaek had a certain chemistry with emotional and occasionally impulsive Kim Jong-il. There were also instances where Jang caused Kim Jong-il to explode in anger, but after a certain time, the Dear Leader would once again seek Jang out.

Nobody else could imagine doing such things. Jang's usual behavior was different from that of other North Korean officials. Jang wasn't stiff; he had a leisurely air. At times, he even made playful jokes. Therefore, in the eyes of his Southern counterparts, Jang seemed to have a peculiarity about him that was not present in the working demeanor of any other North Korean official. When economists who were part of the presidential delegations to the North upon the Summit meetings in 2000 with President Kim Dae-jung and 2007 with President Roh Moo-hyun made any suggestion to Jang, he made sure that it was conveyed to Kim Jong-il right away. Seemingly with much ease, Jang led the delegation and arranged their meetings with Kim.

There are two major reasons why Jang Song-thaek reached the position of number two under Kim Jong-il. First, as everyone knew, it was the fact that he was Kim Jong-il's brother-in-law—what is more, he was the husband of the younger sister whom Kim Jong-il personally adored. In a country valuing lineage by blood, although he wasn't born of the prestigious "Mt. Paektu lineage" (a descendant of anti-Japanese resistance heroes who fought with Kim Il-sung on Mt. Paektu), he was in some form dependent on that bloodline. Being outside the Paektu bloodline actually worked to his advantage; had he been a direct descendant of Kim Il-sung, Kim Jong-il would have never placed Jang or any other direct relative of the sort anywhere nearly as close to the core state power.

There was another reason why Jang enjoyed special status. It was his personal qualities, a good and noble character, and capabilities. Almost everyone on friendly terms with him said he was gifted not only in his work, but also a man of good character, who was tolerant, embraced humanity, and displayed remarkable leadership. Japanese chef Kenji Fujimoto, who as Kim Jong Il's personal chef had a great number of opportunities to observe him up close, as well as Hwang Jang-yop, one of the highest ranking North Korean officials ever to defect to the South, pin-pointed Jang Song-thaek as the obvious number two of the Kim Jong-il era.

More often than not, Jang Song-thaek went by titles that differed from his actual official position; specifically, "Number One Comrade," or "Dear General on the Road." Jang definitely had a different perspective from any other high government official. Once, the usually calm Jang stepped over a red line and confronted Kim Jong-il face-to-face. As a marginal man in Kim's regime, crossing the line was very dangerous.

The argument was about state reform and the so-called "open-door" policy.

Kim Jong-il was well aware of the necessity of reform and opening the door to trade. However, for the Kim regime, which is by fate in competition with the South, to switch to a reform and opening system, whether it be in the Chinese or the Vietnamese style, would be tantamount to demolishing its own legitimacy; its raison d'être.[2] It could signal a great transformation of the government system, and a transition reminiscent of that from Josef Stalin to Nikita Khrushchev, Mao Zedong to Deng Xiaoping, or Leonid Brezhnev to Mikhail Gorbachev (via Yuri Andropov and Konstantin Chernenko).

In the mid-1990s when the food distribution system collapsed in the North and the number of deaths from starvation reached the many tens of thousands, Jang Song-thaek proposed to Kim Jong-il an era-defining transition. This incident occurred around the first-year commemoration of Kim Il-sung's death.

Some thirty highest government officials were gathered for a party on the second floor of the No. 8 Receptional Hall within Kim Jong-il's residence. Seated alone with Kim Jong-il, separate from the others, Jang Song-thaek bluntly listed the pathetic reality of the country, and suggested wide-ranging changes in policy. It would have been impossible for others to do, and was an unwise move for Jang even from a political reasoning point of view: it opposed the rational principle that water flows downhill by trying to make things work the other way around.

What mattered to Kim Jong-il was not the fact that tens and thousands of his people had died of hunger; what mattered was the idea that if he were were unable to maintain power, the entire world should fall with him. Of course, Kim Jong-il vented in ire.

The unexpected diversion of Jang Song-thaek was an act of treason. It wasn't one of those occasions where Kim Jong-il could present Jang with some logical disputation. Kim Jong-il abruptly shouted out, and, seizing a stainless-steel napkin holder from the table in front of him, tried to attack his brother-in-law. Kim Jong-il's wife Ko Yong-hui clutched at his arms, but the situation had already turned violent.

Jang Song-thaek immediately realized his misdeed. For a split second, he felt the incredible truth lying dormant in the destructive force of Kim Jong-il's anger. Jang stood up and said, "Forgive me!" And he then continued, "I shall sing a song.

He quickly changed the atmosphere by singing *Sahyangga*, a song about longing for one's hometown.[3] Kim, who had moments ago been unable to cool his rage, soon regained his composure and seemed to change mood.

But was that repentance, remorse, or sorrow?

In any case, Kim Jong-il seemed to be in deep thought, asking himself why he had exploded in anger, and all the more for behaving in such a manner in front of his men, which would hurt his reputation. The people present were dumbstruck.

Following the incident, Jang Song-thaek was demoted in official terms. However, his status was maintained without much damage. As before, he went by the name, "Comrade Director Jang."

Could Kim Jong-il have felt it too much of a burden to make the incident official? He regarded Jang as essential personnel. Although on and off he did things that were disagreeable, and had fundamentally different opinions regarding major policies, in various ways Jang was someone he needed in his regime. Besides being an outstanding manager and administrator, he was a man of flexible leadership with the capacity to soften the atmosphere wherever he went, and also to bring people together to cooperate in fulfilling State projects.

Jang Song-thaek stayed in Italy for about a month in the late 1990s, and it was his job to buy and to send back to Pyongyang construction materials required for projects as well as Kim Jong-il's personal consumer goods: the so-called "100 Items," or "Longevity Goods," ranging from luxury items to children's toys and ice cream.

One day the Party International Department's first deputy director, Ji Jae-ryong came to Italy at the invitation of the Italian Communist

Party. The day he was returning, the North Korean embassy held a farewell drinks party, but after drinks and trivial small talk for formality's sake, the air in the room became stale and dull. Yet it instantly changed when Jang Song-thaek, who had been quietly sipping wine, suddenly got up from his chair.

"You call this a party? People should know how to party!"

Jang, who became master of ceremonies, cried, "Bring an accordion if there is one at this embassy." The one presented to him was beaten up and had air leaking out of it, but paying no heed, Jang held the instrument in his arms and started to play a South Korean song, "The Island-Village Teacher" and encouraged everyone to sing along.

For a moment, all those present forgot their duties, politics, the famine back home, the revolution, and the Great Leader, and joined in the lively singing party. The ambassador, Ji Jae-ryong, and the younger diplomats all fought over one another to sing a song, and the party reached its climax. They had a good time forgetting about their plight, even if only for a short moment. Those who remained posted there would recall the party for a long time thereafter.

There is a story from another embassy in Western Europe in the late 1990s. With just a day left until his departure, Jang insisted that he would personally prepare his own farewell dinner party. Taking along a junior diplomat's wife as his guide, he went to a big supermarket and bought some ingredients. From there he went to the ambassador's residence, put on a borrowed apron, headed into the kitchen and started to cook.

He only had the junior diplomat and his wife as helpers to prepare a dinner for twenty people. But Jang made all the preparations with agility and seemingly without much difficulty. When someone asked him, "When and where did you acquire such skills?" he merely smiled and replied, "One learns all sorts of things when one lives here and there."

That evening, everyone ate and drank heartily until the early hours, and all slept in late the following morning. That is, except for Jang, who got up early and again went into the kitchen, threw on an apron, and made egg soup for the men suffering from hangovers.[4] It goes without saying that Jang left a huge impression on the people he met, who were astonished to see the so-called number two guy be so modest, free, and easy-going.[5]

Kim Jong-il's chef, Kenji Fujimoto also spoke of Jang's genuineness. After losing a huge sum in a forced gambling game during one of Kim Jong-il's dinner parties, in spite of himself Fujimoto muttered a most common four-letter-word in Japanese (*chikusho-*), and he believed nobody had heard him. However, the following day when he accidentally ran into Jang, the latter quietly advised the chef at a place where no one was about, to take precaution from then on so that he may not to be harmed for such verbal utterance. In his memoir, Fujimoto wrote how greatly touched he was at Jang's earnest consideration for the Japanese chef's personal safety.[6]

At one point Jang sojourned in Vienna. One late night he went to see a young diplomat, his local aide, to use the telephone. "What could be the matter?" the junior official asked himself. At the other end of the line he heard a young woman's voice, and with that, a loud wail. Jang calmed and consoled the woman, saying, "I'll be there soon. I will."

The young woman was no other than Ri Ok-dol, the only daughter of Kim Jong-il's wife Song Hye-rim and her ex-husband Ri Pyong. It is a well-known story [outside the North] that as a young man, Kim Jong-il went to the house of his friend Ri Jong-hyok, and was so strongly attracted to his friend's sister-in-law, Song Hye-rim, that he took her to live with him. It was in that relationship that Kim Jong-il's first son Kim Jong-nam was born. Ri Pyong was the oldest son of writer Ri Ki-yong (who went to the North [soon after Korea's independence from Japan in 1945] and in later years served as chair of the North Korean Writers League) and the older brother of Ri Jong-hyok, deputy chairman of an organization well-known in the South, the Korean Asia-Pacific Peace Committee. After losing his wife to Kim Jong-il, Ri Pyong disappeared without leaving a trace. Ri's father, the author Ri Ki-yong is also said to have stopped writing, as he was too shocked to work.

However, Kim Jong-il paid significant consideration to Song Hye-rim's former husband and her former in-laws. Suffering from high blood pressure and psychological problems, Ri Pyong was unable to go outdoors, but he could live in one of the two apartments his father Ri Ki-yong had received as a present from Kim Il-sung years before. Ri Pyong's five-years younger brother Ri Jong-hyok was co-seated as vice minister of the Central Party and president of Korean Central News Agency (KCNA), then as he moved to the Central Party's apartment complex in the central district of Pyongyang, he gave his house to his second son, Ri Soe-dol.

There are some people who call the relationship between Kim Jong-il and Song Hye-rim "love," and others who call it, borrowing Fujimoto's expression, "a looted marriage." Either way, it caused trouble for innocent bystanders. Among them were Ri Pyong, Ri Ki-yong, and one more: Ri Pyong and Song Hye-rim's only child, Ri Ok-dol, the woman on the phone to Jang. Her family was shattered when she turned four years old. She was left all alone after her mother left, and her father became an invalid.[7] It was Jang Song-thaek and Kim Kyong-hui who raised the little girl.

This couple also came to act as foster parents for Kim Jong-nam.[8] Kim Il-sung, who learned of his son's relationship with Song after the birth of Kim Jong-nam, strongly reproached Kim Jong-il. To think that the son who was to succeed him as leader was an adulterer. The relationship had to end, at once! The mediator who came forward to solve the problem was Kim Kyong-hui. She first explained the situation to Song Hye-rim, and persuaded her to give up Kim Jong-il and to leave the country since she (Kim Kyong-hui) would take care of Jong-nam. Song Hye-rim naturally protested, but in the end she had no other choice but to go along with the decision.[9]

Kim Jong-il then ordered Jang Song-thaek to send Ri Ok-dol abroad, and to see to it that she never returned to the fatherland. Since then, Ok-dol attended schools in Sweden and Austria, and finally found a job with the United Nations Industrial Development Organization (UNIDO) in Vienna. To her, home was a complex memory, a country she would never be able to visit.

Along with his local aide, Jang Song-thaek went to the house where Ok-dol was living. It was the middle of the night. Ok-dol, who came outside barely dressed, embraced Jang and the two lamented sorrowfully. It was as if they were expressing in the most primitive way possible their endless story, which they did not know how to tell in words: what to recollect, what to grieve about. The two only cried together. The young aide quietly watched from a corner, but as if the emotions the two felt were contagious, he felt a painful heartache.

Ok-dol finally calmed down and started to spill her heart out: "Why was I born with this fate to live in another country? Even the embassy here treats me coldly. What did I do wrong?"

Once she opened her mouth, a cascade of repressed grudges poured out. Jang Song-thaek also stopped crying, and counseling Ok-dol gently he told her past stories and memories of amusing moments. Thus, he soothed his foster daughter.

"If you wait just a little bit longer, won't the day come when you can return home and end these years of hardship?"

As they parted, Jang Song-thaek tried to pass her an envelope of bank notes, but Ok-dol refused to accept it, saying she had a job and was not short of money. But still Jang Song-thaek forcibly thrust the envelope at Ok-dol and left her place. On the way back, Jang remained in deep thought and low spirits, an after-effect of the brief reunion.[10]

In his tasks, Jang Song-thaek showed traits extreme precision and promptness. One of his acquaintances witnessed how Jang frightfully reprimanded a major general, the commanding officer of a military unit Jang had mobilized for a construction project, as the military officer was making his report. The major general submitted his report, but Jang commented on errors in it in detail even though he had only skimmed through the document. The officer failed to answer properly and, at a loss what to do, finally left after saying he would correct highlighted areas and resubmit the report. Following the verbal lashing, the military man realized his mistakes and said he would correct them. Jang changed his attitude, advised him in a gentle tone, and told the officer to do a good job.[11]

Around that period, Jang started to leak views that could be seen as critical of the North Korean domestic situation. He often spoke in this way, particularly when he was inebriated. Were it anybody else, such words would normally reach the ears of Kim Jong-il, and the result would be re-education if one were very lucky; if not, a trip straight to a political prison camp.

But that did not happen. First, because he was Jang Song-thaek. Second, perhaps those who heard Jang's critical babble agreed with him to a certain extent and decided to protect each other. Jang Song-thaek's imprudent utterances usually were about the ordinary people's food situation, but taken a step further, they were small indictments of the North Korean regime's basic policies. That is, he was arguing that North Korea should completely change its economic policies and adopt Chinese-style reforms right away.

In a way, he was contradicting himself. Jang benefitted from status and privilege many others could not enjoy, despite not being of Paektu lineage himself. He was directly involved, and was known to be key player, in Kim Jong-il's decadent lifestyle.

Jang was at the same time critical of the regime in which he played a big role. These utterances were more detailed and clear when he was drunk, especially when completely drunk. Even in North Korea, he shared his inner thoughts with close friends, but most of these conversations happened while he was visiting other countries. The fact that there were not instances of the diplomats, who heard him, leaking it or filing any report to their headquarters about Jang could have been a greater mystery. That suggests indirectly that North Koreans, who are exposed to the realities overseas, have to a certain extent an area of critical consensus when it comes to discussing the situation back home.

The same was true among South Korean diplomats during the years of authoritarian government. There was an enormous gap in knowledge and awareness between the people confined within the country and those who had exposure to trends overseas, and to communicate with foreign counterparts. In the South back then, although it was rare, there were a number of diplomats who chose political asylum in another country for various reasons.

Jang Song-thaek would appear at North Korea's overseas hubs without notice. He mostly travelled to Europe, especially France, Italy, Switzerland, and Northern Europe. He hardly went to the United Kingdom, where there weren't any bases. During business trips to Europe, Jang Song-thaek or the late Kim Yong-sun (who passed away in 2003) were registered as counselors of the North Korean delegation to the United Nations Educational, Scientific, and Cultural Organization (UNESCO), so they used diplomatic passports under those titles. In such cases, they would alter one or two syllables of their names. For instance, Jang Song-thaek became Jang Sang-thaek.

When travelling abroad, other North Korean officials as a custom stayed at accommodations provided by the respective embassies or consulates; however, Jang Song-thaek did not, instead going to five-star hotels. He would have the local North Korean representatives make several reservations, including a suite, and he would sleep in one of them: usually a single or twin-bed room.

When he was abroad, Jang Song-thaek took a keen interest in his host country's red light districts or decadent aspects. Upon his visit to Paris in the summer of 1990, he went to the city's nightlife center, Place Pigalle, or to bars where women did the serving, and he would demand to be served by pretty young women. The locally posted diplomats tried hard to host this VIP well even if they had to cover huge expenses. Jang Song-thaek drank like a fish: he would drink at one sitting both a bottle of champagne and a bottle of cognac. Could it have been a reward to himself for life in Pyongyang, which was under constant surveillance and control? Or would it have been cultural curiosity of a certain aspect of being abroad, which did not exist in his country?

South Korean officials and businessmen posted overseas for the first time were also keenly interested in red light districts. Those are the recollections of the 1960s and 1970s. Back then the most popular issue in the private conversations of men who had returned from a trip abroad wasn't about the Louvre, or Covent Garden. For both the North and the South Korean men, freed from their narrow and heavy actualities and turned loose in the big, wide world, the freedom they indulged in was nightlife. All the same, it was only Jang Song-thaek who openly sought this freedom.

Meanwhile, Jang Song-thaek spoke without reservation his preeminent concern regarding the situation of the fatherland. Drunk as a skunk, he would cry out that people are starving to death, and deeply sigh, "What can we do?"

On one occasion, he drank heavily after attending a dinner hosted by a North Korean embassy. The diplomat who carried him back to his hotel room was flabbergasted upon hearing the words Jang spilled out. Believing the man was completely knocked out, the junior officer tried to untie Jang's necktie when the latter suddenly opened his eyes, and before the startled junior officer could say anything, started to yap away.

"Comrade, I'm in deep trouble. I cannot go on without booze. The fatherland is in an abominable state right now. People are dying of hunger by the tens and thousands! It is indeed an Arduous March. If I think of the Party members, officials, and our countrymen who are starving to death back home, I cannot sleep at night. Therefore, I have to at least drink. What can we do for the pitiful people who have died so miserably? How good it would be if we also reformed and opened our doors to trade like China? It's only a matter of one decision from the top, so why can't that be done?"

The diplomat who heard Jang say this felt a cold shiver run down his spine. If this had made it to the ears of the State Security

Department, and as a result reported to Kim Jong-il, even if he was the Great Leader's son-in-law, he would never have avoided the firing squad. What's more, he would be severely punished for not reporting that he had heard such a thing. To avoid that dreadful hazard from falling upon him, he had to report to his superiors. Even if not directly to the State Security Department, at least to his ambassador.

However, this diplomat decided not to disclose it to anyone. It was a daring, difficult decision to make considering the social norms of the North Korean regime.

In late 1996, Jang Song-thaek and Kim Yong-sun took turns making appearances in Europe. If they were notified that Jang Song-thaek, who was staying in Paris, had arrived, local diplomats went to meet him at the border. The official purpose of his visits was to prepare funds and technology for North Korea's highway construction project. A couple of officials from the general bureau for engineering and the roads bureau of the Public Security Department would come with him, but Jang would leave the official duties to those delegates, and he mainly went out to procure the 100 Items and send them back to Pyongyang. Staying as long as a month in one country at a time, Jang travelled to various places and scooped up mysterious and rare luxuries, including truffles.

Kim Yong-sun also once had to procure European mullets. Kim Kyong-hui's health had started to deteriorate, and someone had suggested that the blood of a live mullet is good for women's health. Therefore, mullet was added to the top of the purchase list. And the mullets had to be transported back alive. So, a specially ordered fish tank holding five mullets was flown to Beijing International Airport. From there, a North Korean carrier flew the five live mullets to Pyongyang that same day.

Each country's premium ice creams were also packed in boxes filled with frozen ice and through Beijing Airport got delivered to Pyongyang.[12] Besides these, medical supplies, pharmaceuticals, toys, Omega Swiss watches, yachts, and automobiles were all flown in.

The local diplomats conducted this work according to Jang's orders without any complaint, as though they were a matter of grave importance for their fatherland. Even Stalin feasted on luxurious food while Soviet citizens were starving. The North Korean diplomats remained taciturn, but deep down in their hearts they could not help feeling uneasy.

Jang Song-thaek and the diplomats who attended him did not speak a word of these particular missions of theirs. Yet they could, even if vaguely, read the true thoughts of one another.

Around that time, Jang Song-thaek drank to excess almost every day. A day's schedule ended only once he was catatonic. At times, he wet himself. Diplomats had to carry him to his room, undress him, and change him into dry garments. All the while, Jang was in extreme agony.

He was worried about the situation of his country. Back home people were starving to death, but nothing was being done. "What can we do? China's population is 1.2 billion yet the Chinese government has no problem feeding them. What on earth will happening to our Republic? What can be done, and how?"

He was far from his usual self. He invariably gave an impeccable and pristine impression from his attire to his demeanor. He himself was a non-smoker, and loathed it if someone smoked near him. Therefore, nobody was allowed to smoke in his car, so officers dreaded to ride with him.[13] The unconventional behavior he demonstrated overseas revealed the depth of his mental anguish.

The morning after his insobriety, he would be all freshened up and sober, smiling and joking, bringing about laughter. Even on the road, he would entertain his driver throughout the journey with his comical stories. When travelling late at night, he woud engage in endless conversation in case the person behind the wheel fell asleep. Then, when he was inebriated again, he grieved over the state his country was in.

"The factories aren't running. How can you mine coal without electricity? Without gas, how can you go out to sea to fish? The people are starving! No food in the house, families are falling apart as they each go out to look for food on their own: fathers, mothers, children wandering alone in search of things to eat. Only the old remain home, waiting for their last moment to come. There are instances where the family can't afford a coffin so they roll the deceased in a blanket and bury them just like that in the ground. The whole country is full of wanderers. It is even hard to maintain the transit control system."

Younger diplomats were the most patient audience for Jang's mutterings, and after a whole month they had his lamentations memorized, yet there were none who thought politically ill of Jang. And no one reported him to the State Security Department either.

Although North Koreans feared bringing up the subject when they were with close acquaintances, the fatherland's sad plight would always become the topic of conversation within families. Married couples discussed the matter in detail, keeping their voices low, close to whispers in case their children overheard. Nevertheless, there was nothing they could do.

Back home, he wasn't as free as he was abroad, yet still Jang Song-thaek often brought up the hopeless topic of prospects for the North Korean economy. In addition, he spoke of his aspiration that the economy could be revived and turn a corner to new development. His close acquaintances agreed with him at heart, but they also worried for him.

Some worried what might happen to him in the future, and some feared for their own safety because just being close to him could eventually put them in danger. Some feared that even though Jang Song-thaek himself could be spared the worst punishment by virtue of being Kim Kyong-hui's husband, they would enjoy no such protection.[14]

Even Jang Song-thaek never said that the South is more developed than the North, no matter how drunk he got. Instead, he spoke of China.

At the end of the year, an urgent message arrived from Pyongyang. It was a telegraph telling Jang to return immediately. Even as he was heading back, Jang grabbed hold of the young local diplomats while he was sober and shed still more tears.

"Whatever it takes, shouldn't the priority be caring for the people who are starving to death? Engage in some activities that will produce more food and send it back. Rice is the most important of all. Sending rice back to the fatherland is most pressing. How can China make it so well?"

That part Kim Jong-il also knew. Upon one of his visits to China, Kim Jong-il marveled at the development of Shanghai. "It's heaven on earth!"

Like Jang Song-thaek, Kim Jong-il knew what he had to do in order to make China-style progress, but unlike Jang, he had no intention of doing anything of the kind. Kim Il-sung had made a similar statement back in the '80s upon seeing the changes in Shanghai, but he never took action. Chinese Premier Zhu Rongji personally accompanied Kim Jong-il on his visit to Shanghai and tried to have a discussion about Chinese-style reform and opening, but the North Korean leader gave no reply.

There were factors Jang Song-thaek may not have fully understood. The reason the Kims could not risk Chinese-style reforms was tightly bound with the North's fatal rivalry with the South, which had been going on for more than half a century. It was a question of the ultimate reunification of the peninsula, and a matter of who would have the legitimacy to represent all Koreans.

Reform and opening would inevitably cause instability within the regime and place the North in an inferior position in the framework of inter-Korean relations. The South would become the generous teacher, and the North the student. Voices raised about legitimacy would tilt favorably toward the South, and, more gravely, so would the sentiment of the North Korean people.

Based on the economic development achieved by previous governments, the South sought a reunification that was advantageous to them, while the North Korean regime believed it could overcome its economic weaknesses with political strengths. North Korea believed that the South, despite its economic achievements, would repeatedly fall into chaos due to political immaturity and that that chaos would ultimately enable the North to lead the way to reunification on its terms. Inter-Korean reconciliation and exchanges would only be possible when both sides believed it to be in their interest. It could be seen, figuratively, as a marriage full of misunderstandings, miscalculations, and communication failure.

Were it not for the existence of the South, and had the North not been in a pre-ordained state of inter-Korean confrontation, both Kim Il-sung and Kim Jong-il would have followed China or Vietnam's example much earlier on. In the 1970s, while the Park Chung-hee regime turned the crisis it was facing into a success story through active investment and internationalization, the North doubled down on the command economy, socialism, and anti-Americanism. Thus, there developed an imbalance between the two Koreas that would be hard to reconcile. As the South began to eagerly look forward to the failure of the North's economy, the North looked forward to political chaos and a leadership crisis in the South.

Jang Song-thaek did not have a deep understanding of the regime's reservations, indicating that his status and thinking did not belong to the true core of the regime. He was at once the number two of the Kim dynasty, and an outsider.

Even as problems worsened elsewhere, Kim Jong-il's evening parties became all the more colorful. His parties were of various types;

depending on who the participants were, sometimes influential women were present, and it was also possible to attend with one's spouse. Sometimes the invitees attended with their daughters.

Kim Kyong-hui also came. She would enjoy singing, or dancing, and then watch a performance. That was pretty much all. Naturally, imported wine would be served and a rare feast laid out. After the party was over, the Dear Leader would give U.S. dollars or electronic goods like video cameras and MP3 players, permitting each person to choose what they wanted.

On extremely special occasions, Kim Jong-il's dinner parties were held at one of his villas scattered across the country, and would last from Friday through Sunday afternoon. When a small number of key influential officials attended, performances based on special themes would be held. For instance, if a party's theme was Chinese, the waitresses would all wear Chinese soldier uniforms, and the food would also be Chinese cuisine. If the theme was "The Night in New York," attractive women dressed up like Americans would sing and dance to jazz or country songs. On "A Night in Paris," the can-can dancers of the Moulin Rouge would make an appearance. At times, the singers or dancers were ordered to take all their clothes off in order to heighten the excitement. The performers then had to continue serving while naked, as the male guests looked on with sardonic smiles.[15]

Mostly, the secretive parties were held at the Taedonggang Guesthouse. However, when they were held at Kim Jong-il's villas, guests were asked to stay overnight, ostensibly to avoid road accidents. Each guest had a partner arranged for him.

As a matter of fact, the high number of road accidents involving high government officials in the North could be directly attributed to Kim Jong-il's special parties. The guests who were invited to his parties had to drive personally to the party venue without the help of a chauffeur, and driving was bound to be deadly after excessive drinking. Moreover, there was little concern for traffic safety since there weren't that many vehicles on the road. Officials hardly ever wore seat belts, and road accidents caused more damage. A former first vice minister of the Foreign Ministry Ri Jong-mok, and deputy director of the Party's Organization and Guidance Department Ri Hwa-yong and others died in traffic accidents after such parties.

Even at the special villa parties, Jang Song-thaek couldn't be left out. Like Ho Dam, O Jin-u, and Kim Yong-sun, he was a regular.

Kim Jong-un, who would years later rise to power, received help from his uncle Jang Song-thaek during his own succession. However, Kim did not look favorably upon the man known as the regime's number two. One reason for it was his strong distaste for the so-called Pleasure Troupe parties his own father had thrown, a distaste deeply ingrained in his psyche by his mother.

A father-and-son relationship is not always simple. Within Kim Jong-un there was an awe for Kim Jong-il, but at the same time revulsion for his father's depraved lifestyle. That repugnance was tacitly directed toward his aunt's husband, Jang, rather than his father, because the former organized and seemingly encouraged those events. Jang Song-thaek failed to read the confused mind of his young nephew, who was much more complicated than Jang seemed to imagine.

In such circumstances, there was no way Jang Song-thaek's marriage could go unaffected.

The private life of Jang Song-thaek and his wife became a great source for gossip. Stories about Jang and Kim's private lives spread to everyone who might know, or at least became a focus for gossip among those who pretended to know. The couple did not seem to care about the rumors. It's hard to say who did it first, but both of them found a new partner for extramarital affairs. A widely known rumor about Jang was that besides the Pleasure Troupe, he had affairs with many women, and that he practically lived together with a famous sportswoman.

Kim Kyong-hui's affair partners were mostly artists. The conductor of the Sea of Blood musical Choe Kon, the head of the Mansudae Art Troupe Kim Il-jin, and widely known violinist Kim Song-ho were the names usually thrown around. They were all some twenty years younger than Kim. In addition, she promoted to vice minister one Choe Kwang-ho, an especially loyal staff member at the Department of Light Industry, fueling a rumor that their relationship went beyond the professional.

Kim Kyong-hui's diversion cannot be merely dismissed as debauchery or depravity. She was a passionate woman and someone who could be faithful to her own emotions. She did not even try to hide her deviations. Choe Kon, for one, would bring along photos of Kim Kyong-hui and brag about them to his friends.[16] It did not seem Kim Kyong-hui minded the photos being shown to outsiders.

The violinist, Kim Song-ho never married, and said he would like to carry on attending to the needs of Comrade Kyong-hui, so their relationship went on. There was also a rumor that the two had a child. Royal palaces during the monarchies era in Europe were at once scenes of fierce struggles for the throne, and on the other hand places where all sorts of sexual acts were secretively conducted between royals and nobles. Nevertheless, rarely did marriages lead to separation even after spouses learned of their partner's extramarital affairs. Could the deviations have acted as a new stimulant and energizer to a marriage in a state of ennui, smothered in social privilege and wealth? Among the offspring of nobles or other privileged families, there are always those who are not of the father's family line, yet still it is rare for the parents' marriage to come to an end.

Jang Song-thaek and Kim Kyong-hui's marriage also continued. They both knew of each other's affairs, yet they had affection for each other. They understood each other's circumstances, and continued to feel empathy.

Even under North Korean criminal law, "to be ostentatious and debauched" and acts of destroying families and so forth are subject to criminal punishment. When power and money do not circulate through transparent procedures and is not contained by public observation, especially from a free press, private lives fall into debauchery. Even Choe Ryong-hae, who earned the full trust of Kim Jong-il via his Youth League activities in the late 1990s, started to lead a promiscuous life, holding drinking parties with beautiful women of the Youth League propaganda unit. This continued until the wind of execution blew on to the Youth League after a case known as the so-called Yellow Wind.[17]

In a situation where everything revolves around the political sensitivities of a supreme power, private affairs generally did not become an issue. This was generally the case whether we are talking about the royal courts of the Medieval era or dictatorial regimes of modernity.

When Lavrentii Beriya was executed after the death of Stalin, one of his supposed crimes was sexual deviance. But this became an issue only after he was removed from power and executed for political reasons. More than half a century later, an "ostentatious" and "debauched" private life was mentioned in the ruling statement of Jang Song-thaek's execution. This is reminiscent of the so-called Yun Pil-yong incident, which occurred in the South in 1973. In the ruling on Yun, there are mentions of immoral relations with a "female prostitute" and "adulteress." However, he was sentenced for something other than his "depraved" private lifestyle.[18]

With the New Millennium around the bend, and the country still on the "Arduous March," two major purges swept the country. Even a high government position was no guarantee of safety during these periods.

Jang Song-thaek not only survived without much difficulty, but actually saw some of his political rivals exterminated. It all began with a corruption case for So Kwan-hui, the Party Central Committee secretary in charge of agriculture. So Kwan-hui was to be punished for allegedly embezzling fertilizer given by the Dear Leader. However, the matter rapidly escalated and led to the bloody purge of a great many high government officials. In other words, Secretary So's embezzlement was not merely an individual corruption case but a touchstone for an organized operation of anti-revolutionary forces which conspired with the South to destroy North Korea.

Likewise, in South Korea under authoritarian governments, there were instances of dictators trying to remove political obstacles by fabricating North Korean spy-ring cases. Nevertheless, the Simhwajo incident was incomparable in scope and content. That is because the knife blade was aimed at key Party and administrative officials in the heart of the regime.

As for Secretary So, he was treated as an anti-revolutionary, and not simply personally corrupt. The charges were that during the Korean War he was recruited by the Southern side, like the Northwest Korean Youth Association (*Sobuk Chongnyondan*), and from the beginning he had decided to stay in the North and infiltrate into the Party with the purpose of removing top North Korean officials. It was a way of saying that responsibility for the food shortages and hardships the North Korean people were suffering lay with the South and anti-revolutionaries.

The size of the purge could not be explained by the anti-revolutionary activities of one or two people. The horrendous number of sacrifices in the purge reflects the crisis that the regime was then facing. The sacrifice of So was followed by those of Central Party Agricultural Affairs Director Kim Man-kum, former South Pyongan Provincial Party Chief Secretary Jang Yun-pil, Central Party Committee Secretary Mun Song-sul, then South Pyongan Provincial Party

Chief Secretary So Yun-sok, South Hwanghae Provincial Party Chief Secretary Pi Chang-rin, Central Prosecution Office Party Secretary Kim Ji-sun, Central Party Secretary Kye Ung-tae, and others.

The story didn't end there. What followed was the "Ryongsong Espionage Incident" in which executions were carried out on a massive scale. The accusation was that agents specially trained in the South since the Korean War had infiltrated the Ryongsong district of Pyongyang and were waiting for their moment to begin destroying the regime.

With these incidents, Kim Jong-il ordered the Social Safety Department (today's Ministry of People's Security) to conduct a thorough investigation into the personal history of all citizens nationwide and root out suspects. The organization set up to conduct this job of digging out the past of all personnel on a nationwide scale with the purpose of eliminating them was the Simhwajo. This body was put under the responsibility of Chae Mun-dok. It is said that Kim Jong-il ordered the Social Safety Department to research the situation of each household in the citizens' register, and even told the men to start by checking their own documents.[19]

Chae Mun-dok wielded unfettered power. His group targeted former and current high government officials and not the general public; Chae reported directly to Kim Jong-il, all cases were aimed at "removing the top," and were fabricated or trumped up as "anti-Party, anti-revolutionary acts." Once Kim Jong-il had granted approval, ruthless executions were carried out.[20]

Jang Song-thaek was then the first deputy director of general administrative affairs at the Party Organization and Guidance Department, and his rights included control of the Social Safety Department. The number Simhwajo executions reached some twenty thousand. Then, Mun Song-sul, the chief secretary of the Central Party Comittee, who had at ordinary times kept Jang Song-thaek in check for various reasons, was also arrested on espionage charges.

Some of the South's sources on North Korean affairs interpreted this incident as Kim Jong-il attempting to get clear of the leadership of the Kim Il-sung era; however, evidence was lacking. The high government officials victimized by this incident, such as Mun Song-sul, So Yun-sok, and Kye Ung-tae had stood on Kim Jong-il's side from early on, and it was unnecessary to eliminate them because by the late 1990s, Kim Jong-il's power had already been firmly stabilized for several years.

Since blame for economic failure and the food crisis in particular had been put on the South and the people had turned their dissatisfaction southwards, the mass purge incident would have to be seen as an advance clearing of any domestic dissatisfaction or signs of dissent by imposing a general atmosphere of fear. It is understandable that Kim Jong-il would order further investigations when Chae Mun-dok first raised So Kwan-hui's corruption case as a political issue.

However, seeing how Chae Mun-dok abused the Dear Leader's trust to excessively expand his own political domain, and started to cause a negative effect on the regime's capacity by purging his political rivals, this time Kim Jong-il targeted him as an "ambitious" figure whose risky decisions were made solely for the interest of advancing his personal power.[21] Along with Chae Mun-dok, some six thousand agents of the Simhwajo were also said to have been punished: expelled from the Party or removed from their positions.

As the number of Simhwajo arrests got out of control, even Kim Jong-il's supposedly close aide Kye Ung-tae, the secretary in charge of administration, judiciary, and prosecution, was charged. Kim Jong-il ordered the Military Defense Command to conduct an internal investigation of the Simhwajo. Military Defense Command reported that the Simhwajo was obtaining "confessions" through "facts" and "sins" admitted through extreme torture after arresting the officials who were loyal to the Party and the revolution. Kim Jong-il ordered Military Defense Command to arrest and execute Chae Mun-dok and the Simhwajo leaders, and to punish related personnel. In addition, he restored the honor of the victims of the Simhwajo and their families posthumously, and he closed the incident by reinstating them to their current positions.[22]

Jang Song-thaek did not undergo any close investigation during this period, and moreover, he got rid of Mun Song-sul, who was always on his back in one form or another.[23] Since Jang's position put him in charge of judiciary and prosecution, one could imagine he was deeply involved in this incident, but not so deeply involved as to be reprimanded for this matter years later for failing to respond properly in its early stages.[24]

Then, Jang Song-thaek became once again indirectly involved in another case known as "The Yellow Wind of the Youth League." Those involved in this case, such as Youth League organization secretary Kim Tong-yon, and other secretaries; Youth League charge leader Ri Hak-chol, former Korean resident in Japan Unbyol (Silver Star) Trading Company president Pak Byong-so, were all functionaries who had become successful under Jang's shade while he was working as director of the Party's Youth Activities. The person punished for having direct involvement was Choe Ryong-hae.

While he was chairman of the Central Committee of the North Korean Socialist Workers and Youth League, Choe Ryong-hae was highly praised by Kim Jong-il for suggesting that he rename the organization the Kim Il-sung Socialist Workers and Youth League. Later, after the death of Kim Il-sung, during the Arduous March, he composed, "Without You There is No Us" and had the Youth League sing it first, and thus he further earned Kim's trust.

However, just when Choe Ryong-hae's power reached its peak, Kim Tong-yon, Ri Hak-chol, Pak Byong-so, and Ri Chan came to be questioned by the State Security Department for alleged charges that they travelled around South Korea's Jeju island and received several million U.S. dollars in bribes from the South Korean intelligence agency abroad on a business trip. It was a fact that the men became big spenders of foreign currency after returning from their trip, and their indulgence in promiscuous private lifestyles backed by the influence of money and power was an eyesore. The charges were admitted and they were all executed.

Almost all the victims of this incident had worked with Jang Song-thaek, and were people he had raised. Though he wasn't directly involved in the case, he couldn't in any way be free of responsibility. Nearly all of the executed were secretaries, including Choe Ryong-hae, and among them Ri Hak-chol and Pak Byong-so were former junior officers who Jang Song-thaek had raised as "Effort Heroes" while he was the Party's Youth Activities director in the 1980s. Based on Jang Song-thaek's human networking, the two played key roles in the City of Pyongyang's construction and foreign trade sections respectively, until they were named as main culprits in the "Yellow Wind" case and eliminated.

The Party Organization and Guidance Department had recapitulated the case at the time, and it thoroughly examined the related details, but when Jang Song-thaek's past human network was brought forward the matter grew to a "fractional act" and "enemy line liaison charges," the punishment level augmented, and thus ended up with an execution sentencing.[25] Whether these men were indeed recruited by the South's intelligence, visited Jeju island, and received operations funding cannot be confirmed. However, interestingly, in these men's list of charges, there is hardly any mention of their conducting operations or activities related to the South's intelligence's orders after their return to the North. It merely states that the men received several million U.S. dollars from the South's spy agency, and received the duty to reinforce the local conditions by bribing high government officials, including the military.

If they had really conducted activities connected with the South's intelligence, one cannot help thinking that the men would have avoided standing out so visibly. Just maybe, couldn't they have merely wasted some foreign currency left over from trading or immense construction projects, and spent it on decadent lifestyle? Nevertheless, that high government officials, especially those affiliated with organizations with the Great Leader's name in them, showed corrupt and depraved behavior especially when nationwide the country was in such a difficult state undoubtedly, which would have had a negative impact on the government. On such occasions, it was convenient for the North to aim all of its blame at the South, especially the South's intelligence agency's conspiracies and operations.

With this case as a turning point, the word spread among the Pyongyang ruling class that being affiliated with Jang Song-thaek was fatal. This incident wasn't one in which Jang directly intervened, or one which he fabricated. However, the general understanding was that the Youth League's senior officials were punished because of their connections with Jang. If Jang Song-thaek and Kim Jong-il were on good terms, being an acquaintance of Jang could be great news for oneself, but if the two were on bad terms, then simply knowing Jang could be bad news.[26]

The Yellow Wind incident suggests that the regime's leadership was mindful of Jang's people advancing. Even before the Yellow Wind incident, there were cases where people experienced disadvantages since they were taken for Jang Song-thaek's people, but this was by far the biggest and most famous case. In the same context, after Kim Jong-un's appearance, many prominent individuals met the same fate as Jang Song-thaek.

Jang Song-thaek himself received revolutionization (re-education) once again. However, the revolutionization by then was no longer so hard. This time he was sent to a farm in Kangwon province, and surveillance was not as severe. The president of that region's university even looked after him to the extent that he was given a whole chicken every day. Jang would recall later on that it felt like he was on vacation there, and that he had a great relaxing time in the fresh air.

After his revolutionization program was over and he was called back to Pyongyang, he asked the university president, who had taken such good care of him, what he would like Jang to do for him in return? The university president replied, asking him to please look after his son. Within a month after his return, Jang Song-thaek called the son, Kim Dong-won, treated him to dinner and wine and asked him, "What is your wish?" The man replied that he would like to work in trade. In one month, he became the head of the Wonsan branch, and the head of the Chinese branch of a subsidiary of Taesong General Department, the trading company run by the Central Party.

However, Kim Dong-won in the end defected from the North.[27]

The 1990s in North Korea passed into the pages of history with the Arduous March and massive executions. One of the remedies the regime had chosen to overcome its internal crisis was to order a large-scale purge, blaming the country's exterior enemy, the South, especially the conspiracies and operations of its intelligence agency.

In 1990 with ten years left until the New Millennium, Kim Jong-il made some two dozen "Millennium Rings" of pure gold, and presented them to twenty of his close aides, adding the word that they should all meet again in the year 2000. However, when the time did come, six had disappeared. Three were arrested and executed on espionage charges, two died of illness, and finally, one of Kim Jong-il's closest aides, illicit funds chief manager Choe Bong-man was arrested for accounting violations.[28]

7

Sunshine, Shade, and Shadows

> Sunshine is more threatening than artillery.
>
> —Kim Jong-il

After having become supreme leader in his mid-fifties, Kim Jong-il soon reached sixty. His rule had been a continuation of the hardship that preceded it. However, finally there came a way for Kim Jong-il to overcome his situation.

For the first time in fifty years, the main opposition party won a presidential election in the South, bringing a new phase of inter-Korean relations. This was at once a huge crisis and also a great opportunity. The main proponent of the so-called Sunshine Policy, Kim Dae-jung, was president in the South! Kim Jong-il knew perfectly well what a threat the Sunshine Policy could be to his regime, and now that the lifelong opposition had become the actual leader of South Korea, Sunshine was sure to become its foreign policy orientation. In the name of reconciliation, exchanges, cooperation, and ultimately reunification, he would try to break down the North.

However, Kim Jong-il was adept at using the odds to his advantage. He crafted a basic strategy that would be fleshed out by Song Ho-kyong and Ri Jong-hyok. Kim Dae-jung emphasized the need for inter-Korean reconciliation and cooperation in a public speech in Berlin, then followed it up by proposing an inter-Korean Summit during the third year of his presidential term. Kim Jong-il was ready to respond.

One of the peculiarities of inter-Korean relations is that they only move forward when both sides calculate (or miscalculate) that it is favorable to them for there to be a functioning bilateral relationship. For example, what made the first inter-Korean Summit of June 2000 possible was essentially Kim Jong-il's creative thinking.

However, just because both North and South Korea surmised that renewed North-South ties to be to their own advantage, the so-called Sunshine Policy, or the reality that was based on it, should not be regarded only with cynicism. In the world of politics, motive doesn't matter. You can start out with bad intentions but still achieve good results, and bring about catastrophe despite having the best of intentions.

Kim Dae-jung may have believed that the Sunshine Policy would bring about change in North Korea, and in the long run lead to the two Koreas realizing reunification, yet he did not set "achieving immediate results" as his goal. He never imagined that reunification would be actualized suddenly and, even if that did happen, he did not think that it would be advantageous for the South. He saw a lesson in the case of Germany, which suffered economic difficulties after reunification. The design of his policy was that after a long period of inter-Korean exchanges and cooperation, and when the North Korean economy and other aspects of North Korean society had reached a certain level of development, a relatively low-risk reunification would be realized. That would be the final stage. In contrast, Kim Jong-il's design was much more complicated: a mixture of short-run economic interests and mid- to long-term military and political ones.

Around this time, Jang Song-thaek was working both construction projects in Pyongyang and overseas trade, neither of which was directly related to Kim Jong-il's anti-South strategy. In 1998 and 2003, he became a full member of the 10th and 11th sessions of the Supreme People's Assembly, but that only had to do with personal status; there was no power attached to the position. Nevertheless, Jang was always present at key inter-Korean meetings.

In the last year of Kim Dae-jung's single five-year term, a delegation headed by Lim Dong-won visited the North to discuss several pending issues, including the North Korean nuclear program. Kim Jong-il did not grant Lim a personal meeting. Kim Dae-jung was very upset that Kim Jong-il had refused to meet his last special envoy,[1] but for Kim Jong-il, the delegation's visit had no particular meaning. For Kim Dae-jung, the incident showed how wide the gap really was between the North Korean leader's mind and his own.

Instead of a personal meeting, Kim Jong-il threw a grand feast combined with a song and dance troupe performance and all kinds of delicacies. The person he sent to greet the Southern visitors in his place was Jang Song-thaek. Jang did not say anything important dinner, although he was perfectly polite. Yet even still, he managed to leave a positive impression on the Southern delegation. As usual, dinner was followed by heavy drinking, and though one of the Southern members could not handle his drink and retched, Jang was perfectly unperturbed. He quietly had the situation taken care of, and had the nauseated guest looked after. His calm and thoughtful gesture left a deep impression.

Jang Song-thaek's most prominent role in North Korea's relations with the South at this time was to lead a large North Korean economic delegation to the South in October 2002, where they visited factories owned by some of the country's largest corporations. It was important that Jang Song-thaek was part of the delegation.

At the time, the North needed to revive its economy at all costs. It is also true that in the aftermath of the 2000 inter-Korean Summit, the regime anticipated cooperation with the South. In 2001, the year after the first summit, Kim Jong-il visited Shanghai and was so impressed that he left behind his famous quote, "Heaven on Earth." However, at home he could not even attempt drastic reforms or open the doors to trade. Instead, the North reacted with slogans such as, "New Millennium Pyongyang Construction Boom." It may have seemed like a passable plan with a superficial frame, but it was not backed by any actual strategy for economic development.

In any event, North Korea's effort to actualize that hope could be seen in the dispatch of the largest government economic delegation sent to the South since the division of the two Koreas in 1948. It was quite possible that Kim Jong-il hoped to take advantage of a rare moment of inter-Korean reconciliation and cooperation, sensing an extraordinary chance to develop the North Korean economy.

Jang Song-thaek's official position was as first deputy director of the Administrative Department of the Party Organization and Guidance Department, so actually he did not have any direct relation to the economy. That he was included in the delegation to the South in spite of this reflected the North's hopes, as well as raising the status of the delegation and placing political importance on it. Additionally, Jang Song-thaek was knowledgeable about the situation overseas, and was an open character, so he may have been seen as capable of observing the South more objectively.

In July of that year, the Kim Jong-il government issued a package of economic "improvements." For the time, it was a very innovative step. Dispatching an economic delegation to the South, and including in it Jang Song-thaek, was part of a related thought process; that there could be something to learn from the South about economic development. But as the story always seems to go, the long-awaited reforms soon withered and faded away. Starting the following year, the Economic Management Improvement Measure started to be revoked bit by bit. The State Security and Party Organization and Guidance departments reported that "a wave of Capitalist ideology is threatening the roots and the trunk of Socialism," signaling the death knell for reform.

But the real problem lay with Kim Jong-il himself. Any leader intending on reform should expect to face resistance and opposition of some kind. Kim Jong-il was aware of that. Yet, he himself was only half committed. In a corner of his mind, there remained the fear that economic reform could one day turn into instability. The report, which concluded that reform is a threat, was a mere reminder. Even without such a report, Kim Jong-il's reformist rhetoric was bound to wax and wane.

Economic reform meant opening the country's doors to foreign capital. That opening would bring in not just foreign capital and technology, but also the distribution of information. However, in order to maintain the monolithic leader system based on the myth of the Paektu bloodline, the North had to block the inflow of outside information at all costs. In a nation that propagates the notion that Kim Il-sung commanded his soldiers to defeat the Imperial Japanese military and liberated then-occupied Joseon, and the Korean War broke out because the United States and the South invaded the North first, it was unthinkable to be inundated with information from all directions. The Kim regime could be maintained only if the doors were kept locked and the nation isolated from the outside world. Jang Song-thaek was in the shadow of Kim Jong-il's dilemma, but he feigned not to know it.

The 18-strong economic delegation visit was a rare event, and had there been more in-depth bilateral adjustments beforehand, there could have been a better outcome. When the visit was being discussed, the Northern side expressed their hope to visit mainly small and medium-sized businesses (SMEs). However, the Southern side wanted to make use of this rare opportunity and prepared an itinerary which involved mainly going to Chaebol corporations, in order to emphasize the South's economic capacity.

The actual event was conducted according to the desires of the host country. And indeed, it was evaluated as having left a profound impression on the Northern officials, certainly as far as the South's heavy chemical, car, shipbuilding, and electronics industries were concerned. Incheon International Airport, which had just opened, would also have been in sharp contrast with Pyongyang's Sunan International Airport, which was reminiscent of airports of the 1950s.[2]

However, it is open to question whether the visit contributed much in terms of actual inter-Korean cooperation. Wouldn't it have been better for the delegation to visit mainly SMEs and factories that corresponded better to North Korea's actual situation (and from which the visitors could deduce actual and practical policy steps to take home)? This was what they had requested, after all. It is worth wondering whether demonstrating the huge difference between the two economies to the North's first, biggest and, it turns out, only economic delegation to the South in the end had a negative effect.

Jang Song-thaek drank like a fish even during his visit to the South, and after he was inebriated, he would babble away depressingly on the economic gap between the North and the South. He would often sigh, "Now you really can't even call it competition."

Jang's drinking habit, especially his mumblings on North-South economic development, was to cause a huge problem for him. Two years later in 2004, he was sent away for his third and last period of revolutionization, and one of the faults pointed out to him there was his verbal conduct in the South. During the re-education course, it became a subject of criticism particularly when he had to go through sessions of self-criticism at Kim Il-sung Higher Party School. Nevertheless, the fact is that the economic difference between the two Koreas had not been news to Jang for many years. It was yet another occasion that reconfirmed his firm belief in the vital importance of economic reform.

The official leader of the delegation was Pak Nam-ki. Jang Song-thaek behaved just like one of the ordinary subordinate members and did not allow himself to stand out at any of the official events.

Nevertheless, everyone could tell that he was the true leader. Jang was flexible and leisurely in his manner, even when he came into contact with news reporters. However, when asked for a meaningful answer, he'd cut the reporter off by telling him or her to direct their question to the leader of the delegation, Pak.

Even in the few anecdotes left after the Northerners' visit, it is clearly revealed who was the true key character in the delegation. On one occasion during their stay, leader Pak Nam-ki became interested in a vending machine that accepted credit-card payments. Standing in front of a vending machine, he was trying out various experiments and listening to the explanations, when Jang Song-thaek, who had been standing behind Pak, leaned forward and said to him in a low voice, "Let's get a move on." Pak jumped as if terror-stricken, ceased what he was doing, and the delegation promptly left the site.

On another day, the delegation was housed at the Hotel Inter-Burgo in Gyeongju, where they had come to observe the city's ancient relics. The North Korean delegation all woke up in the morning and headed to the breakfast hall together, but Jang Song-thaek did not show up. They were all standing in front of his door waiting, but nothing happened even after the agreed upon meeting time, as though Jang was still sleeping. Yet no one dared knock on his door, nor did they try to think of another way to get him up. Despite the South delegation's urging to call him, no one would do it.

Frustrated, a Southern counterpart put a call through to Jang's room and conveyed the message that everybody was waiting for him. When Jang finally opened his door, the whole delegation immediately came to attention to greet him, and stood against the wall so that he could pass. The South Korean delegation was stunned.

In the South, Jang sought wine and women, just as he had on his visits to Europe. The South Korean government was happy to treat the delegation to karaoke parties at their hotels. However, when the delegation was travelling in provincial areas, Jang would ask his South Korean counterparts to take him to so-called "room salons," expensive, comparatively luxurious bars with female hostesses. The South Korean civil servant declined, saying that unlike at his hotels, which are not open to outsiders, room salons were open to the public, and if reporters got in they could generate very unpleasant stories about the situation.

All in all, the historic visit of the biggest ever Northern economic delegation to the South could have been a sensational opportunity, but turned out to be a one-off with no particular influence on the North's economic policy.[3]

Two years later, in 2005, there was a change of government in the South, Unification Minister Chung Dong-young visited the North, and upon meeting with Kim Jong-il asked after Jang Song-thaek. Kim Jong-il replied caustically that Jang was then "taking a rest" because he had consumed so many depth charges[4] in the South. In fact, Jang was then in the middle of his third period of revolutionization. Certainly, Kim Jong-il's excuse was not groundless, or entirely humorous. He had received reports about Jang's behavior in the South, and had doubtless kept it in mind.

To non-North Korean outsiders, the origins of the cases themselves would be so trivial as to be almost comical. However, in the North, trivial matters can take on enormous meaning. The punishment of important officials was not important per se. Most of the time, trivialities were simply an excuse used to punish a big fish and bring him to heel. Every now and then, some key individual would be punished on a one-time basis, but that was quite rare.

Detailed punishment plans were made by the State Security and Party Organization and Guidance Departments, as information on the target person would be gathered. With the punishment of Jang Song-thaek in 2003, one explanation has it that one of his junior officials held an overly extravagant wedding for his son. Another argues it was because of trouble with the Guest Hall building, which Jang managed.

One day there was a second-marriage wedding ceremony for the daughter of the Party's Organization and Guidance Department's deputy director Pak Chang-son at a restaurant on Kyonghung Street in the Potonggang district of Pyongyang. On that street, there was an imported-goods store as well as restaurants managed by the Central Party's accounting department.

Jang Song-thaek attended the wedding for his own reasons. Conscious of Ri Je-kang, a colleague with whom Jang was always in conflict, he wanted to express his congratulations to deputy director Pak in order to maintain good relations with him.

However, something went wrong. The assistant director working with Pak had called around and notified a great number of people about the wedding. That was a very peculiar thing to do in North Korea, where wedding invitations cannot be sent out since it is a private event. What's more, what kind of place was the Party Organization and Guidance Department? It was where all government officials had their personal histories scrutinized and their career trajectories determined. Announcing the wedding of the Pak family was the equivalent of, if one were to use a lowly term, sending out an invoice. It was natural for a wedding ceremony to be extravagant; however, this was so luxurious as to draw people's attention more than usual. The guests were well-known personnel, including party and government officials and military officers, dropped off by imported vehicles that filled up the area. Jang Song-thaek was among them.

The wedding drew such a crowd and sparked so much talk that State Security Department agents in the area reported it to the Organization and Guidance Department. Making matters worse, one of the guests crashed his car in a drunk-driving accident. Coincidentally, Kim Jong-il had just issued a warning to his "close" men not to drink and drive, so this accident became the main reason the wedding news went all the way up to Kim Jong-il.

From the wedding invitations, the fanciness of the wedding, and in particular, Jang Song-thaek's attendance without notifying Kim Jong-il—everything about the wedding disturbed the Dear Leader. Under Kim Jong-il, close aides gathering on their own, or partying by themselves without his knowledge, was a political liability.

As a result, Jang Song-thaek and many officials who attended that wedding were penalized: removed from their posts, dismissed altogether, or sent for revolutionization.

The second time, Jang Song-thaek allegedly earned himself an enormously grandiose-sounding charge called, "breach of the Party's monolithic leadership." Previously, Kim Jong-il had permitted Jang Song-thaek and his wife to use a guesthouse near Taesongho, a lake in Kangso County, South Pyongan Province. Jang Song-thaek put the dilapidated building under his jurisdiction, refurbished it, and then managed it.

Then one day an expatriate Korean for whom Kim Jong-il cared deeply came to stay in the North for a while, and Kim Jong-il gave orders to accommodate his guest at the above guesthouse as a vacation spot. But when the people who had come on Kim Jong-il's orders to check the guesthouse got there, the Social Safety Department agents forbade entrance, saying they did not have orders from Jang Song-thaek. In other words, Jang Song-thaek's authority mattered more than Kim Jong-il's when it came to the building.

When this was reported, Kim Jong-il was infuriated and, jumping on the bandwagon—a partial group within the Organization and Guidance Department, including his enemy Ri Je-kang—raised as a pressing matter his "breach of the Party's monolithic leadership." Jang Song-thaek was travelling in Europe with Kim Kyong-hui at the time, and he returned immediately upon receiving notice, but he was escorted home the moment he landed at the airport and put under house arrest. He then went through his third revolutionization period. But the ones who really suffered were the comparatively innocent bystanders around Jang. The Administration Section of the Organization and Guidance Department was dissolved, and its employees scattered among regional governments. The guards who had prevented Kim Jong-il's guests from entering the guesthouse for not having "the permit of Deputy Director Comrade Jang" were all thrown in political prison camps. Social Safety Department Division 25 was also demobilized and its senior officers became subject to punishment—both by law and Party. Social Safety Department head Choe Yong-su was also punished on joint liability and was banished to a remote rural area. This was a case that could only occur in a regime where no alternative to the authority of Supreme Leader Kim Jong-il is permitted to exist, no matter how trivial and isolated it may be.

However, the explanation of another person, who was in a position to know about the case very well, was quite different. According to this person, in 2003 Jang Song-thaek and his wife were on a long sojourn in France. Kim Jong-il had issued some orders to the Administration Section, but the official in charge did not execute the work, instead reporting that it would be dealt with after consultation with Jang upon the latter's return to Pyongyang. This reply provoked Kim Jong-il, who responded by dissolving the department in its entirety. When Jang returned at year's end, he was immediately ordered to write a self-criticism, and was once again sent for revolutionization. This time Kim Kyong-hui was so shocked that she was unable to work for a prolonged period, and employees of the Light Industries Department had great difficulty getting her signature on official documents.[5]

When you hear a same story from several different people, certain common denominators emerge regardless of the truth of each narrative. When you hear that Kim Jong-il senses that his authority has been minimized, it is his reaction that is more important than the specifics of the case itself. It is Kim's feelings that matter. Some cases get brushed off without any measures being taken. Kim Jong-il treated different cases differently according to the relative gravity of the case as he felt it.

In contrast to leaders who obtain and exercise power according to sensible rules and/or tradition, Kim Jong-il's "feelings-based" governance gave him almighty power yet left him in a constant state of anxiety. Because it was hard to predict what his reactions to general circumstances might be, the people around him were every bit as anxious as he was—all the time. Of course, this is a fairly typical phenomenon with tyrants.

A similar situation occurred nine years later in 2013, upon Jang Song-thaek's final punishment under his nephew Kim Jong-un. The word was that this latest immense series of executions was once again triggered by a low-ranking person denying Kim Jong-un's authority and instead demanding the permission of Jang Song-thaek. The difference this time, however, was that there weren't several other cases leading slowly to his punishment and execution. For a considerable period of time Jang Song-thaek had been under observation by several organizations, as well as by Kim Jong-un himself.

For as long as two years after the third revolutionization, Jang Song-thaek was put under house arrest, and had to go through self-criticism and re-education courses at Kim Il-sung Higher Party School. One of the most prominent subjects in his self-criticism was how careless he had been in his "revolutionary tasks" when in the South in 2002, and how easily blinded he had been by the materialism that the "enemy" showed him. He praised the South for its affluence and showed a depraved side under the influence of alcohol.

Of course, Jang Song-thaek voluntarily conducted self-criticism on all these charges.

During this period, Jang lived without any official status or role, as a socially and politically meaningless man. Only in early 2006 was he able to resume his former position.

Jang Song-thaek and his wife Kim Kyong-hui suffered another ordeal that year. Their one and only child Kum-song, who was studying in Paris, took her own life.

Jang Kum-song (literally, golden pine) was the only biological offspring of Jang and Kim. Rumors that Kum-song wasn't their own child were untrue. Before having Kum-song, Kim Kyong-hui went through two miscarriages. So, when she carried Kum-song, even Kim

Jong-il was highly concerned, and did not hesitate to pay the fees to fly in obstetricians from Germany to ensure her wellbeing. They were ordered to take good care of the dictator's sister, who delivered her daughter safely in 1977 at the Ponghwa Clinic, an exclusive facility for the privileged class in the Shinwol-dong area of Pyongyang. A precious only daughter, her parents doted on her and she grew up with everything. Blossoming into a talented and beautiful girl, she was loved by her parents and the people around her. Taking after her father, she was tall and her features lent her an exotic Western air. Possibly from her paternal genes, she was musically gifted, especially at the piano. From middle school, she was educated overseas.[6]

One difference between Kim Jong-il's era and that of his father was that his family's offspring were all educated overseas. Kim Il-sung raised all of his children in the North. Kim Jong-il and Kim Kyong-hui, Kim Yong-il, Kim Pyong-il, and Kim Kyong-jin all attended Pyongyang Namsan Middle and High School, and later Kim Il-sung University.

However, Kim Jong-il's children were all put into schools abroad—not in socialist countries like Russia or China, but in Western European countries, where everything was totally different from North Korea. What's more, they were sent abroad from a very young age. This was an unusual thing in a country that puts so much emphasis on indigenous identity in all aspects of life.

This is an important point. There is a huge difference, on the one hand, between receiving basic education in one's country and then later going overseas to study professional fields or conduct research, and on the other hand, beginning student life abroad and spending one's whole character formation period away from home.

Kim Jong-il may have had a number of reasons for sending his children to study abroad. North Korean education may simply have been too limited for his standards. However, Kim Jong-il himself may, in his heart, have felt some longing for life in non-socialist Europe. He had previously wished to visit several Western European countries.

Kim may have also had the desire to turn his family into a royal dynasty, and may have feared that if he let his offspring grow up mingling freely with ordinary North Korean children, it might secularize the sacred "Paektu lineage."

Kim's family lineage had become imbued with such politically important meaning that there was indeed the need to isolate his offspring from other North Korean families. If Kim Jong-il's children had started to present a friendly image to ordinary people, and seemed little or no different from any other kid, they might well have eroded the sense of mysticism or awe suitable for a theocracy. Perhaps worse, if Kim's offspring caused some kind of accident, or fell short in scholastic aptitude, and had to go through an awkward experience or situation in front of commoners, it could affect the image and authority of the Kim regime.

The same concerns applied to all of Kim Jong-il's sons, Jong-nam, Jong-chol, and Jong-un. They grew up without a single friend or classmate in the North, and were always kept inside the compound. In the case of his oldest son Jong-nam, a sort of mini school was made within Kim Jong-il's residence, and the boy was home-schooled there. Under the supervision of Kim Jong-il's security unit, five women and four men were selected—thoroughly screened for family background, health, and looks—to live in the residence and take charge of the eldest son's education. However, as this gradually became known to outsiders and generated gossip, the scholastic venture came to an end.[7]

North Korean affairs experts have not paid much heed to this aspect, but it was a fundamental difference between Kim Il-sung's and Kim Jong-il's era. Kim Jong-il seems not to have spared much thought for the difficulty of the children, who likely felt confused or lost, detached from family at a young age and forced to live and stay in another country where everything was so foreign to them.

Kum-song went to middle school and high school at an international school in Sweden, and afterwards registered at Kim Il-sung University, but never attended a single class. Instead, she moved between several schools in Sweden and in Paris. Her parents gave all their love to their daughter. They travelled at least once a year to see her, and Kum-song returned home during school breaks.

She had nothing to envy in her daily life, enjoying the kind of privilege which paradoxically may have deepened her worries during her most sensitive years. Whether she was abroad or back home, she was surrounded by an invisible fence. For Kum-song, it was hard to tell whether it was to keep others away from her, or to keep her inside.

During her adolescence, she did not have a single close friend. Wherever she went she was alone; she was a special person receiving special protection. Both her father and her mother were always busy with their own schedules and, more importantly, they each had extramarital partners whom they would swap out periodically. Her special status began to feel like restraint, and privilege to seem like a curse. Unlike almost everyone else, she did not have a friend in the true sense, someone who she could rely on and talk to, nor a family that would warmly embrace her.

Even when she came home after a long while for a vacation, nothing pleased her. Exalted status with no trace of material shortage was a kind of ennui that was hard to bear for even a few days. Every time she returned to the fatherland, she would pack her bags again within a fortnight.

Seeing North Korea's domestic situation depicted in the Western media was another burden for Kum-song when she was abroad. The foreign press described her country as a cruel and ridiculous society. There were also occasional reports of how the impoverished state received international aid, yet a great number of people died of famine, and all the while a small number of the privileged class lived like kings. Whenever she came across these stories, she would be startled, feeling that the reporters were directly addressing her. Had she lived her whole life only in the North, she may have been relatively free from this inner conflict, since the regime is not seriously exposed to outside information. The more she became used to life in Western Europe, however, the more she felt the situation within North Korea was abnormal.

It was the same story with some other North Koreans in similar shoes, like Song Hye-rang's daughter Nam-ok. Whenever she returned to Pyongyang, Nam-ok would suffer dreadful boredom. As she reached the age to marry, everyone set out to look for a husband for her, and even Kim Jong-il took an interest. After a painstaking selection process, she finally got engaged, but it was done only semi-willingly, with one eye on Kim Jong-il's thoughts. In the end, she did not make it to the altar. One of the reasons for breaking off the engagement was because her fiancé was somewhat uncivilized—for instance, he spat in a park. However, she needed Kim Jong-il's permission to break off the engagement because he had personally searched for her future husband in the first place. She needed the help of her maternal aunt Song Hye-rim, and it was not easy to get Kim's consent.[8]

Going through puberty, Kum-song was confused between the two drastically different worlds in which she lived. In one reality, all information was controlled and the collective rule for frugal consumption was the norm. In the other reality, all information was open and free, and individualistic life was the generally accepted norm.

Like Nam-ok, when Kum-song graduated university and reached the appropriate age for marriage, the Party started to look for a spouse for her. This goes far beyond the the notion of a private family's "arranged marriage," but rather might be described as selecting a kind of "royal consort," which was very definitely the business of the state. The party started making a list of prospective candidates, choosing from among the elite ruling class bachelors "suitable" to be Kum-song's partner. Both Jang Song-thaek and Kim Kyong-hui received reports about project progress.

Of course, what mattered most was not Kum-song's paternal side, it was her maternal (Kim family) side; that is, the maintenance of the "Paektu lineage." Kum-song was also informed by her parents about this plan. Her mother and father made it sound as though it was great news, but for Kum-song it was yet another dreadful trial. Hearing this "great news," Kum-song could only sigh.

The fact is that Kum-song had a boyfriend she was considering marrying. He was a young Frenchman. She was in her late twenties. However, this news was passed on to her parents back home through her driver/bodyguard. Flabbergasted, her parents ordered her immediate return, but Kum-song refused and wrote a letter that said she'd live by her own will. Kim Jong-il also came to learn of the contents of this letter, and he ordered the North Korean representative of the UNESCO office in Paris to send Kum-song back home by whatever means necessary.

If she returned, she would be doomed to ordinary life in North Korea. However, Kum-song did not have the courage to cut off her past and start a new life in a foreign country. In this sense, she differed from Song Hye-rang's daughter Nam-ok, who had escaped the North and cultivated a life on her own. Could it have been their differing social status, or was it simply a matter of character?

Regardelss, one day in August 2006, in the scorching heat of the Paris summer, Kum-song took a lethal overdose of sleeping pills. Her body was found two days later by her aides. The police found her will and concluded it was suicide.

A victim caught between two paradoxical realities, Kum-song's corpse was sent straight to Pyongyang. It was an indescribable shock for Jang and Kim Kyong-hui. Upon hearing the news, Kim fainted and was rushed to the elite Ponghwa Clinic. Jang Song-thaek also fell into deep despair, although he held himself together well enough to look after his wife.

Strangely, the couple found a kind of mutual understanding and empathy for one another after their daughter's death. There is a Korean word, *wensu*, which evokes a complex emotion of antipathy and sympathy, grudge and regret, resentment and attachment. The closest Western corollary might be "love-hate," as relationships are sometimes described. Indeed, many Korean married couples are said to be involved in a love-hate, or *wensu*, relationship.

Jang Song-thaek and Kim Kyong-hui had lived in the shadow of absolute power ever since they fell in love as youthful university students, and the couple overcame all sorts of difficulties to get to an age where they could share feelings of pity and compassion with one another. In the end, it was the regime's peculiar power system that led their one and only daughter to take her life. The couple may have been at once the regime's greatest beneficiaries and its worst victims. Maybe the same is true of those around them, like Kum-song.

Kim Jong-il never understood why the people around him, who received all sorts of benefits and privileges, would flee to third countries and seek political asylum. His first partner Song Hye-rim's older sister Song Hye-rang; his second partner Ko Yong-hui's younger sister Ko Yong-suk and her husband; his diplomat brother-in-law Ko Dong-hun;[9] and the abducted South Korean actress Choe Eun-hee and her director husband. Why on earth did they all flee from the Republic?

He failed to understand that no one could live cultivating their own domain in a system that is centered only on Kim Jong-il, nor that people cannot live like another's pet, regardless of the benefits offered. It did not occur to him that his system ran contrary to human nature. Isn't it said in the Bible that the first two humans, Adam and Eve, turned their backs on the limitless abundance of Eden and instead ate the fruit of knowledge, willfully choosing for themselves a road full of trial and tribulation?

In the early stage of his rule, third-generation hereditary ruler Kim Jong-un allegedly made the macabre comment that he would "exterminate [up to] three generations" of those who escaped from the country. When this word spread, another rumor was added: that the largest number of escapees came from the Kim family itself. This is not just black humor. Whether it be Kim Jong-un or anyone in a position of responsibility in the North Korean regime, thought must be given to the matter: why do so many asylum seekers come from the country's most privileged family?

Jang Song-thaek and Kim Kyong-hui regularly travelled overseas together. Sometimes they would be away for several months. When they were outside the Republic, it felt like they had returned to the good old days when they were young and happy. But, once they returned, the same old reality would be awaiting them.

Neither Jang Song-thaek nor Kim Kyong-hui ever spoke of their colorful lives, or told their past anecdotes. Actually, they did not feel any need to tell anyone, or to clearly gather their thoughts about their history. There was no lingering resentment between the two. It is one of the traits one can see in married couples who have spent their whole lives together.

Both Jang Song-thaek and Kim Kyong-hui liked to drink, and they drank often. If Kim Kyong-hui got drunk at Kim Jong-il's parties, she would behave rudely to Jang Song-thaek. She would call her husband by his name, "Jang Song-thaek! Wine, drink more!"[10] However, Kim Kyong-hui wasn't looking down upon her husband in public. Rather, she was showing a special relation fundamentally different from what existed between other people. This was a unique method of putting on a display of affection in the special circumstances in which the two would find themselves.

There are many people who believe that had Kum-song simply been a more flexible woman, able to avoid despairing at the two paradoxical realities she was in, she might have married a handsome and capable young man of good family and Jang's end would have been different. Personnel well informed of the situation inside the North Korean upper class say that if Kum-song and her spouse had been in charge of key positions within the Party, and on top of that maintained good relations with Kim Jong-un, Jang's end wouldn't have been as miserable as it was, or at least he might not have ended up dead.[11]

There may be value in the above argument; however, Kum-song was not such a tactful person. Since she was raised in a specially protected environment, she had no ability to manage herself or her surroundings. Just as her father was active only on the fringes of Kim Jong-il's theocratic monarchy, Kum-song also had to live at the intersection between the two different realities that she knew. Perhaps father and daughter were in a position more similar than they realized.

The offspring between Kim Jong-il and Ko Yong-hui—the three siblings Kim Jong-chol, Kim Jong-un, and Kim Yo-jong—were sent overseas for five years between approximately ten and fifteen to an international school in Bern, Switzerland. However, their stay abroad ceased quickly due to a report that their whereabouts "could have been exposed to the enemy." The report could have been made because either the then-North Korean ambassador to Switzerland Ri Chol (Ri Su-yong), who had the massive responsibility of looking after the three children, was too sensitive, or because he believed this would be an excellent excuse to take the burden off his shoulders. In any case, because the children stayed for a relatively short period of time abroad, they may have been comparatively free from the emotional effects of experiencing two different realities.

During this period, Jang Song-thaek and Kim Kyong-hui both continued a married life based on a peculiar understanding and empathy which they did not verbally express. A special emotion grew between the two, one which others could not possibly comprehend. There were frequent instances where if they happened to be alone, they'd glance at each other and burst into laughter. There was no grudge or jealousy. They both could transcend those kinds of emotions.

However, Kim Kyong-hui was an alcoholic, so much so that no part of her body—liver, heart, lungs and kidneys—remained unimpaired. Like most high-class North Koreans, she mostly received treatment in Paris. Jang Song-thaek, on the other hand, maintained fairly good health until the very end. He also used to go for check-ups and treatment overseas, mostly in France or Switzerland, if he felt signs of physical illness. Nearing his final years, he went to Singapore for a dental implant treatment.[12]

Completing his third revolutionization course, and returning to his official position, Jang Song-thaek once again was given an important role. His became the first deputy director of the Working Organization Department and the Capital Construction Department, which put him in charge of construction in the capital Pyongyang as well as foreign trade. It was a position newly created for Jang, involving two activities in which Kim Jong-il was directly involved.

That same year, Jang came to be in charge of another new department, the Party Administrative Department, which had been newly established as a separate department in early 2007. He thus commanded the regime's security, judiciary, and prosecution. The State Security Department, however, was carved out of his jurisdiction.

In the year that Jang returned to public service after two years of punishment, Kim Jong-il finally succeeded in his long-fostered ambition, the development of nuclear arms. The first nuclear test was a success. The earlier-than-expected timing of the test, as well as the regime's actual carrying through of its nuclear development program, surprised North Korea's neighbors.

Even up to one or two weeks before the nuclear test, high government officials in North Korea's neighbors had been skeptical as to whether a test would be possible in such a small territory like the Korean peninsula. In particular, South Korean opposition was greater than expected. The liberal government's North Korea policy had emphasized reconciliation and cooperation, but it was now in dismay, as leaders realized how difficult it would be to continue arguing their peaceful approach.

Of course, Kim Jong-il expected the test might be followed by international sanctions. A seasoned professional in controlling and maintaining political power, Kim Jong-il was well aware of what mattered and what didn't. What mattered wasn't the other person's (as well as his own) goodwill or trust, but the power to force or compel. Whoever might try to confront him would first have to think of what power they might use to do it.

"The reconciliations, exchanges and cooperation with the South will continue as they are. Yet some aspects will change greatly. The North will in one hand see economic interest, and in the other continue to create fissures in the South–U.S. bilateral alliance. It will receive aid from the South, while the balance of realistic force remains with the North, and thereby it will keep its political superiority." This was Kim Jong-il's thinking, and, strategically, it was superb. However, it overlooked one contingency, which came to pass in February 2008: conservatives took back power in the South.

When the South held presidential elections in December 2007, the North's anti-South intelligence agencies reported that the conservative candidate, Lee Myung-bak, was leading. However, they forecast that even if Lee took power, the Sunshine Policy's direction would be maintained, and exchanges and cooperation with the North would not deviate from the existing framework. The outcome, though, was far from what they had predicted. Lee, who won the election in a landslide, adopted a Northern policy that completely capsized the Sunshine Policy.

Nevertheless, Kim Jong-il did not despair of lost cooperation with the South, for he had already obtained the military force to destabilize the South, and without the cooperation of the North, the South would not be able to live in peace. Despite this, the Lee government's attitude was not that of a sitting duck.[13] Lee Myung-bak refused to concede to the North's demands of aid in exchange for a summit, and instead demanded an unconditional summit at which they would discuss nuclear disarmament. Looking back on North Korea's acts around this period, even though there was an extremely high degree of inter-Korean intelligence activity, it is clear that the two sides still harbored huge misunderstandings about each another.

What offended Kim Jong-il was the Lee Myung-bak government's North Korea policy slogan, "Vision 3000: Denuclearization and Openness." For Kim Jong-il, that was absolute nonsense, impossible to discuss; no, not even thinkable. The numeric figure 3000 was especially disturbing. Among scholars majoring in political science, it is said that if per capita income reaches USD 3,000 in any country, democratization movements arise.

The Lee Myung-bak government's North Korea policy was the same as telling Kim Jong-il to abandon the most important card of the ones he still held, and to simply wait for the fall of his regime.

Amongst all this, there was one more victim. It was Choe Sung-chol, a deputy director in the Party United Front Department. Choe had continued to file optimistic reports on the future of inter-Korean relations. He had reported that the Sunshine Policy's basic direction would continue under the new Lee government. Frustrated at the South's unexpected attitude, Kim Jong-il ordered the Party Organization and Guidance Department to audit the activities of the United Front Department. What the audit team found at Choe's house was not evidence that the deputy director was conspiring with the South to cloud Kim Jong-il's judgment, but the unbelievably huge sum of USD 300,000 under the floor of his bedroom. Choe Sung-chol was executed, and the United Front Department was drastically reshuffled.

In the summer of 2008, a South Korean woman on a tour of Mt. Kumgang in Kangwon province, the only Korean province to be divided in the middle by the inter-Korean border, was shot and killed by a North Korean soldier. The North argued that the tourist had trespassed on a military base area, while the South objected and requested that a fact-finding mission be allowed to inspect the scene.

However, the North refused and brazenly claimed the South should apologize. In the end, the Mt. Kumgang tours were suspended.

The South's reaction was disbelief—why was it necessary to kill a woman tourist who briefly entered a military base compound? But from the North Korean soldier's view, the victim was not a tourist. During the decade of the Sunshine Policy, many South Koreans started to think of North Korea as a country with which one could be friends, and one which they must help. But to North Korean soldiers, who are trained to be hostile toward the South, the female tourist was an enemy who could be a threat to the security of the Republic. For Kim Jong-il, the unfolding of the incident was a severe blow, much more serious than losing regular infusions of foreign currency. He would have to reconsider his anti-South strategy, which was based around the Sunshine Policy. As inter-Korean relations became rigid, various aid streams it had received were severed. Kim Jong-il was ill at ease seeking a new exit strategy.

His final years did not amount to much in the way of leisure or pleasure, for various reasons. Health was his most pressing problem.

Late in the summer of 2008, Kim Jong-il suddenly collapsed during a discussion concerning practical issues related to the regime slogan that it would bring about a "Strong and Prosperous Nation" by 2012. No one expected this to happen, including Kim himself. Close to half a century of gourmet food consumption and heavy drinking had resulted in cerebral thrombosis. The diagnosis: a brain hemorrhage. Kim Jong-il's condition was critical, perched between life and death. It was a problem to try to run a country which, since its foundation, had only been controlled by one exalted ruler at a time. Were Kim Jong-il not to recuperate, stabilizing a successor plan would become an urgent matter.

Jang Song-thaek and Kim Kyong-hui took action on all fronts, from taking care of Kim Jong-il at his bedside to managing a contingency countermeasure system to run state affairs. Had Jang Song-thaek not been there at the time, and had he not promptly handled the situation, North Korea might have fallen into chaos. Jang organized a small emergency management team containing key personnel such as his political rivals Party Organization and Guidance Department's first deputy director Ri Je-kang and Ri Yong-chol, and senior deputy director of State Security, U Tong-chuk.

At the time, the Republic was facing the sixtieth anniversary of its foundation and the people were highly interested in the event. The group stopped news of Kim Jong-il's illness from leaking out and stirring popular sentiment. It can be said to be Jang Song-thaek's greatest contribution to North Korean politics that he got the whole government to respond to the Worker's Party Organization and Guidance Department management system even without Kim Jong-il's direct orders.

The news of Kim Jong-il's illness was conveyed to very few core personnel; otherwise it was kept completely classified, so much so that even the department in charge of the annual September 9th foundation day ceremony was unaware of Kim Jong-il's inability to attend the event. There being no proper communication between Jang Song-thaek's team and the ceremony preparation department, the officials in charge waited for Kim Jong-il's arrival and caused a row by continuously delaying the event, which was slated to begin at 10 o'clock in the morning.

Some two hours later, when Kim Jong-il's absence became a reality, naturally the people present started to wonder whether something bad had happened to the Dear Leader. In the end, the scale of the event was reduced: the North Korean military was omitted from the military parade, and only the Workers and Peasant Red Guard and the Red Youth Guards participated.[14] It was in a sense a trivial matter, yet it confirms the weakness of the North Korean regime, wholly dependent on a single person.

As for Kim Jong-il's treatment, in the early stages the dominant view was to depend on domestic medical staff, mainly from Ponghwa Clinic. The main reason for that was maintenance of secrecy and security. However, Jang Song-thaek firmly opposed this and hurriedly invited doctors from overseas, notably China and France, mobilizing the presidential plane to fly them in. He wanted the doctors to treat Kim immediately.

The French doctors examined the patient and immediately went into surgery. Showing good progress, Kim Jong-il regained consciousness. Had something gone wrong with the operation and Kim never woken up, it would have been a huge problem for Jang. However, if North Korean doctors had been in charge of the treatment, then Kim Jong-il might not ever have regained consciousness. It was a decision only Jang Song-thaek could have taken, for he knew of the different medical standards between the North and other countries, and what's more he was in a position to take major decisions.

The other person who played a key role in bringing in the best foreign doctors was an overseas resident: Kim Jong-nam. After regaining consciousness and hearing what had happened, Kim Jong-il thanked Jang Song-thaek profusely and expressed his trust in his brother-in-law. It was indeed only his family that he could trust.[15]

Kim Jong-il was under a strict health management plan for the next three months. During that period, the regime ran under the emergency management system Jang had established, which was centered on himself. Even once Kim Jong-il had regained consciousness, he was frequently incapable of seeing to pending matters. A handful of individuals watched at his bedside: Jang Song-thaek and Kim Kyong-hui, Kim Ok (Kim Jong-il's fourth wife), and the late Ryu Kyong-su's wife Hwang Sun-hui.[16]

From October, Kim Jong-il's recovery began to speed up, and he began to cautiously engage in outside activities as part of his rehabilitation. However, he would never fully regain his health.[17] Still, he went out even though it was a risk to his health, such as to a closed-door tour of the newly built recreation resort on Mt. Ryongak in Pyongyang, and a soccer match between Kim Il-sung University and Pyongyang Railway College.

Kim Jong-il's daily schedule was also taken care of mainly by Jang Song-thaek and Kim Kyong-hui. From this time, the couple's status unprecedentedly changed. To Kim Kyong-hui was endowed the title of military general, and Jang Song-thaek was finally given a concurrent post, the one he had no luck earning until then: member of the National Defense Commission.

Although in appearance he seemed worn out, Kim Jong-il started to go out more and gained strength. In August of the following year, when former U.S. President Bill Clinton visited Pyongyang to negotiate the release of two American female journalists held in the North, Kim Jong-il attended a meeting that ran over 75 minutes, and also hosted a two-hour-long dinner.

Nevertheless, an American doctor who accompanied Clinton on the trip said he thought he observed many problems in Kim Jong-il's health. The diagnosis was that his illness was quite likely to recur in two to three years, and then it might be impossible for him to recover.

This diagnosis was incredibly prophetic.

One of the most difficult dilemmas shared by supreme power holders is the matter of choosing a successor. Choosing a successor early can help in stabilizing the government, but it might also siphon power from the current ruler. Frequently, people who relish absolute power tend to misconceive that their power will last for eternity.

In Kim Jong-il's case, he settled himself as the only successor to his father. Rather than becoming successor by top-down nomination, one could say he built the position using his own abilities.

However, Kim Jong-il did not take measures with regard to his successor until he collapsed. The person who first showed keen interest in the successor matter was Ko Yong-hui in her final years, but that was because she sensed that she did not have much longer to live. Entering the New Millennium, Ko once raised the idea of nominating her first son Jong-chol as successor.

After Ko, a second person to mention the successor issue was reporter Rang Sun of the *Rodong Sinmun*. Rang was an editorial writer and a political desk reporter at the head office of the party bulletin. The political desk was the section in charge of the latest news on Kim Jong-il. Rang was known for her looks and impeccable writing, but especially for receiving information enabling her to write scoops that other reporters couldn't dream of getting. Rang wrote so many articles on worshipping the Great Leader that she earned the trust of Kim Jong-il, and she was also invited to his evening parties. Her husband Kim Man-yong, who worked at the same company, was a recipient of the Kim Il-sung Award and an automobile from Kim Jong-il. One of Rang's scoops was an article entitled, "Short naps and rice balls," an ode to the Dear Leader for sacrificing his sleep, and having mere rice balls as his meals to continue his guidance for the nation. The story touched many North Koreans.[18]

It was Rang who first raised the matter of designating a successor to Kim Jong-il among the Great Leader's family. However, Kim Jong-il then did not consider succession to be an urgent matter. He brushed off the subject saying that his children were still too young, and asked back, "what was the need when he was still in good health." Even until the mid-2000s, Kim Jong-il's was disinclined to so much as mention the word succession.

However, Kim Jong-il had long since been well disposed toward Kim Jong-un, his second son with Ko Yong-hui. He judged that Jong-un's aggressive and strong disposition was optimal for a leader. He stopped trusting Jong-nam, his oldest son with Song Hye-rim, after

Japanese immigration authorities caught him trying to visit Japan on a fake passport.

Kim Jong-nam made numerous attempts to regain his father's trust, but he never could restore the father-and-son relationship, especially after the bad news reached Pyongyang that his maternal aunt Song Hye-rang and her daughter Nam-ok had defected. The one person who might speak on his behalf, his mother Song Hye-rim, was long gone from Kim Jong-il's side.

Fortunately, Kim Jong-il's condition was manageable thanks to the surgical prowess of the doctor. But he still couldn't move his body at will. He also had chronic illnesses, diabetes, and high blood pressure, and needed dialysis twice a week due to kidney failure. But since his heart had weakened as well, he could only receive dialysis once a week or every ten days. He would often be out of touch with reality.

One day Kim abruptly said he was going to the February 8th Vinylon Factory in Hamhung and ordered the preparations to leave. The factory, built by South Korean defector chemist Ri Sung-ki on the orders of Kim Il-sung, made a synthetic fiber called vinylon (or vinalon) out of limestone. But the quality of vinylon textile was poor, and production consumed an impractical amount of electricity, so it was already considered a failure.

Nevertheless, to liven up Kim Jong-il's mood, the February 8th Factory made it look as if the production lines were producing an overabundance of goods.

Upon his arrival at the factory, Kim Jong-il was pleased to see that all was running perfectly and satisfied to see the end products piled up like a mountain, but then said something that shocked everyone within hearing range.

"Comrades, wrap this vinylon up. How glad the Great Leader will be when I show it to him!"[19]

The people who were around Kim could only stare at each other. When his illness was aggravated, Kim Jong-il sometimes responded excessively. At times, he'd be full of suspicion and in such a state of anxiety that he'd give orders that did not make any sense. But soon he'd turn around, regret the order he had just given, and apologize. Recollecting his past, he'd become sentimental and often shed tears.[20]

As the successor matter grew urgent in late 2008, secretive chatter took place among high government officials. The rumor was that Jang Song-thaek and Kim Kyong-hui were pushing for Kim Jong-nam;

while the Party Organization and Guidance Department's first deputy director Ri Je-kang and the Party Administrative Department deputy director Ri Su-yong (Ri Chol) both recommmended Kim Jong-un. And it was added in low whispers that depending on who became the successor, one group would rise to the top, and the other would become traitors.

However, no one was in a position to raise the issue of a successor, not even Jang Song-thaek. It was only Kim Jong-il who could bring up the subject. For instance, if Kim Jong-il asked in the form of a question, "I'm thinking of designating Jong-un as successor. What do you think?" officials would express their full support, or if he asked, "Who do you think would be suitable?" they might reply with the utmost caution, trying to read his mind and feelings.[21]

The very first thing Kim Jong-il did after regaining consciousness was to see to the matter of his successor. One day, Kim Jong-il had the people standing by his bedside all leave; that is Hwang Sun-hui, Kim Ok, and his sons Jong-chol and Jong-un, and daughter Yo-jong. All except for Jang Song-thaek and Kim Kyong-hui.

Then Kim Jong-il asked the couple: who must he appoint as the "revolution's successor"?

Kim Kyong-hui was already debilitated in both mind and body from alcohol and drug addiction. She merely glanced at her husband.

Jang Song-thaek already knew who Kim Jong-il had in mind.

And he himself thought, rather than Jong-nam, who lived an uninhibited life abroad, or fainthearted Jong-chol, Jong-un would be better. Jang believed that he could well assist young Jong-un and gradually realize the reforms he had in mind. Jang Song-thaek cautiously started to speak.

"How about your youngest son?"

Kim Jong-il did not show an immediate response, but a slight expression of relief and satisfaction reflected on his face. After a long pause, Kim Jong-il spoke.

"Yes, let's place the youngest one. But keep this classified until I tell you to make it public."

After that, Kim Jong-il started to take Kim Jong-un with him to military bases and Party Central Committee events. Finally, in the following year (2009) on January 8, Kim Jong-un's birthday, the Party, Military, and Administrative Department head officials were told to gather at the Party Central Committee's main complex office and there it was announced, "The next successor of the Juche Revolution, which originated from Comrade Kim Il-sung, will be Comrade Kim Jong-un." The gathered group was asked to express their congratulations, and loud cheers instantaneously roared from the office.[22]

"Long live dear venerable general!"

"Long live the Juche Revolution!"

Jang Song-thaek and Kim Kyong-hui together also cheered.

After Kim Jong-il's illness and relative recovery, the plan for the succession was decided without too much trouble. Besides his youngest son, without any justification, Kim Jong-il suddenly endowed the Korean People's Army titles on Jang Song-thaek, Kim Kyong-hui, Choe Ryong-hae, and Organization and Guidance Department's first deputy director Kim Kyong-ok. The appointments were a non-verbal sign to the four awardees to look after the young supreme leader after his father was gone.

In late 2011, Kim Jong-il finally died. Jang Song-thaek together with Kim Kyong-hui announced the news of the Dear Leader's passing, and the couple prepared the funeral procedures and started to take various measures so that Kim Jong-un could smoothly be appointed as the Korean People's Army's supreme commander, the Korean Worker's Party's first secretary, and the first chairman of the National Defense Commission.[23]

Looking back, for Jang Song-thaek, the period that stood out the most was from when Kim Jong-il was bed-ridden to Kim Jong-un's rise to power. This wasn't a matter of his official positions. Throughout his whole adult life, he lived on the fringes of the Kim regime. He did not belong to the Kim family, but was merely dependent on them. He even heard the expression "a side tree" in reference to him, instead of "a side branch." However, in this last instance, he overcame the limitations of his family background and played a most important role at the core of the regime.

When Kim Jong-il collapsed and was bedridden, there wasn't anyone who could actually take over his tasks in the government. That was because Kim Jong-il had thoroughly prevented the possibility of any challenging force from arising, or anyone trying to replace his power within the Kim family, and he had stigmatized everyone as a bunch of "side branches" and had politically castrated them to be defenseless, except for his own politically ambitionless sister Kyong-hui. Thereby, from Jang Song-thaek's view, it was the first and last time in his life that he played a role overcoming his limitations as a man standing on the borderline. That is, he played a pivotal part standing in a position of quasi-family head despite his status of a son-in-law married into his wife's family.

However, Jang Song-thaek failed to realize that his status would be a temporary and treacherous one. He did not imagine what might happen to him once the family's legitimate prince would succeed to the throne and secure his seat. On the contrary, he was overwhelmed by a lethal illusion that his situation would last forever.

Inexplicably, around this time a good many of Jang Song-thaek's life-long enemies died one after the other. Ri Yong-chol died of chronic illness on April 26, 2010. Ri Je-kang died in a traffic accident on June 2nd of the same year. And Ri Je-kang's successor as first deputy director died of illness in September of that year. These were all coincidences and had nothing whatsoever to do with Jang.[24] Nevertheless, these incidents enabled him to grow in confidence.

> *He shall spurn fate, scorn death, and bear*
> *His hopes 'bove wisdom, grace, and fear.*
> *And you all know, security*
> *Is mortals' chiefest enemy.*
> —Shakespeare, *Macbeth* (Act 3, Scene 5)

It wasn't that Jang Song-thaek focused only on settling the risks of the former regime and solidifying the roots of the successor at the time. In his mind, he was busy pondering ways to realize his ideas under the new regime: he wanted to solve the most imminent of North Korea's economic problems by adapting Chinese-style reforms.

But first, the succession question had to be dealt with. And while helping the new leader, he would have to gather his own people around him so that he could work with them and also thereby increase his power. Then he had to obtain Chinese cooperation. If possible, he had to cooperate with South Korea as well, attracting their capital and technology. Jang was aware of how difficult and perilous a task it all was. However, without extraordinary reforms, he did not believe there would be a tomorrow for North Korea.

Jang Song-thaek not only made a meritorious contribution to the cause of the Kim regime at a time of crisis; he also devised a plan for the country's future. But this ended up placing him in great danger.

It would also have been dangerous in other countries, but especially under North Korea's monolithic leadership structure: to take a role that goes beyond one's limitations means to put one's life on the line.

Jang Song-thaek went up against several of the regime's most precious taboos and began to forge new customs. In 2009, in the name of the Party's administrative director, he conducted an inspection tour of regional parties. That would have been impossible in the past. Upon an event held at Miryong on Mt. Paektu in Samjiyeon County, Yanggang Province (Kim Jong-il's mythical birthplace) on Kim Jong-il's birthday, February 16th of that year, Jang officially participated as an official of the Central presidential group. He then participated in the Yanggang Provincial Party general assembly as a guidance official,[25] which was again against previous regulations.

Through late 2010, the so-called pilot construction projects that received guidance from Kim Jong-il and Kim Jong-un, namely the Taedonggang Tile Factory, Mirim Riding Club, the State Security Department's umbrella Competition Bullets Factory, and Haedanghwagwan in Pyongyang were mostly under the direction of Jang Song-thaek.

Jang's status and influence had amplified enormously. It goes without saying that hubris was now his biggest threat.

8

The Past Is Never Dead

> The past is never dead. It's not even past.
>
> —William Faulkner

Pyongyang in December. It was bitterly cold as Jang Song-thaek waited for his final moment.

His fate had been decided long, long ago. Indeed, his end began with Kim Jong-il's death and Kim Jong-un's rise. Actually, his destiny may have been preordained decades ago, when he was passionately courted by Kim Kyong-hui, or when the two got married and, selected by Kim Jong-il, he took the road to power. In the frame of the monolithic leadership system, where he would inevitably stand, became a sensitive issue. And his position grew all the more precarious the more the new leader settled in as the absolute leader.

Jang Song-thaek was an outstanding man wherever and whenever he went. He was talented in virtually all fields. He was even good looking. He could be the life of a party, singing and dancing, drinking and playing cards. He was skillful in management and processing tasks. Most of the main buildings in Pyongyang were his work in one way or another. He drew people's attention wherever he went.

Most important of all was the fact that people would always gather around him. It wasn't just because he was the Great Leader's son-in-law and the Dear Leader's brother-in-law and close aide. Nor was it only because of the power he held. Wherever he went, whatever he did, he was one of those exceptional people who naturally drew others to him. He was earnestly empathetic toward people in difficulty. His popularity was by no means merely attributable to his attractiveness.

"This is a great man," was the impression Kim Jong-il's former chef had of Jang.[1] Having lived in the North for thirteen long years, Fujimoto had met countless North Korean officials and other members of elite families. But the only one who impressed him as a genuine person was Jang.

Jang Song-thaek sought power, but not merely for power's sake, or for his survival. The power he sought came with the vision of a solution to the North's totally closed reality. That is, he did not seek power like others did—simply for his own wellbeing, for his own interest, or for personal glory.

Such qualities naturally were of the utmost concern to the young and, more importantly, inexperienced new leader. The man, who had felt like a reliable supporter and tutor in the early stages of his rise to power, was gradually becoming a burden. The man was the Great Leader's son-in-law, the Dear Leader's brother-in-law, the Dear General's beloved sister's husband, the Supreme Leader Kim Jong-un's aunt's husband: a man who transcended the borders of the core leadership, and was in an important but also somehow uncomfortable and sensitive position.

Jang Song-thaek had a fundamentally different view regarding the country's future: reform and opening. It wasn't simply a difference of policy orientation. Ultimately, it was about the continuous governance of one line, one family. Jang believed the North ought to open up to the outside world and thoroughly reform from the inside out. Such a complete change of policy had little to do with the maintenance of the monolithic leadership of the Paektu lineage or guaranteeing the safety of the regime.

Jang could never become someone like Ri Jae-il or Kim Yong-nam. The first deputy director of the Propaganda and Agitation Department, Ri Jae-il endlessly humbled himself and never stood out, and so he remained a close aide to the Supreme Leader from the time of the Kim Jong-il regime. Such functionaries did not choose their own people as secretaries, or even chauffeurs, but requested that the Party make recommendations. If Jang had behaved like Ri Jae-il or Kim Yong-nam, he would still be alive today.[2] However, even if Jang had tried to behave so, he couldn't have kept it up for long.

There are several rationales put forward for Jang Song-thaek's execution. A political struggle for power was taking place within the regime, especially vis-à-vis Jang's relationship with Choe Ryong-hae, a known competitor. Some viewed the conflict as one between distinguished loyalists, led by Choe Ryong-hae, and "the in-laws" represented by Jang. Others saw it as tension between conservatives, mainly the military, and economically minded reformists. Still others regarded it as a struggle over vested economic interests. One North Korean official, speaking anonymously, explained that Jang was executed because he conspired with China, handing them classified information at a wretched price.[3]

The above views may all serve to explain and/or describe his execution. However, if we step back and look at the big picture, we find that Jang's fate was already determined before any of these scenarios played out.

Jang Song-thaek was held in check when Kim Jong-il was alive. Among the four organizations responsible for the security of the regime—State Security, People's Security, the Central Prosecutors' Office, and the Central Court—the most important, State Security, did not fall under the Party Administrative Department, which was Jang's sole jurisdiction. The measure was taken to keep Jang under control. And just as the leader of the day had intended, Jang's fall began there. Moreover, in addition to State Security, Jang also had no access to the military and munitions departments.

In his last days, Kim Jong-il took his successor Kim Jong-un on a tour of a children's hospital built with aid from South Korea situated in front of Pyongyang Medical College. One of the large structures nearby was used by an organization working on espionage in South Korea. Kim Jong-il remarked that he didn't particularly like the building, and that its maintenance was lousy.

Everyone immediately looked at the Party Central Committee Pyongyang Party Secretary, Mun Kyong-dok, who was on the tour. As quick as a flash, he gave an excuse, "That building was built under the responsibility of the Party Administrative Department." In other words, it wasn't the city of Pyongyang's responsibility. To this, Jang Song-thaek could not remain silent. There was emotion in his words, since Jang had appointed Mun in the first place. Jang countered Mun's claim, and the two ended up quarreling.

But instead of settling the dispute, Kim Jong-il watched the scene, amused, even quietly encouraging Mun. The sight would have been a lesson to the successor, Kim Jong-un.[4]

Nevertheless, Kim Jong-un and his uncle Jang Song-thaek would have seemed very close in the eyes of outsiders. Upon hosting a dinner for an important foreign delegate a few days before Kim Jong-il's death, Kim Jong-un showed signs of being closer to Jang Song-thaek than to anybody else. The relationship between the two was qualitatively different from that with ordinary North Korean senior officials. When the time came to bid the guests farewell, Kim Jong-un and Ri Yong-ho both stepped aside to make way for Kim Jong-il. Ri Yong-ho first yielded to Kim Jong-un, but Kim insisted and in the end Ri stood on that spot. Conversely, Kim Jong-un and Jang Song-thaek were beyond that level. Smiling at each other, they behaved naturally, as if they were close.

People were surprised to hear not long after Kim Jong-un took power that Ri Yong-ho had been purged. But they were even more shocked when they learned that Jang Song-thaek had been killed.

In spring of 2013, Jang Song-thaek was quite anxious about the crisis of inter-Korean economic cooperation, as the Kaesong Industrial Complex faced permanent closure. Jang asked Kim Kyong-hui to propose to Kim Jong-un that he ought not close the Complex.

Jang could not openly oppose the third nuclear test in February that year, or the launch of the Unha-3 rocket a few months later, yet he did make his negativity evident. He did not confront the adoption by the Party Central Committee of the so-called *pyongjin* line of "building the economy and nuclear arms in parallel" either, but he was not well disposed to the idea and expressed his concerns to people close to him, including Kim Kyong-hui.

"Almost every country in the whole world, including China and Russia, opposes North Korea's nuclear arms program and is sanctioning us, so how are we supposed to simultaneously develop nuclear arms and develop the economy?" In short, Jang diverted from the official policy line of the new leadership, and thus ended up isolating himself.

However, the execution of Jang Song-thaek did not arise from politics or conflicting interests between departments. It was all about firmly erecting the newly emerging power center as the "monolithic" origin of all power. Had it been a matter of simple conflict, the like of which frequently crops up between departments or individuals, his execution would not have been done in such a grave manner.

As the procedure of conviction and execution makes clear, Jang's sentencing was tantamount to a top-down coup. The Choson Sinbo, published in Japan commented, "If the ordinary people living in Joseon (North Korea) were shocked by this incident (. . .) the fact is that someone, who attempted a political coup against the fatherland's Party's monolithic leadership, was hiding there."[5]

There is another story from the time when Jang Song-thaek visited the South some ten years earlier at the head of a large economic delegation. Hwang Jang-yop, who was then living in asylum in the South, urgently sought another exiled elite with whom Hwang was on good terms. Handing over two envelopes to the man, Hwang urged him not to open them until he was back home alone.

The first envelope contained a memo with orders to secretly approach Jang Song-thaek and pass him the second envelope. The memo in the second envelope read as follows:

> Jang Song-thaek, it is not too late even now. Will you become the fatherland's traitor? If not, remain in the South![6]

Of course, the second memo never reached the hands of its designated recipient. Even had it been delivered, there was no possibility at that time for Jang Song-thaek to seek asylum in the South. Nevertheless, the anecdote suggests a number of interesting things. It indicated that at least Hwang Jang-yop believed he and Jang Song-thaek were in considerable agreement vis-à-vis the Kim Jong-il regime. Otherwise, Hwang had no reason to suggest defection, not to a man higher on the totem pole than Hwang had ever been.

Meanwhile, Kim Kyong-hui never took the road of power, nor did she play an important role politically. She had no need to: her status and influence were guaranteed by her father and her brother. Even if she did not play any special role in Kim Jong-il's regime, her actual influence was next to that of the supreme leader.

In any regime, there is a "power that is invisible to the eye" though unofficial. But all the more so in theocratic North Korea; there it was reality. Kim Kyong-hui was part of the system and structure that ruled. As long as her brother was alive, she did not need to care about the world of power.

However, once power went over to her nephew Kim Jong-un, things changed. In the first year that her nephew newly appeared as the supreme leader, Kim Kyong-hui accompanied Kim Jong-un on an onsite guidance trip. If you look at the photos taken that day, it clearly reveals how dramatically her status had collapsed. Her previously proud and upright posture had become a humble, cautious crouch as she walked next to her 31-year-old nephew. In the following year, along with Kim Kyong-hui, the influence of Jang Song-thaek started to decline. The number of times the couple accompanied Kim Jong-un on his onsite guidance visits noticeably dropped.[7]

Nevertheless, Jang Song-thaek did accompany Kim Jong-un off and on until late autumn 2013. He even accompanied Kim to a sports event: the finals of the public sports field of the pan-national provincial sports competition in October that year. Participating in a meeting on November 6 between the Japanese House of Councilors delegation and North Korea's sports university representatives was the last official schedule of Jang Song-thaek's close to four decades of service.

An uneasy presentiment lingered. But the final moment came abruptly.

Once Kim Jong-un inherited the regime, Jang Song-thaek vastly widened the scope of his activities, all in accordance with the line of the late Kim Jong-il era.

Jang had been doing the same things since the late Kim Jong-il era, but it all became public at the 3rd Party Delegates' Conference in 2010, where Kim Jong-un was revealed as the successor. The main aims were to reduce the status and role of the oversized military, and to have the Party take over at the center of government.

Jang Song-thaek actively expanded his role in the process of having the Party return to the core of governance; however, along the way he inevitably ran into conflict with other organizations. It was unavoidable: he ran headlong into the military, State Security, and the Party Organization and Guidance Department. As the person in charge of the Party Administrative Department, Jang controlled public security—the judiciary, prosecution, and police. In addition, he established new umbrellas of the Party's Administrative Department in provincial and county Party committees. He also set up a sub-organization of the Party Administrative Department, a research institute for strategic studies, by which he wanted to propose economic policies. In fact, he might well have waited his whole life to set up this very research institute.

But Jang unfailingly violated the rights of not only the military, the State Security Department, and the Party Organization and Guidance Department, but also of Cabinet members' vested interests.[8] The cutthroat collisions surrounded the economic interests of all these organizations.

Jang Song-thaek made full use of his positions at the head of the Party Administrative Department and deputy chair of the National Defense Commission. He expanded construction projects which had been ordered by Kim Jong-il, including Pyongyang city housing, Munsu Water Park, Ryugyongwon, Rungna Dolphinarium, Haedanghwagwan, Potonggang Department Store, and Mirim Riding center.

The projects were necessary in the early stages of the new supreme leader Kim Jong-un. The best symbol of immense power is monumental construction. The problem is that such mega projects are often extremely expensive, and foreign currency is involved. Moreover, wherever there is money and power, whether one wishes it or not, people gather like flies, and close acquaintances tag along, swearing loyalty. Costs rise.

In truth, the construction projects that Jang Song-thaek thought of as top priorities were of a different order from the ones listed above. He was more interested in social infrastructure that could help rebuild the North Korean economy, such as railways, airports, seaports, roads, communication facilities, and an energy industry. But Kim Jong-il always ordered exhibition projects within the boundaries of existing capital. It was a constant problem: orders for development were shortsighted and focused only on achievements that would be visible almost immediately. They never looked ahead to the future.

Jang was dissatisfied. There were more than a hundred ideas in his mind, but he couldn't openly talk about them. Jang was aware that to build infrastructure, one required investment capital and preparations of a totally different scale from the construction projects he was then conducting. But neither of the supreme leaders, Kim Jong-il nor Kim Jong-un, had any desire to agree to those projects, and more importantly, the Republic was not ready to engage in civil engineering projects on such a massive size.[9]

Any huge project in a Socialist country requires the State to mobilize State organizations to provide resources and do the construction. In that sense, if much of the power is centered in one organization, others feel naturally daunted. While he was alive, Kim Jong-il merged the former 7th and the 8th general bureaus of the Ministry of People's Security into the 2nd and the 3rd corps under the Construction Department of the Korean People's Army; and to ease the burden of the Party Administrative Department's major construction projects, Kim endowed Jang with the title of deputy chairman of the

National Defense Committee, giving him the commander rights of the unit. In the name of his new additional title, Jang mobilized the KPA construction staff's 2nd and 3rd corps to carry out the capital's construction plans.

Many followers were attracted to Jang, under the illusion that being close to a man in charge of so many big construction projects overflowing with resources and people throughout the city of Pyongyang could be their ticket to success. Jang's memory of his revolutionization experience but seven or eight years ago was dim, stored in a distant corner of his consciousness.

Jang did not focus on his position and influence, or on ways to enhance them. The more projects he engaged in, the more he perceived the limits of what could be done with such a restricted budget. That is, what work was possible was already determined by the state's foreign currency reserves, North Korea's limited human resources, and its technological capacity. If one organization launched a project, that meant another organization would face restrictions. This brought about dissatisfaction, jealousy, and even political conflict.

Jang's plan was China.

> China is not only doing a fine job of feeding its 1.3 billion people, it is achieving development not short of, or perhaps even more advanced than Japan and the United States, isn't it?
>
> If we changed our minds just slightly, North Korea could also attract an infinite amount of foreign capital and technology very quickly, and achieve development comparable to the South.

Jang's thoughts were not out of the blue; not recent ideas devised in a day or two. He had held them in his heart for at least twenty years.

> Why can't we do that? We should do that, shouldn't we?

Notwithstanding the need for change, there was an underlying problem that plagued his mind. Even if the regime opened its doors to foreign investment and actively engaged in trade with other countries, it could maintain its system, just like China had done with its one Party dictatorship, and so had Vietnam. However, could the North hold on to its monolithic leadership system dominated by the Kim family, as it had at present? Wouldn't Kim Jong-un believe that it would be better for him to seek political stability through nuclear arms than risk his power via economic development?

If developing a nuclear program meant North Korea would be isolated from the international community, even that wouldn't be bad news for the security of his government. North Korea's supreme leader is a demigod figure, at least within the country. There is a great difference between the stature of the supreme leader in the North and leaders in other countries. And that difference is an obstacle. It stops North Korea from exposing itself in the way other countries do in the international arena.

Jang Song-thaek believed there was a need to persuade the young new leader of this point. He believed it could be done: that after all, military power was in the long term impossible without economic power. Whereas by keeping the present system while conducting limited reforms and opening the door to trade, one could build the powerful nation desired by Kim Jong-un's predecessor.

It could be possible if he stressed the importance of cooperation with China. And Kim Jong-un easily understood Jang's plan to visit China. However, it of course was a mistake, one that only hastened Jang's end. Only Jang was unaware of that.

In August 2012, a scorching hot summer in Northeast Asia, Jang Song-thaek led a fifty-man delegation to China upon the occasion of the 3rd Meeting of the DPRK–China Joint Steering Committee for the Development of Hwanggumpyong and Rason Districts. China gave a highly cordial reception to the influential man from a most unstable state. From President Hu Jintao on down, he met all senior government officials.

Jang Song-thaek's main task was to arrange cooperation with China at a meeting for the development of Hwanggumpyong and Rason, two special economic zones. He ran into no difficulty on that front. Jang and Chinese Minister of Commerce Chen Deming signed an agreement for the joint development.

However, Jang failed in another respect, which was arguably North Korea's most pressing need: urgent assistance worth one billion USD. It was a countermeasure to make up for the shortage of foreign currency North Korea had been experiencing since inter-Korean economic exchanges were cut off. One other pressing interest was expanding Chinese investment in North Korea. China's attitude toward these two agenda items was not at all positive. The money was not possible in the short term. China saw it as something to be negotiated in connection with the North Korean nuclear program. As for more investment, the North would have to meet certain prerequisites to get support for the idea.

Premier of the State Council Wen Jiabao listed failed examples of Chinese corporations' investments in North Korea, and remarked on the importance of North Korea's investment climate if it wanted to win foreign investment. He said that the Law on Foreign Investment in particular would have to be revised. It couldn't have been a more embarrassing moment for Jang. But at the same time, he knew it all perfectly well already.

Many foreign corporations had done business in the North down through the years, making the mistake of thinking it was like other countries and then experiencing bitter failure. It was true that the North has many restrictions, starting with entry permits. Another problem is the poor condition of North Korean social infrastructure, most significantly energy, which is essential for any business. Then there is the exasperating attitude of petty officialdom, who see foreign companies as easy prey. Jang was aware of many cases of failed foreign investment, including those made by ethnic Korean businessmen from Japan, who came with a generally favorable view of the North, and the Xiyang Group, one of the top 500 Chinese conglomerate companies.[10]

After his return to Pyongyang, Jang Song-thaek reported to Kim Jong-un on the meeting with Wen Jiabao, and initiated revisions of the Law on Foreign Investment. One of the measures taken was to assign international trade mediation to the National Defense Commission. In other words, Jang Song-thaek was put in charge of the government agency in charge of regulating foreign investment.

The Party Administrative Department, which Jang managed, put in place measures to legalize housing transactions. Houses had previously been sold in secret, and if dealings were detected by the authorities, the house was turned over to the state. Despite this, the demand for housing increased throughout North Korea, and in Pyongyang housing prices soared, surpassing 50,000 USD, 100,000 USD, and even occasionally 200,000 USD in places. The situation was such that housing deals could not be kept secret anymore. In the end, the Party Administrative Department took steps to legalize the sale of housing. It was a dramatic sea change, as marketization expanded into new areas of the North Korean economy.

Elsewhere, the number of taxi companies in Pyongyang jumped fourfold, from one or two companies to seven or eight. The previously passive official attitude toward tourism, full of criticisms that it would bring about an air of capitalism, changed; suddenly everyone believed tourists must be attracted and the tourism industry promoted. Then the government permitted extensions of sojourns abroad for company executives, and even granted direct permission for family members to join their heads of household abroad. In Pyongyang, more facilities were built to accept hard currency, such as Potonggang Department Store and Haedanghwagwan. A debit card called Koryo was introduced and accepted at overseas service organizations and foreign currency shops.

Jang Song-thaek vastly expanded the country's special economic zones, too. In 2010, five special economic zones were added to the previous Rason SEZ. Mere days before he was executed, on November 22, 2013, a total of thirteen more special economic zones were added. As a result, the total number of special economic zones in North Korea grew to twenty. Despite these measures, Jang was not able to lead North Korea onto the road of reform.

Jang also played a decisive role in improving the food security situation of ordinary families. In 2012, food security was still dire. Kim Jong-un gave a special order to Jang Song-thaek to solve it. Jang convened a planning meeting, and in order to immediately obtain the necessary 800,000 tons of food, he released 300,000 tons of stored food and allotted quotas for the remaining 500,000 tons to various parts of the overseas trade and commercial sector. Thanks to these measures, a pressing food crisis was averted.[11]

Younger officials, who were opening their eyes to foreign goods around this time, began to harbor high expectations for the future of the North Korean economy. There were optimistic prognostications that in about ten years, there would be a clear change, be it in the Chinese way or another form. There was even word that an era of private car ownership would be possible in the North in a decade or so. These rosy outlooks withered with the execution of Jang Song-thaek. The main reason for that was that with his death, there was no longer a character with the political magnitude, personal conviction, and vision to get the job done.[12]

As Jang Song-thaek expanded his clout and forged ever closer relations with China, he received warnings from a good number of places. Kim Jong-un started to think negatively of Jang. Of course, in the first year that he appeared as the third-generation leader, he depended on Jang for many things. When Kim Jong-un received reports, he would sometimes ask Jang's opinion: seeking his advice and asking him how his father Kim Jong-il would deal with such cases.[13] Although theirs was strictly a monarch-servant relationship, on many occasions the young tyrant would feel awkward or find it difficult to give orders to the veteran, infinitely more experienced Jang.

Unlike Kim Jong-il, who had university classmates, the new leader Kim Jong-un had no close friends of the same age. All his offspring had grown up in a sealed-off environment with hardly any contact with their peers. Years before, the Japanese sushi chef Fujimoto had been puzzled when he received Kim Jong-il's orders to play with his children.

"Why is he asking me, a middle-aged foreigner who can't even speak Korean, to play with his children who are now only six and seven?"

But the Japanese chef soon realized why. There were no other children around.

Fujimoto, who spent a lot of time with Kim Jong-un when he was young, described the future leader as egoistic, ambitious, and violent. Once the boy went on a fishing trip with his parents on Kim Jong-il's presidential boat, and the group wagered on who would catch more fish. Fujimoto recalled how whenever he'd catch a fish, Kim Jong-un would dash next to him, snatch his rod, and excitedly cry out that he, in fact, had caught it.[14] Fujimoto wrote that the young boy was violent by nature; when he'd become angry, he'd rage even at his older brother Jong-chol, who most of the time would just tolerate the Jong-un's outbursts.

This phenomenon is common in second sons. We need not borrow the words of psychologists to know that second sons are normally more violent and have stronger cravings for the limelight than their older brothers. At any rate, Kim Jong-un was never an easy personality, and would never be intimidated by someone just because he was younger than they. He was used to power from a very young age and grew up seeing everyone tremble before him.

Fujimoto witnessed the teenage Kim Jong-un kick and tease a person called An Shin, a former aide to Kim Il-sung, who was well past sixty.[15] Kim Jong-un made fun of him, demanding to know "why the Great Leader used that pudgy guy as his adjutant!" His behavior would not have been normal even from a prince or crown prince in the ancient dynasties era. An Shin just accepted the humiliation without even thinking of scolding the Great Leader's grandson. Unable to bear the scene any longer, Fujimoto conceived a scheme to end it. An gave a modest grin and bowed his head deeply to the Japanese cook.

In North Korea, where a great many old men are still in government service, the new leader was considered young. However, a person in their early thirties is not so young as to be unable to make judgments. So, after a year had passed and Kim Jong-un entered his second year in power, he gradually grew conscious of his true authority. And on many occasions, Jang Song-thaek's presence felt like a burden.

Disturbing rumors would reach the new ruler's ears. There were people around who would feed Kim Jong-un information to trouble his mind.

"Isn't Jang Song-thaek's relationship with China a bit too close?"

His father, Kim Jong-il had once said that the regime had more to fear from China than from the United States or South Korea. When North Korea first succeeded in developing nuclear arms, one of Kim Jong-il's first reactions had been, "Now we won't have to be interfered with by China."[16] "The republic must maintain close and friendly relations with China, yet watch out for its policy of favoring great powers."

But here was Jang Song-thaek trying to lead the regime to open its doors to foreign capital and technology, backed by China.

Years later, a Chinese high government official who is a close acquaintance of the writer remarked once that from China's point of view, the execution of Jang Song-thaek was "an attempt to eliminate China's influence over North Korea."

There were more troublesome reports than that. One aide showed Kim Jong-un a leaflet flown across the DMZ from the South. "In North Korea, the Kim monarchy will soon come to an end and the Jang monarchy will begin."

On the leaflet was a low-quality yet meaningful cartoon drawing of himself and Jang Song-thaek. Soon after New Year's Day in

2013, the Intelligence Headquarters of the South Korean Ministry of National Defense issued a special press release:

> From this year, Jang Song-thaek has often been seen taking little account of First Secretary Kim Jong-un, so we are hearing rumors that the actual supreme power within the North is Jang Song-thaek, not Kim Jong-un.

The report pointed out that Jang Song-thaek did not attend an official gathering organized by Kim Jong-un; and that he did not keep a straight posture, but sat tilted sideways without paying full attention as Kim Jong-un made a speech at the 4th Conference of Cell Secretaries of the Worker's Party. In the two photos that the South Korean Ministry of National Defense published as evidence, Jang Song-thaek was indeed either sitting slanted, or glancing in a different direction from the front while Kim Jong-un was giving his speech.

These things touched sensitive nerves in the Party Organization and Guidance and State Security Departments.[17] But more than that, the fact that the South Korean military distributed such a press release couldn't have been better news for Jang Song-thaek's enemies. Kim Jong-un also knew very well that this was psychological warfare intended to stir anxiety and conflict in the North Korean ruling class, yet he couldn't help thinking about it.

Then, toward the year end of 2012, an incident occurred that truly grated on Kim Jong-un's nerves. In Pyongyang on November 3, the day Kim Jong-un was due to visit Ryukyongwon prior to completion, a rumor spread that Kim's bodyguards were checking the site and found a loaded machine gun under a tree.[18] Although wide-ranging investigations were conducted, it was not revealed how that weapon had ended up in such a place. The machine gun had no serial number that could identify its unit or owner. Could it have been left there by mistake? No chance.

One thing that was certain was the facilities Kim Jong-un was to tour that day: Ryukyongwon, and an ice rink and roller skating rink all built by soldiers of the KPA under the command of Jang Song-thaek. Could it have been an act by someone trying to frame Jang? Whether such a rumor was true or not, it is a fact that around that time an incident occurred that made Kim Jong-un fear for his life.

After that event, Kim Jong-un reinforced his personal security. The team responsible for his up-close security changed from Escort

Command under Yun Jong-rin to Security Commmand under Cho Kyong-chol. Armored vehicles were placed not only at Kim Jong-un's residence, but also at some thirty of his villas and personal facilities; Cho Kyong-chol personally carried a pistol with him and protected Kim by remaining at his side. The bodyguards not only wore pistols, but also put on helmets and were deployed with machine guns and grenade launchers.

After the machine gun incident, Kim Jong-un visited the State Security Department not once but *twice* and ordered it to eradicate all hostile elements. Mulitple meetings of law enforcement officials were convened, mostly for the first time in more than a decade. All of North Korea's military chiefs were removed and, by July 2013 the following year, more than half of army corps commanders had been replaced.[19]

His second year in power just around the bend and feeling tense about his personal safety, Kim Jong-un may have kept on thinking of his aunt's husband Jang Song-thaek. Or Kim Jong-un could have been devising how to destroy Jang, and perhaps even imagined Jang's faction venturing a preemptive attack.

Two groups were keeping an eye on Jang. One was the military, dissatisfied at Jang's practical monopoly on limited resources. The other was the faction made up of those nervously watching Jang's influence grow thanks to his young nephew. In the latter group were State Security Department's first deputy director U Tong-chuk, and Party Organization and Guidance Department first deputy directors Cho Yon-jun, and Kim Kyong-ok. Hwang Pyong-so and Kim Won-hong also tried to restrain Jang's forces from growing.

It goes without saying that Jang was not in the dark about what was happening. After all, he had survived all those years on the battlefield of palace politics. First of all, the State Security Department's U Tong-chuk was a problem. Jang Song-thaek made a great effort to try and take control of that department, or to bring them to his side. But this angered U Tong-chuk, who accumulated considerable information on Jang's corrupt activities and was biding his time for an opportunity to use it. After all, U was appointed to command the Ministry and had special orders from Kim Jong-il to "Protect the Successor." U was no easy opponent for Jang.

But Jang was expecting a battle. He instantly mobilized the Ministry of People's Security and Supreme Prosecutors Office to gather documents on U Tong-chuk and submit a report to Kim Jong-un.

This time Kim Jong-un immediately gave orders to arrest U; however, learning of the news through his affiliates, U penned a suicide note before taking his own life with a pistol. The arrest team that had gone out to fetch U reported what happened to Jang Song-thaek and passed on the note, but Jang destroyed it and told Kim Jong-un that U killed himself out of fear of punishment.

Jang had not only failed to seize the State Security Department, but he had caused deep resentment within the organization. Of course, in the end it would be this very organization that arrested and executed Jang.[20]

The next organization that broke with Jang was the military, led by Ri Yong-ho. As far as the military was concerned, it was an eyesore for Jang to be suddenly appearing in public in a general's uniform, not to mention that his mobilization of military manpower for personal projects was a conflict of interest in the distribution of resources. Chief of Staff Ri had been appointed to the Worker's Party's Politburo and the Party Central Military Commission back in 2010 when Kim Jong-il promoted him from General to Vice Marshal. Ri was under orders to protect the successor with force of arms.

Ri Yong-ho was greatly displeased with Jang actively expanding his own territory. Ri would often comment that he was different from the reckless "quack star (fake general)," a thinly veiled reference to Jang. The situation had reached a point that Jang could no longer ignore.

Mobilizing the Party Administrative Department and the Prosecutors' Office, Jang started to dig into Ri Yong-ho's corruption; it was not hard to do. Few high government officials in the North Korean regime have clean backgrounds. The key problem wasn't the corruption, but the political judgment of the regime.

Jang Song-thaek reported on Ri to Kim Jong-un, who immediately ordered Ri's arrest. Naturally, Ri's corruption was not what mattered. The most important factor was that Kim Jong-un ordered Ri to hand over to the Party the rights of military-owned trade and commerce organizations, which earned foreign currency, but Ri allegedly refused to do so. To be exact, he did not refuse per se, but did complain.[21]

At dawn on July 17, 2012, a Korean People's Army Security Command arrest team surrounded Ri Yong-ho's residence, and at first there was a light clash with Ri's guards. However, the clash ended after Ri came out of his own accord and submitted to arrest. For Jang, it seemed like one more extreme conservative political enemy had been eliminated. However, Jang did not realize that these small victories were actually creating a very hostile environment against him.

To lay the groundwork for reform, Jang Song-thaek contained the State Security Department and the KPA, and lined up the Party Politiburo and the the Secretariat with personnel of an open disposition. At the same time, he started to deeply involve himself in the 3rd Economy; that is, foreign-currency earning businesses. He did so to obtain the capital needed for reform. But in the process, there were conflicts of ideas, and ultimately, he got on Kim Jong-un's nerves.

In the second half of 2013, some top military commanders accompanied Kim Jong-un on a visit to a military base on the west coast. On site, those senior military officers told Kim that the military was in extreme difficulty due to financial shortages, and blamed the Party Administrative Department, which was in charge of all the foreign-currency earning fish farms in the Yellow Sea. After hearing this, Kim Jong-un gave orders that the facilities be returned to the military, but the orders were not well executed because Jang stalled for time.[22]

The case ended with the arrest of one of Jang's close aides, but a bigger case was waiting for him. The slush funds collected during Kim Jong-il's life were ordered to be transferred from Office 39 to an umbrella of the Party Administrative Department, Bureau 54, which was to then support the oil business of the Sungni Trading Company that was managed by the Administrative Department.

One summer day in 2013, Kim Jong-un was looking at the accounts, and noticed that the amount of capital available to him was very limited. He summoned the deputy director of the Secretariat.

> Why are the expenses so petty? How was it managed during my father's and grandfather's times?

The Secretariat, which was unhappy with Jang anyway, reported as follows, pouring oil on the fire.

> The Dear General kept the funds in Room 39 and spent them on revolutionary projects; but now the Party's Administrative Department is managing the funds and spending as it pleases. Something must be done about this.

The funds that the Party Administrative Department was managing used to be handled by Department 54 of the KPA, but that duty had been transferred to the Administrative Department while Kim Jong-il was still alive. Therefore, it wasn't a matter that Kim Jong-un was in a position to know about in much detail. However, being already upset with Jang Song-thaek for a number of things, Kim Jong-un fulminated and, citing the Sungni Trading Company's fuel oil business as an example, had all funds immediately restored to Room 39.

Despite the orders, when staff arrived at the site and tried to enter the fuel oil depot, they were stopped by armed guards. It was no use trying to tell them that it was "the Marshal's Orders."

> If you want to go in, bring the approval of Comrade Number One.

Who on earth is Comrade Number One?

> Comrade Director Jang. You can go in only if you have his orders.

The festering wound finally burst out into the open. Upon hearing this report, Kim Jong-un lost his temper. He gave orders to Escort Command to mobilize arms and seize the site and then report back to him. A fully armed Escort Command unit headed to the fuel oil company, occupied the place, and reported back.

The incident was an opportunity for Kim Jong-un to clear once and for all a complex mixture of deeply imbedded feelings. The big picture was already settled. The only remaining question was when and in what situation to take care of the matter.

And now was that time. Once he had made up his mind, he was far from indecisive. He immediately called Party Organization and Guidance Department first deputy director Cho Yon-jun, and ordered him to audit Jang Song-thaek. For Cho, it was the opportunity of a lifetime, the one that he had been waiting for. The Party Organization and Guidance Department and the Administrative Department had a long history of hostility and conflict. The mission of the Organization and Guidance Department was to search for any element that threatened the monolithic leadership. The department had only ever been daunted by Jang Song-thaek's influence. Kim Won-hong of the

State Security Department joined in the audit, and started to file reports that meticulously pointed out Jang Song-thaek's corruption and factional activities.[23]

Testimonies about Jang Song-thaek's final days contradict one another to an extent that it is hard to ascertain their authenticity. One cannot assert whether the above actually occurred, much less whether they were the cause of Jang's execution. Even among well-informed North Korea watchers, opinions vary about the cause of Jang's purge. That there was no system that could mediate the conflicts rising from limited resources and power struggles between organizations and personnel, and that Kim Jong-un lacked the leadership to act as mediator of the conflicts between powerful institutions, were all reasonable theories.

However, what really mattered does not lie in these detailed facts. If conflicts of this magnitude were what brought about Jang's end, that end wouldn't have been so inhumane. The basic problem was determined before the discord was created, and the case was heading toward a prearranged conclusion.

The most important clue can be found in a speech Kim Jong-un gave in front of officials in June, 2013. The subject of the speech was "The Ten Principles for the Establishment of the Party Monolithic Leadership System." Changes to the previous version of the "Ten Principles" saw Kim Il-sung's revolutionary ideology changed to "Kim Il-sung-Kim Jong-il-ism," and the terminology "Paektu lineage" make an appearance, in effect stipulating the Kim family hereditary system as the highest authority, and stating any remote disturbance or threat should be dealt with mercilessly.

Taking a closer look, in Article 6, the phrase, "The phenomenon of idolization, such as having illusions or practicing flattery towards individual officials is strictly opposed," was changed to, "illusions, flattery, and idolization on individual officials is denounced, and the phenomena of acting blindly or against the principle daunted by the authority of individual officials must be abolished." In addition, in Clause 5, Article 6, it is said that the following phrase is inserted, "[One must] oppose the phenomena of people of a same group split apart, each striving for a different objective, and being seemingly obedient only, as well as all sorts of anti-Party elements, such as factionalism, regionalism, and familism, which gnaw at and destroy the Party's unified solidarity.[24]

This was almost exactly what was written in the court ruling prior to Jang Song-thaek's execution.

His fate was already determined. Not even a "side branch," but a "side tree" had to be uprooted so that the "main tree" could grow well. The merits and mistakes of the "side tree" were of no importance whatsoever; not in whatever way one might look at the situation,

Jang had no chance of surviving in a system where his young nephew appeared as the supreme leader.

Jang's end, which approached him slowly and gradually over many years, finally hit him abruptly when the moment came. Once Kim Jong-un had made up his mind and drew his sword, all organizations and officials moved on the tip of his blade.

Nobody stood up for Jang Song-thaek. Even if anyone had wanted to, they could not.

Kim Jong-un promptly placed the Party and Military on alert, and suspended all work of the Party Administrative Department. Hee ordered the arrest of Jang's closest two aides, Administrative Department's first deputy director Ri Ryong-ha, and deputy director Jang Su-kil. The two arrested men did not last a day before confessing to all of Jang Song-thaek's violations. Upon receiving their written confessions, Kim Jong-un ordered them to be executed in front of Jang's eyes. Jang Song-thaek was also immediately arrested and put under house arrest.

Winter had already arrived in Pyongyang in late November 2013. Jang Song-thaek was present with hundreds of party and government officials as well as military officers on the military training ground of Kangkon Military Academy on the outskirts of the capital near Sunan International Airport. At around 10 a.m., a military vehicle approached and stopped in front of the stage. From the vehicle descended Ri Ryong-ha and Jang Su-kil, their whole bodies bound in rope. A special tribunal of the State Security Department read their sentence.

"For blindly following and blindly acting after a personal officer (Jang Song-thaek), and thereby committing anti-Party, anti-revolution, and sectarian acts, first deputy director of the (Korea Workers Party) Administrative Department Ri Ryong-ha and deputy director Jang Su-kil are sentenced the death penalty and the execution is to be enforced immediately."

The minute the sentence was announced, the firing squad that had been aiming at the two men unleashed a volley of bullets.

The weapon used for the two men's execution was a 14.5mm quad-barrel anti-aircraft gun. Frequently reported recently as the weapon used for executions in North Korea, it is a pirated version of the Soviet-made 14.5mm ZSU series of air-defense AA machine gun. Generally, these guns are installed at important facilities for defense, but in North Korea they were used for executions from around this time.[25] It is entirely unnecessary. Executions can be done with a fire extinguisher as long as you are close enough. The purpose of using an anti-aircraft machine gun is to impose fear on the audience.

In India in the mid-nineteenth century, British troops suppressing an uprising by local soldiers called Sepoys also used cannons to execute their foes. In the twentieth century when the Soviet Union military invaded Afghanistan, the local resistance called the Mujahideen, who resisted the Soviets' advance, used an assortment of special methods to execute Soviet prisoners and maximize their fear.

The bodies of Jang's two men were torn to pieces. What remained was burned with a flamethrower. Seeing his closest aides killed in such a vicious manner right before his eyes, Jang lost consciousness in his seat.[26] He had seen much cruelty throughout his life, but this was too shocking to bear.

A week or so later on December 8, an enlarged meeting of the Politburo of the Central Committee of the Workers' Party was held, and it was here that Jang Song-thaek became the target of public criticism. Video footage of security guards dragging him out was aired on North Korea's state-owned television channel. But Jang remained indifferent to the charges filed against him, even as more charges were listed in succession by Cho Yon-jun, Kang Sok-ju, and Pak Pong-ju.

Even then Jang may not have been aware of the fate that was waiting for him. As his men were charged one after another, one day he struck a ballpoint pen that he was holding in his fist down onto his project notebook on his desk. When all the charges came to an end, he was dragged away from the hall. On his desk where he had sat was a ballpoint pen split in two.[27]

Four days later, Jang Song-thaek received the death penalty. The trial was held behind closed doors and conducted in a most strange form: with no presentation of evidence or testimony to prove the charges, no attorney, nor any testimony. There was nothing else besides two photos of the guilty at the trial with his hands tied together and an indirect quote that the guilty "admitted all charges." The statement was also unusual in that the charged was referred to in vulgar terms, as "this bastard," or "that bastard." From a normal country's perspective, the trial could not be seen as proper. Jang's "trial" and execution was, in essence, a murder contract put out by a despot.

Even with Joseph Stalin, or with Pak Hon-yong's men of the South Korean Worker's Party in the 1950s, there were public trials and defendant testimonies. But the only evidence of Jang Song-thaek's trial is one photograph of him in an extremely withered state being taken away by a soldier. Judging from his the photo, it seems probable that Jang was tortured under interrogation.

On December 13, Jang Song-thaek was placed where his men Ri Ryong-ha and Jang Su-kil had stood not many days before, and his body was also torn to pieces with a quad-barrel AA machine gun. What remained of him, too, was incinerated with a flamethrower. Of course, no one planned to collect the remaining parts of his corpse and preserve it.[28] The only trace Jang left in the world was the split ballpoint pen where he sat during the enlarged meeting of the Party's Central Committee's Politiburo.

While in custody waiting for his sentencing, Jang Song-thaek asked to meet Kim Kyong-hui. Naturally, his wish was not granted. Even Kim Kyong-hui couldn't be of any help to him by then. Not because she had gathered her thoughts and made a decision in her own way, but because she was virtually an invalid due to alcohol and drug abuse, and was suffering from heart disease and other illnesses. This was surely the most painful period in Kim Kyong-hui's otherwise wild and colorful life.

Jang's purge meant the end of Kim Kyong-hui's mortal life, and her political life, too. She was someone who never kept her own political circle. Her influence only derived from her special family connections. But her older brother was now no more, all authoritative power was in the hands of her nephew and, once her husband was executed and gone, her influence would be nonexistent. With Jang's death, the foundation of Kim Jong-un's power solidified, and Kim Kyong-hui's position became meaningless.

Despite being physically and mentally emaciated, Kim Kyong-hui would look back on her life and at intervals be wrought with tension, but then turn emotional and fall into deep sorrow. On and off she would recall the years she spent with Jang Song-thaek: alone, she would shed a tear, then burst into laughter, in an endlessly repeating cycle of crying and laughing.

A few days after Jang's execution, Kim Jong-un visited his aunt's house with several aides. It was to pay his sick aunt a visit as well as to report the latest news. Though it was for formality's sake, he thought it was the right thing to do so since, after all, his aunt was no side branch.

Before the young leader could even offer his greetings, Kim Kyong-hui took a pistol out from beneath her chair and aimed at her nephew. Terror-stricken, Kim Jong-un dodged to safety, and his aides jumped onto the woman and snatched her gun. The aunt did not put up much of a struggle or protest. She merely smirked. In her expression, there was no anger. It seemed she felt something closer to contempt, mockery, or even sympathy.

> I know everything: this power game; you will seize the power you so anxiously long for, but see a miserable end after living a pitiful life as a slave to power. Pathetic things! You flies caught on a spider web. But now you're rejoicing, loving that web.

After Kim Jong-un and his men had gone, Kim Kyong-hui's stream of thoughts continued. There was a man, a down-to-earth man who used to set her heart on fire. But where had that man gone? Where is his eloquent speech, laughter, songs that could liven up people's hearts so easily? His romance and love; where had they all gone?

Even for that exceptional man, everything completely changed once he became entangled in the web of power. All became futile. He wandered aimlessly trying to look for something to replace power. But all was meaningless. The only thing that remained was her weak body, and her companions that could help her forget the endless memories of the past: alcohol and drugs.

Another torrent of blood inevitably followed. First were the officials either already arrested or executed at the time of Jang's purge. These were mostly his close people who had directly or indirectly managed the foreign-currency earning sector, the "Party's Funds." Deputy director Jang Su-kil, who was executed with the first deputy director Ri Yong-ha, was a so-called deputy director, but in reality, he was working as the head of a trading company under the Ministry of People's Security and was in charge of managing funds.

Jang Su-kil accompanied Jang Song-thaek upon his China visit in 2012, and was deeply involved in the overseas economic joint project with China. Toward the end of the Kim Jong-il era, he won Chinese investment in buildings such as the Hapyong building-materials factory[29] in Nampo, and Haedanghwagwan in Pyongyang. Other officials purged with him, such as Administrative Department deputy director Ryang Chong-song (in charge of land), Ministry of People's Security 7th General Bureau head and construction manager deputy director Pak Chun-hong were personnel related to the Party's Funds, running small and large foreign-currency-earning organizations, as they were in charge of the construction of the capital and various target project constructions.

Some ten officials were executed for the same list of crimes as Jang Song-thaek; treason, anti-revolutionary activities, and factionalism. The officials who perished were Ministry of People's Security 7th General Bureau Chief Pak Chun-hong, Korean People's Army Lieutenant General Ryang Chong-song, Jang Song-thaek's brother-in-law and Ambassador to Cuba Jon Yong-jin, Jang Song-thaek's nephew, Ambassador to Malaysia Jang Yong-chol, Ambassador to Sweden Pak Kwan-chol, and Deputy Delegate to UNESCO Hong Yong.[30]

Mun Kyong-dok, who was in the second round of executions, was a candidate member of the Party Central Committee Politiburo, secretary and concurrently Pyongyang municipal Party secretary, not to mention former winner of the Republic Hero title (in 2009) and the Kim Jong-il Medal (in 2012). Ri Yong-su, who also had the same credentials, was the Central Party's working group director and the deputy chairman of the State Sports Guidance Committee. Once he received a thorough trust of Kim Il-sung father and son, and served consecutive terms as the head of the League of the Socialist Working Youth.

Unexpectedly, most of the people who were known as Jang Song-thaek's close personnel made appearances at official events upon the second anniversary of the death of Kim Jong-il. Some North Korea experts analyzed this as an intentional event aimed at visibly reducing the aftermath of Jang's execution, but that by fate they would all gradually disappear. Executions of key figures carried on, all unknown to the public.[31] In the end, the number of dead is estimated to be as high as 400.

Both domestically and internationally, some people grieved the death of Jang Song-thaek. They believed North Korea had lost the one person who could ameliorate the hardships of his people and take the role of leading North Korea toward reform and opening so that it might come out into the international community as a normal country. The mourners knew well that in the foreseeable future there would not be a chance for a second Jang to be born. They estimated that it would be difficult for such a person to appear again: one who is not only of high caliber, but who is also so close to the Kim family, thoroughly experienced and well-connected with actual authoritative power, and what is more, acutely knowledgeable of internal and foreign affairs.[32]

It goes without saying that reform, which was Jang's line, would inevitably face huge obstacles. Current Prime Minister Pak Pong-ju is also an exceptional figure, but ever since he went through several periods of revolutionization, he became tamed and conscious of others around him as well as the thoughts of his boss(es) above. It has become hard to expect him to conduct bold reforms. One must wait at least a decade for another character like Jang to appear in North Korea. But ten years is a long time, long enough to fit the expression (in Korean), "Even the mountains and the rivers change," and during that time the frame of reality, which is what people today are interested in, could also alter. One thing is certain, however: no matter how the world changes, people will remember a man who died in his boots after living an extremely peculiar life in the exceptional system in the northern half of the Korean peninsula.

One rumor in North Korea had it that Jang Song-thaek was in fact not dead but still alive. The rumor went that there was only an announcement made that Jang was executed; there were no stories of witnesses to his execution, nor of people who checked Jang's corpse. Another rumor, which is still spreading, went that Jang was still alive and living somewhere, and is engaged in a very special job. Curiously, while the rumors that Jang was still alive spread, at once rumors on Kim Kyong-hui claimed that she was already dead.[33] Could the reason perhaps be her private sentiment for an exceptional man being sent to his death, and the sense of duty of a member of the royal family conflicting with one another, and thus being destroyed from within?

One Pyongyang citizen once said that you are inevitably reminded of Jang Song-thaek whenever you look at the buildings in the capital. One of those people who is destined to remember the structures Jang built is Kim Jong-un. Whenever he saw one such building, Pyongyang Folk Park, Kim is said to have expressed his discomfort, saying, "It reminds me of Jang Song-thaek." Ultimately, construction work to demolish the facility began. Thereby, North Korea's Tourism General Bureau informed a travel agency based in Beijing that from now on visits to the Pyongyang Folk Park are unavailable, and the Worker's Party's Propaganda and Agitation Department recalled brochures on the park. However, the memories of Jang do not solely remain in the buildings that he built. People will remember his genuineness, his passion, masculine charm, romance, love, and the effort he put in to trying to help those around him until the very end of his life. Most of all, he will be remembered all the more clearly because of the people who committed unimaginable atrocities just to erase him from the world.

But the past is never dead. It is not even past.

Notes

Preface

1. In this book, commonly accepted English spellings of Korean names, places, government policies and others are used. Both North and South Korean names are hyphenated for the reader's comfort.

2. Former South Korean President Roh Tae-woo (1988–1993) is an extremely rare case of a regime number two successfully succeeding to power. In that respect, former President Roh's political ability was impressive.

3. North Korea brought in the so-called *pyongjin* (parallel development, or parallelism) line in April 2013, replacing/augmenting the *songun*, or military-first, line of the Kim Jong-il era.

4. Among those I then conversed with was Christopher Green, who was working on his Doctorate on North Korean affairs at Cambridge University in the UK (at present, a researcher at Leiden University in the Netherlands). When the international media reported on Jang Song-thaek's execution, Green recalled our conversation made two years prior to the event and sent me an email.

5. Long ago, I read an article on North Korea in a British newspaper. Written by a progressive reporter, the title was a satire of North Korea's official name: "Neither democratic, nor people's, nor republic."

6. Irish novelist James Joyce wrote in *A Portrait of the Artist as a Young Man* that the weapons of an artist in difficulty were "silence, exile, and cunning." Jang Song-thaek could not use any of them. James Joyce, *A Portrait of the Artist as a Young Man* (Ware, Herts: Wordsworth Classics, 1992), p. 191.

7. This story was reported partially in the Korean media immediately after Jang Song-thaek's death (although the quote was not accurate.). One foreign reporter based in Korea told me that he heard a friend back home say, "Professor Ra's prediction was exact with a single week's error."

8. The following work gave the author a great deal of insight in writing this work: Michael Kumpfmueller, "The Glory of Life (Die Herrenlichkeit des Lesbens)," *Times Literary Supplement*, February 6, 2015, p. 6.

9. Several years ago, I felt it my duty to write a book on the case of a North Korean agent caught after the Rangoon Bombing in 1983, who died in prison there after 25 years' imprisonment. 라종일, 아웅산 테러리스트 강민철 (파주: 창비, 2013) [Ra Jong-yil, *Aung San Terrorist Kang Min-chol* (Paju: Changbi, 2013)]. English version planned.

10. The Korean title of this book is 장성택의 길: 신정의 불온한 경계인.

Chapter 1

1. Sheila Fitzpatrick, *On Stalin's Team: The Years of Living Dangerously in Soviet Politics* (Princeton, NJ: Princeton University Press, 2015), p. 9.

2. 김현식, 80년, 7만리: 통일 한반도를 향한 생명의 전주곡 (서울: 홍성사, 2013), 196쪽 [Kim Hyun-sik, *Eighty Years, and Seventeen Thousand Miles* (Seoul: Hongsongsa, 2013), p 196]. In this book, the author recalls that Kim Il-sung was passionate about education, and that the Great Leader's interests in the subject were specific and down to earth.

3. Rumor has it that the direct cause of Kim Il-sung's death was a disagreement between father and son. According to an anonymous source, Kim Il-sung called the Cabinet members in charge of government administration to his villa at the foot of the picturesque Mt. Myohyang, but Kim Jong-il promptly summoned the men back to Pyongyang while his elderly father was taking a nap. When he woke up, Kim Il-sung looked for his men but learned belatedly that they had all left. He exploded in rage, and promptly collapsed.

4. A traditional Korean taboo has it that one must not say to a third party any words of praise about oneself, or of people close to oneself; namely, one's children or spouse. The man who does so is stigmatized as half-witted, or simply shameless. Nevertheless, on a big rock by the *kuryongp'okp'o* (Nine Dragons Waterfall) in the Mt. Kumgang region of North Korea is engraved Kim Il-sung's "Poem of Praise," which he wrote for his oldest son Kim Jong-il upon his 50th birthday. The poem is also published in one of the volumes of the *Kim Il-sung's Works* collection.

5. Kim Il-sung's poem, published in Rodong Sinmun on February 16, 1992.

6. 최은희, 최은희의 고백 영화보다 더 영화같은 삶 (서울: 랜덤하우스코리아, 2004), 212쪽 [Choi Eun-hee, *Choi Eun-hee's Confession: A Life More Like Film than Film Itself* (Seoul: Random House Korea, 2004), p. 212].

7. President Kim Dae-jung, who attended a summit with Kim Jong-il in June 2000, once casually said during an unofficial gathering, "How come Kim Jong-il did not take after his father's good looks?"

8. A conversation with Hwang Jang-yop one day in 1998.

9. The South Korean government statistics agency estimated 330,000 dead, based on UN census data. Other official estimates hover around 400,000.

This of course could change greatly depending on the data gathered and methods used, and also what period one chooses to delineate as the period of famine.

10. 최은희.신상옥, 조국은 저하늘 저멀리 (Monterey: Pacific Artist Cooperation, 1988) 226쪽 [Choi Eun-hee and Shin Sang-ok, *Fatherland is Afar over that Sky* (Monterey: Pacific Artist Cooperation, 1998), p. 226].

11. The North Korean regime calls the United States its irreconcilable "enemy," however, what it really cannot tolerate is the existence of its brethren country, South Korea. The Ubuted States is the enemy only as long as it backs the South militarily and diplomatically; without that singular restriction, the North could befriend it at any time. But South Korea is a fundamentally different matter. North and South Korea are unable to coexist over the long term.

12. Advisor K's testimony. Another, slightly different testimony also exists. It is agreed in both testimonies that Kim Il-sung called in ten close personnel, placed a rifle in front of them, and announced his will. However, the alternative testimony says that the purpose of the summons was to have those present pledge loyalties to the son, Kim Jong-il. However, if the latter were the case, there would have been no reason for the story to be kept secret. Based on several testimonies, and objective circumstances, it is thought Advisor K's testimony is closer to the truth.

13. See, for example: Xenophon et al., *Hiero the Tyrant and Other Treaties* (London: Penguin Books, 1997).

14. Ko Yong-hui also had an official name, Kim Son-sil (pronounced Seon-sil). The person who appeared as Kim Son-sil on state funeral committee members' lists is said to have been Ko Yong-hui.

15. Ko Yong-hui's younger sister Ko Yong-suk lived in Switzerland in this guise of a diplomat to take care of Ko Yong-hui's three children. Her husband Pak Kon also sojourned as a diplomat of the North Korean embassy in Switzerland, where he mainly worked on matters concerning trade and commerce (in Korean, lit. "foreign currency-earning businesses"). U.S. and Swiss intelligence are said to have closely cooperated in actualizing this family's asylum in the Unied States in May, 1998.

16. 성혜랑, 등나무집 (서울: 지식나라, 2001) 407–09쪽 [Song Hye-rang, *The Wisteria House* (Seoul: Jisiknara, 2001), pp. 407–09].

17. Choi Eun-hee and Shin Sang-ok, op. cit., p. 27.

18. 후지모토겐지 김정일의 요리사 (서울: 월간조선사, 2003) 152–53쪽. [Fujimto Kenji, *Kim Jong-il's Cook* (Seoul: Monthly Chosun, 2003), pp. 152–53].

19. High-end brothels popular with the political and commercial elites of South Korea.

20. Fujimoto Kenji, op. cit., p. 31.

21. Former unification minister, intelligence chief and foreign affairs and national security adviser to President Kim Dae-jung.

22. 임동원, 피스 메이커: 남북관계와 북핵문제 25년 (서울: 중앙북스, 2008), 133쪽 [Lim Dong-won, *Peacemaker: 25 years of South-North relations and the North Korean nuclear problem* (Seoul: JoongAng Books, 2008), p. 133].

23. 곽중혁, 마키아벨리 다시 읽기 (서울: 민음사, 2014) [Kwak Jun-hyok, *Re-reading Machiavelli* (Seoul: Minumsa, 2014)]. The differentiation of two terms, despot and tyrant, is based on the explanation of Professor Kwak, who says that since Kim Jong-il seized power via a certain institutional procedure, it is correct to use the expression tyrant but not despot.

24. "The Crack-Up," a series of essays by F. Scott Fitzgerald published in Esquire Magazine in February, March, and April 1936.

25. Advisor L's testimony. The writer also spoke once of there being no match for Kim Jong-il at a private meeting with non-Koreans in Washington, DC.

26. Advisor A's testimony. Upon hearing this, the author couldn't help recalling Park Chung-hee.

27. Pasquale Villari, *Life and Times of Girolamo Savonarola* (London: T. Fisher Unwin Ltd., 1918).

28. One upper-class North Korean made this assessment of the Sunshine Policy. Non-Koreans regard the policy as a friendly and reasonable one, but within the peninsula it was an "ideological" political issue. In other words, this suggests that even while the Sunshine Policy was underway (during President Kim Dae-jung and President Roh Moo-hyun's governments, namely from February 1998 to February 2008), inter-Korean confrontation continued to exist, but in a different shape to that of previous years. The official added that had the South not hurried for achievements, but instead initiated gradual, long-term projects, and at the same time negotiated fully on monitoring existing agreements, including food aid, there would have been better results. In the 1990s it was highly probably that North Korea would have agreed to South Korea sending staff to monitor field sites, but now it is impossible. (From Advisor D's testimony)

29. Fujimoto Kenji, op. cit., pp. 108–09.

30. Song Hye-rang, op. cit., p. 394.

31. Song Hye-rang, ibid., pp. 380–81, 412.

32. Song Hye-rang, ibid., pp. 335–36.

33. It is said that in the Second Hall of the Three Great Revolutions Exhibition in Yonmot-dong, Pyongyang, there hangs the following passage: "'The Earth without Joseon (North Korea) is not needed at all.' Kim Jong-il."

34. Close to his death, the founder and first shogun of the Tokugawa shogunate of Japan, Tokugawa Ieyasu (1543–1616) is said to have sent his personal doctor into exile so that the latter may be free from having to take responsibility for his fate and thus commit ritual suicide. It seems Kim Jong-il had no such consideration for his doctors.

35. Thomas Friedman, "Are you sure you want the job?" *International New York Times*, Thursday, October 22, 2015, p. 9. The article is on the countless obstacles that exist for the unimaginably competitive seat of the president.

36. A number of South Korean personnel had expected (or hoped) that after Kim Il-sung's death, Kim Jong-il would fail to stabilize the regime and it would eventually fall into chaos. He did not, and it did not.

37. Advisor K's testimony.

38. The North Korean media uses such myths as tools to create the Kim family's "greatness, and Heaven-origin hero image." (Advisor O's testimony)

39. Song Hye-rang, op. cit., p. 418.

40. The author in conversation with President Kim Dae-jung in 2005.

41. In his final years, Stalin often said he ought to retire given his age and declining health. Then the men around him would mostly strongly oppose it, and without properly grasping the situation.

42. Five of the seven men, who escorted the hearse at Kim Jong-il's funeral along with the new young leader Kim Jong-un, have either already been executed, or disappeared.

Chapter 2

1. 황장엽, 난 역사의 진리를 보았다 (서울: 시대정신, 1998), 172쪽 [Hwang Jang-yop, *I Saw The Truth of History* (Seoul: Zeitgeist, 1998), p. 172].

2. 이한영, 김정일 로열 패밀리 (서울: 시대정신, 2004), 94–96쪽 [Yi Han-yong, *Kim Jong-il's Royal Family* (Seoul: Zeitgeist, 2004), pp. 94–96].

3. An extremely pretty, young male, especially an idol singer or actor.

4. South Korean actress abducted to North Korea from Hong Kong in 1978. She escaped in 1986, fleeing to the U.S. embassy in Vienna and requesting political asylum.

5. Choi Eun-hee and Shin Sang-ok, op. cit., p. 117.

6. 정창현, 장성택 사건 숨겨진 이야기 (서울: 선인, 2014) 89쪽 [Chong Chang-hyon, *The Untold Story of the Jang Song-thaek Incident* (Seoul: Sunin, 2014), p. 89].

7. Chong Chang-hyon, op. cit., pp. 90–91.

8. On August 18, 1976, two American soldiers were bludgeoned to death by North Koreans within the demilitarized zone that separates North and South Korea. They had entered the zone to trim a tree that was impacting line-of-sight between observation posts.

9. Chong, Chang-hyon, ibid., p. 90.

10. Chong, Chang-hyon, ibid., p. 91.

11. Advisor C and D's testimony.

12. Advisor N's testimony.

13. Song Hye-rang, op. cit., p. 389.

14. *Gippeumjo* in Korean, this is a group of artistically gifted and beautiful women who provided entertainment at private events hosted by Kim Jong-il, initially for his father Kim Il-sung.

15. 후지모토겐지, 북한의 후계자 왜 김정은인가? (서우리: 맥스미디어, 2010). 156–57쪽 [Fujimoto Kenji, *Why is North Korea's Successor Kim Jong-un?* (Seoul: MaxMedia, 2010), pp. 156–57].

16. Advisor M's testimony.

17. Advisors B's and M's testimonies on the atmosphere of Kim Il-sung University at the time.

18. Bruce Bueno de Mesquita and Alastair Smith, *The Dictator's Handbook: Why bad behavior is almost always good politics* (New York City: PublicAffairs, 2011), p. 54.

19. 김성보, 북한의 역사1: 건국과 인민민주주의의 경험, *1945–1960* (서울: 역사비평사) 202쪽 [Kim, Song-bo, *North Korean History 1: foundation and experience of people's democracy, 1945–1960* (Seoul: Yukbi, 2011), p. 202.

20. Advisor B's testimony.

21. Chong Chang-hyon, op. cit., pp. 94–95.

22. British jurist Sir Henry Maine (1822–1888) characterized modern times as the movement "from status to contract." If class mattered in pre-modern days, in modern times contracts formed between free individuals became important. It is possible to see North Korea as an anachronistic society in that status still matters the most there.

23. Regarding this matter, refer to Kim Su-am et al., "Quality of North Korean Residents Lives: Situation and Understanding," *Korea Institute of National Unification Research Series* 11-06 (2011), p. 211 onward. However, there are observations that songbun, the system of ascribed status used in North Korea, is far more complicated than three classes. That is, they say it is constituted of five classes: special, core, basic (restless), complex, and antagonistic. As for its origin, there are views of it starting soon after Independence from 1946, while others argue the full-fledged start was after the Korean War in 1956. In any case, classification is very important to the North Korean people as it determines a wealth of things, from residential area to opportunities for education and work. Data for the North Korean classification system is stored at four locations, and is almost impossible to change or to correct. However, in case of actual changes, for instance when there is a North Korean escapee within the family, or there is a change in one's political status, the classification can be changed, and on occasions it can become difficult to classify simply.

24. The blood kindship ideology is a phenomenon where ideological struggle can be defined even in terms of the individual or among family. In other words, the enemy who killed one's parents becomes identified as the ideological enemy.

25. 와다 하루키, 북한 현대사 (서울: 창비, 2014) 151-52쪽 [Wada Haruki, *Modern North Korean History* (Seoul: Changbi, 2014), pp. 151-52].

Chapter 3

1. In discussion with Hwang Jang-yop during 1998.

2. 김현식, 나는 21세기 이념의 유목민 (서울: 김영사, 2010) 215-18쪽 [Kim Hyon-sik, *I am a 21st century ideology nomad* (Seoul: Gimmyoungsa, 2010) pp. 215-18].

3. In later years, when Hye-rim visited Russia for medical treatment, she stayed at this same apartment. It is said that Song used all five apartments on the third floor.

4. The marriage of Hwang and Pak would eventually end in tragedy. Some three decades later, after Hwang Jang-yop defected to the South, his whole family was thrown into a political prison camp, and on the way there Pak threw herself from a moving train, taking her own life. See also: Kim Hyon-sik, ibid., pp. 159-60.

5. East German Foreign Ministry document C1025/73, cited in Haruki Wada, ibid., pp. 172-73.

6. Yi Han-yong, op. cit., p. 65.

7. 이종석, 북한의 역사2: 주체사상과 유일체제, 1960-1994 (서울: 역사비평사, 2011), 116쪽 [Lee Jong-seok, *North Korean History 2: Juche Ideology and Monolithic System, 1960-1994* (Seoul: Yukbi, 2011), p. 116.

8. After this period, it is mentioned in North Korean official media as well as even school textbooks that supernatural phenomena appeared related to Kim Il-sung, Kim Jong-il, and Kim Jong-un.

9. Heonik Kwon and Chung Byung-ho, *Beyond Charismatic Poltics* (Lanham, MD: Rowman and Littlefield, 2012); Wada Haruki, op. cit., p. 181. Monique Macias from Equatorial Guinea, who lived in North Korea receiving the utmost care of Kim Il-sung from early childhood, calls the North "one big theatrical play." That is, the supreme leader is writer, director, and actor; high government officials are supporting actors; and the people are extras and audience.

10. The so-called Pleasure Troupe (Gippeumjo) is one of the numerous political terms originating in North Korea that has spread throughout the world. It is not official terminology, and wasn't coined in South Korea or any other country. It is not used by the North Korean government or the Party, but is used unofficially. Originally, the name was the "troupe that gives pleasure" to Kim Il-sung, but it came to be called simply, "Pleasure Troupe." At any rate, the fact that an official organization of a state in modern times was mobilized to select, train, and manage women to serve the sexual pleasure of a leader is certainly a weird fact that runs contrary to basic reason.

11. Kim Hyon-sik, op. cit., pp. 91–92.
12. Kim Hyon-sik, ibid. pp. 218–19.
13. Kim Hyon-sik, ibid. p. 124.

Chapter 4

1. Chong Chang-hyon, op. cit., p. 60.
2. Everything said to date about Kim Kyong-hui is derived from Advisor O's testimony.
3. The foreign movies for Kim Jong-il, and all foreign foods and products consumed by Kim Jong-il and his family.
4. Simon Jenkins, "A believer's guide to the architecture of Communism, a legacy that is set in concrete," *Times Literary Supplement*, September 4, 2015, p. 3.
5. Advisor E's testimony.
6. Advisor E's testimony.
7. The first person to reveal the existence of the Pleasure Troupe to the outside world was former North Korean diplomat Ko Yong-hwan, the first North Korean diplomat to seek political asylum and defection to the South (from Congo) in May 1991.
8. Kenji Fujimoto, *Why is North Korea's Successor Kim Jong-un?* p. 91.
9. A very strong drinker within a company, who is usually in charge of sales and entertaining clients or prospective business partners
10. Kenji Fujimoto, ibid. pp. 157–58.
11. Kenji Fujimoto, ibid. pp. 97–98.
12. After the execution of Jang Song-thaek, it was suggested that Kim Jong-un harbored antagonistic feelings toward Jang from childhood because Jang was the man who organized the Pleasure Troupe. To a child, growing up mainly influenced by his mother, the depraved lifestyle of his father would not leave a good impression. This of course may not be the main reason why Jang was purged; however, it is convincing that owing to such a history and personal feelings, Jang could have become a target of Kim Jong-un's emotions.
13. Kenji Fujimoto, *Kim Jong-il's Cook*, p. 201.
14. When important personnel attended this gathering, no matter how urgent an incident, Kim Jong-il was not available to sign reports or to make decisions. As a result, an expedient solution, "FAX Wire" appeared. When there was an urgent case at the Foreign Ministry, they obtained the signature of the vice minister, took the document to the office that distributed official materials, and reported to Kim Jong-il by facsimile.
15. Advisor E's testimony.
16. Advisor O's testimony.

17. Considering the fact that there are still surviving families in the North, no actual names are revealed. The children are said to be alive, still bearing a huge grudge against their father (Advisor O's testimony).

18. Advisor D's testimony.

19. Advisors C and D's testimonies. Only on official instances, such as on important funeral members' lists, Ko Yong-hui made appearance in the name of Kim Son-sil.

Chapter 5

1. Lee Jong-seok, op. cit., from p. 122.

2. The author's own work: Ra Jong-yil, *Worldly Discoveries* (Seoul: Kyunghee University Publishing Cultural Center, 2010); 라종일, 아웅산 테러리스트 강민철 (파주: 창비, 2013) [Ra Jong-yil, *Aung San Terrorist Kang Min-chol* (Paju: Changbi, 2013)].

3. Song Hye-rang, op. cit., pp. 468–69.

4. Advisor I's testimony.

5. Advisor E's testimony.

6. Kim Jong-nam, born to Song Hye-rim, was Kim Jong-il's only son at the time.

7. Yi Han-yong, op. cit., p. 97.

8. The Olympic Games of 1980 in Moscow and 1984 in Los Angeles suffered from boycotts that reduced the competitive edge of many events.

9. Immediately after the Korean Air bombing incident in 1987, Kim Jong-il said to Japanese chef Kenji Fujimoto, "Do you think North Korea is responsible for this?" The chef added that when he replied in the negative, Ko Yong-hui who was sitting beside him said, "Whenever those kinds of incidents occur, they always blame only us!" (Kenji Fujimoto, *Why is North Korea's Successor Kim Jong-un?* p. 64).

10. The working-level person who organized the repatriation of Kim Won-sok was Ko Yong-hwan, then-assistant director of the sixth section of North Korea's Foreign Ministry. Less than seven years later, Ko defected to the South and had a dramatic reunion with Kim Hyon-hui in Seoul. Ko apologized to Kim as he told her what happened to her father and family, but Kim Hyon-hui was understanding, saying, "How can it be your fault when you merely followed orders given from above?" The most famous North Korean spy in the South cried sorrowfully (Ko Yong-hwan's testimony, June 2010).

11. It is said that agent Kim Sung-il complained to one Assistant Director Choe, otherwise unknown but in charge of giving operational orders. "If something goes wrong, it won't be only comrade Ok-hwa and me who will be in deep waters, but possibly also the whole Republic. Will you take

responsibility?" But assistant director Choe cut Kim's complaint short, saying, "Do not raise any questions whatsoever about this operation. We also merely follow orders." Kim Sung-il would always be discouraged whenever he heard this. 김현희, 이제 여자가 되고 싶어요, 제1부 (서울: 고려원, 1991), 215–16쪽 [Kim Hyon-hui, *I want to be a woman now*, Pt. 1 (Seoul: Koryowon, 1991) pp. 215–16].

Chapter 6

1. Kenji Fujimoto, *Why is North Korea's Successor Kim Jong-un?* p. 153.

2. It is a well-known fact, but North Korea scholar Andrei Lankov summarized the matter as follows, "Among strategic choices, the most important decision the North Korean regime made during Kim Jong-il's era was that it did not imitate China and moreover did not decide to reform or open trade doors." Andrei Lankov, "Prospects for reform under the Kim Jong-un regime and South Korea's North Korea policy," *Korean Foreign Policy* No. 108 (January 2014), p. 54.

3. Kenji Fujimoto, *Why is North Korea's Successor Kim Jong-un?* p. 153.

4. Such an instance like this is possible because North Korean diplomats posted overseas usually share accommodation and live together as a community.

5. Advisor C's testimony. Defector professor of Russian Kim Hyun-sik recalls how he suffered a stroke at a conference in Moscow and was hospitalized. When by chance Jang Song-thaek stopped by Russia on other business and heard the news, he brought Kim all the musk deer gland medicine he could collect from embassy staff, and helped to hasten the cure. One day in the mid-1970s, Kim could not go home because it was too late at night, but Jang took the professor to his mother's house and treated him to tofu and fresh pollack soup. Kim says, "Jang Song-thaek's unique power is that once you meet him, the relationship with him never breaks but becomes stronger, like that with one's child." Kim concludes, "[This] was out of wise, warm comradeship emitted from his manly physique and body." Kim Hyun-sik, op. cit., p. 229.

6. Kenji Fujimoto, *Why is North Korea's Successor Kim Jong-un?* pp. 152–53.

7. Ri Pyong graduated from the Physics department of Kim Il-sung University, and was once a promising brain. After graduation, he was posted in the Social Sciences Institute. After his divorce from Song Hye-rim, he was somewhat forcibly remarried to an older unmarried woman working at the same office, and had two more children, but in the end illness befell him and he could not go on normally.

Kim Jong-il treated well every member of the Ri family except for Ri Pyong. Ri Ki-yong became chairman of the Writer's League, and lived in a "gift house" in Pyongyang presented to him by Kim Il-sung, which was designed as two households on one floor. After Ri Ki-yong's death, the Ri Pyong and Ri Jong-hyok brothers each lived in the apartments. Then years later, as Ri Jong-hyok moved to a Central Party apartment in the central district of Pyongyang, the house was passed on to his second son Ri Soe-dol.

Ri Soe-dol, who is five years younger than Ri Pyong, served in numerous government positions, unimaginable for a descendant of a family originally from the South (his father having moved to the North after liberation from Japan), and later became a familiar name to South Koreans as he became the deputy chairman of the Korean Asia-Pacific Peace Committee.

The Ri family's grandchildren's first names all end with a same last syllable, "dol." Ri Pyong's daughter's name is Ok-dol, and Ri Jong-hyok's oldest son is Cha-dol, second son, Soe-dol. Ri Cha-dol is an administrative official at the Overseas Economy Ministry, and Ri Soe-dol is the First Secretary of the North Korean embassy in France. He is married to Kim Sun-yong, and they are living together in Paris with their daughter Ri Ok-byol, and son Ri Hyok-chol.

8. Regarding Kim Jong-il's heir, the reason there was a rumor that Jang Song-thaek backed Kim Jong-nam would probably be because Jang and Kim Kyong-hui took the role of Kim Jong-nam's foster parents.

9. The scene of Kim Kyong-hui persuading Song Hye-rim to leave for a foreign country is recorded by Yi Han-yong (Yi Han-yong, op. cit. p. 105). After this decision, Kim Il-sung had his former typist Kim Yong-suk marry Kim Jong-il. Between them were born two daughters.

10. Advisor C's testimony.

11. Advisor C's testimony.

12. Kenji Fujimoto, *Why is North Korea's Successor Kim Jong-un?* p. 157.

13. Kenji Fujimoto, *Kim Jong-il's Cook*, pp. 130–31.

14. There are many, earnest testimonies given in this regard; however, it is regrettable that the witnesses' names and further details of the contents cannot be revealed at the request of the witnesses.

15. Advisor C's testimony.

16. Choe Kon overly abused his relationship with Kim Kyong-hui. He boasted about it indiscriminately, and used it as a pretext to enjoy substantial benefits, including financial ones. Such a rapport could not last long. He was in the end arrested and sentenced to death by firing squad (Advisor C's testimony).

17. On the Simhwajo incident, see: 장진성, "2만 대학살! 北 피바다 만든 김정일의 숙청쇼!" *New Daily*, 2012년 6월 1일 [Jang Jin-sung, "20,000 people

massacred! Kim Jong-il's show purge that turned the North into a sea of blood," *New Daily*, June 1, 2012].

18. On the ethics of power and private life, Hwang Jang-yop recounted the following anecdote. Due to the lack of transportation in the North, young men commonly rode bicycles carrying women on the rear seat, but one day Kim Jong-il saw this and prohibited the act for reasons of "an abuse to public decency." Hwang Jang-yop recalled that in his heart he felt something beyond resistance, that Kim Jong-il was a lousy loser. He himself perpetrated all imaginable acts of depravity as a daily routine, but he could not accept the tiniest accommodation of the ordinary people who didn't have a mode of transportation. Trivial though it was, the incident is one of the instances that disenchanted Hwang of Kim Jong-il.

19. Advisor D's testimony.
20. Advisor D's testimony.
21. Advisor D's testimony.
22. Jang Jin-sung, op. cit.
23. Advisor D's testimony.
24. Advisor F's testimony.
25. Advisor F's testimony.
26. Advisor F's testimony
27. Advisor E's testimony.
28. Fujimoto Kenji, *Why is North Korea's Successor Kim Jong-un?* pp. 185–86.

Chapter 7

1. Lim Dong-won, op. cit., p. 701.

2. Sunan International Aiport has since been refurbished, and is certainly much nicer now. In terms of number of gates and overall passenger numbers, it is still smaller than most South Korean regional airports, let alone Incheon International, which has grown enormously, opening a second large international terminal in early 2018.

3. Jang Song-thaek returned to the North with a copy of a Korea Development Institute (KDI) research report on the development of the Korean economy. During his stay, he showed an interest in the kimchi refrigerator, a South Korean invention for preserving the ubiquitous spicy side dishes, and took one home with him.

4. A mixture of Korean liquor (soju) or whisky with beer.
5. Advisor O's testimony.
6. Advisor D's testimony.
7. Yi Han-yong, op. cit., pp. 175–76.

8. Song Hye-rang, op. cit., pp. 477–80. Song Hye-rang recalls that the reason it was so difficult to choose a husband (for her daughter) was because all the men looked the same. She called this "the socio-historical product of uniformism," and writes that Kim Jong-il deplored that fact also.

9. Advisor E gave testimony of Ko Dong-hun's political asylum. Ko Dong-hun and his wife were sojourning in Switzerland as locally-based North Korean embassy employees, and then escaped to a foreign country.

10. Fujimoto Kenji, *Why is North Korea's Successor Kim Jong-un?* p. 155.

11. Advisor D's testimony.

12. Advisor E's testimony.

13. Upon proposing a summit in the early days of the Lee Myung-bak government, the North demanded considerable material compensation as condition: 100,000 tons of corn, 400,000 tons of rice, 100,000 USD-worth of materials for construction purposes, and 10 billion USD in capital to establish North Korea's state development bank. (이명박, 대통령의 시간 *(2008–2013)* (서울: 알에이치코리아, 2015), 335쪽 [Lee Myung-bak, *The President's Hours: 2008–2013* (Seoul: Random House Korea, 2015), p. 335].

14. Advisor E's testimony.

15. A decade later on February 13, 2017, Kim Jong-nam would be assassinated in a Malaysian airport, seemingly on the orders of his half-brother, Kim Jong-un, whose ruling legitimacy was gravely challenged by the existence of the older son of Kim Jong-il.

16. Ryu Kyong-su was the brigade commander of the 105th Tank Brigade that entered Seoul within days of the outbreak of the Korean War. Ryu Kyong-su and his wife Hwang Sun-hui both fought with Kim Il-sung from their anti-Japanese partisan days, and Hwang Sun-hui in particular was close with Kim Jong-il's mother Kim Jong-suk, and thus had a special relation with the whole family. At the 4th National Conference of War Veterans [in July, 2015] images were aired of the new, third-generation leader Kim Jong-un walking onto the podium with Hwang in her wheelchair (Advisor F's testimony).

17. Advisor E's testimony.

18. Documents provided by Advisors E and F.

19. If one looks at those North Korean media articles that report Kim Jong-il's activitiies on February 9, 2010, he is quoted as saying, gripping a [heaped] handful of vinylon [and raising his right arm up to horizontal level], "Were President Kim Il-sung, who is [currently] at the Kumsusan Memorial Palace, to see this cotton wool, how pleased he would be!" An anonymous critic pointed out that it makes a huge difference whether there is or isn't the precondition, "who is [currently] at the Kumsusan Memorial Palace." This would be a question of which is closer to the truth, the North Korean media or testimonies of people who were there at the time.

20. Documents provided by Advisors E and F.

21. The Japanese chef Kenji Fujimoto wrote that he thought Kim Jong-il had decided on Kim Jong-un as his successor already in the year 2000, even though Kim Jong-il did not make any precise verbal commitment. Before 2000, watching how Kim Jong-il introduced his children to his close aids, Fujimoto recalled how he somehow thought that unlike the other officials, Jang Song-thaek would most likely know Kim's mind in advance.

22. Yonhap News Agency's North Korean defector-reporter Choe Seon-yeong exclusively reported that Kim Jong-un became the new successor for Yonhap on January 15, 2009.

23. Advisor E's testimony.

24. Advisor F's testimony.

25. Selected Central Party secretary and director level officials, who provide guidance at each regional party's general assembly in the qualification of representative plenipotentiary.

Chapter 8

1. Fujimoto Kenji, *Why is North Korea's Successor Kim Jong-un?* pp. 152–53.

2. Advisor C's and D's testimonies.

3. Advisor G's testimony.

4. Advisor D's testimony.

5. Chong Chang-hyon, op. cit., p. 4.

6. Advisor C's testimony.

7. 정창현, "장성택 판결문을 어떻게 읽을 것인가?" 통일뉴스, 2013년 12월 17일 [Chong Chang-hyon, "How to interpret Jang Song-thaek's sentencing," *Tongil News*, December 17, 2013].

8. 최진욱, "장성택 숙청 이후 한반도 정세," 외교 제108호 (2014년. 1월), 41쪽 [Choi, Jin-wook, "The situation of the Korean peninsula after the execution of Jang Song-thaek," *Foreign Affairs* no. 108 (January 2014), p. 41].

9. Advisor C and D's testimonies.

10. Advisor C's and D's testimonies.

11. Advisor D's testimony.

12. Advisor C's and D's testimonies. Despite this, it is estimated that North Korea will continue to pursue modest economic improvements. The decisive element is the limit of a nuclear program conducted at the same time as economic development.

13. Advisor E's testimony. 주성하, "김정은 공포통치," 동아일보, 2015년 7월 6일 [Joo Song-ha, "Kim Jong-un's Rule of Fear," *Donga Ilbo*, July 6, 2015].

14. Fujimoto Kenji, *Kim Jong-il's Cook*, p. 110.

15. Fujimoto Kenji, *Why is North Korea's Successor Kim Jong-un?* p. 132.
16. Advisor C's testimony.
17. Chong Chang-hyon, ibid., 67.
18. 주성하, "장성택 처형 1년: 김정은 권력 안정성 평가 (36)," 동아일보, 2014년 12월 11일 [Joo Song-ha, "One Year after Jang Song-thaek's Execution: Assessment of Kim Jong-un's Power Stability (36)," *Donga Ilbo*, December 11, 2014].
19. Advisor E's testimony.
20. Advisor E's testimony.
21. Advisor E's testimony.
22. There are several accounts regarding this case. One of them is in Choi Jin-wook, op. cit., p. 46.
23. Advisors E's and F's testimonies.
24. 서재준, "김정은, '유일영도 10대 원칙' 간부들앞에서 직접연설," 뉴스1, 2013년, 12월, 22일 [Suh Jae-joon, "Kim Jong-un gives speech on 'Ten Principles of Monolithic Leadership' in front of officials," *News 1*, December 22, 2013].
25. Advisor E's testimony.
26. Advisor E's testimony.
27. Advisor E's testimony.
28. North Korea is not unique in damaging or exterminating corpses in peculiar ways during politically meaningful executions. The United States also killed Osama Bin Laden, the man responsible for the September 11 terrorist attacks, and threw his body deep into the ocean. During the Japanese occupation of Korea, Korean independence movement activists Yun Bong-gil and Ahn Jung-gun were executed, but their bodies either disappeared or were treated in a special way after the sentencing. However, what is noticeable is that in North Korea, these penalties do not occur as rare, exceptional cases; such things happen without exception for so-called political prisoners.
29. The name of this company had been Taedonggang Tile Factory, but after Jang Song-thaek's execution, it was renamed Chollima Tile Factory.
30. In an article carried by the Japanese daily *Yomiuri Shimbun* dated January 31, 2014, which quotes a couple of North Korean sources, a list of sixteen people executed for charges of "breaching the Kim Jong-il Monolithic Leadership System" does not include the names of these four who were hurriedly summoned back to Pyongyang from abroad after Jang Song-thaek's execution.
31. Choi, Jin-wook, ibid., p. 50.
32. Advisor D's testimony.
33. Advisor C's testimony.

English Bibliography

Books and Articles

Bueno de Mesquita, Bruce, and Alastair Smith. *The Dictator's Handbook: Why bad behavior is almost always good politics*. New York City: PublicAffairs, 2011.

Fitzpatrick, Sheila. *On Stalin's Team: The Years of Living Dangerously in Soviet Politics*. Princeton, NJ: Princeton University Press, 2015.

Joyce, James. *A Portrait of the Artist as a Young Man*. Ware, Herts, UK: Wordsworth Classics, 1992.

Kim, Su-am et al. "Quality of North Korean Residents Lives: Situation and Understanding." *Korea Institute of National Unification Research Series* 11-06, 2011.

Kwon, Heonik, and Chung Byung-ho. *Beyond Charismatic Poltics*. Lanham, MD: Rowman and Littlefield, 2012.

Ra, Jong-yil. *Worldly Discoveries*. Seoul: Kyunghee University Publishing Cultural Center, 2010.

Villari, Pasquale. *Life and Times of Girolamo Savonarola*. London: T. Fisher Unwin Ltd., 1918.

Xenophon et al. *Hiero the Tyrant and Other Treaties*. London: Penguin Books, 1997.

Newspapers and Magazines

Fitzgerald, F. Scott. "The Crack-Up." *Esquire*, February–April, 1936.

Friedman, Thomas. "Are you sure you want the job?" *International New York Times*, October 22, 2015.

Jenkins, Simon. "A believer's guide to the architecture of Communism, a legacy that is set in concrete." *Times Literary Supplement*, September 4, 2015.

Kumpfmueller, Michael. "The Glory of Life (Die Herrenlichkeit des Lesbens)." *Times Literary Supplement*, February 6, 2015.

Panero, James. "Hayden Herrera, Listening to Stone, The Art and Life of Isamu Noguchi." *International New York Times*, June 27–28, 2015.

Korean Bibliography

Books and Articles

겐지, 후지모토. 북한의 후계자 왜 김정은인가? 서우리: 맥스미디어, 2010 [Fujimoto Kenji, *Why is North Korea's Successor Kim Jong-un?* Seoul: MaxMedia, 2010].

겐지, 후지모토. 김정일의 요리사. 서울: 월간조선사, 2003 [Kenji, Fujimto. *Kim Jong-il's Cook.* Seoul: Monthly Chosun, 2003].

곽, 준혁. 마키아벨리 다시 읽기. 서울: 민음사, 2014 [Kwak Jun-hyok, *Re-reading Machiavelli.* Seoul: Minumsa, 2014].

김, 성보. 북한의 역사1: 건국과 인민민주주의의 경험, 1945–1960. 서울: 역사비평사 [Kim, Song-bo. *North Korean History 1: foundation and experience of people's democracy, 1945–1960.* Seoul: Yukbi, 2011].

김, 현식. 80년, 7만리: 통일 한반도를 향한 생명의 전주곡. 서울: 홍성사, 2013 [Kim, Hyun-sik. *Eighty Years, and Seventeen Thousand Miles.* Seoul: Hongsongsa, 2013].

김, 현식. 나는 21세기 이념의 유목민. 서울: 김영사, 2010. [Kim, Hyon-sik. *I am a 21st century ideology nomad.* Seoul: Gimmyoungsa, 2010].

김, 현희. 이제 여자가 되고 싶어요, 제1부. 서울: 고려원, 1991 [Kim, Hyon-hui. *I want to be a woman now, Pt. 1.* Seoul: Koryowon, 1991].

라, 종일. 아웅산 테러리스트 강민철. 파주: 창비, 2013 [Ra, Jong-yil. *Aung San Terrorist Kang Min-chol.* Paju: Changbi, 2013].

성, 혜랑. 등나무집. 서울: 지식나라, 2001 [Song, Hye-rang. *The Wisteria House.* Seoul: Jisiknara, 2001].

이, 명박. 대통령의 시간 (2008–2013). 서울: 알에이치코리아, 2015 [Lee, Myung-bak. *The President's Hours: 2008–2013.* Seoul: Random House Korea, 2015].

이, 종석. 북한의 역사2: 주체사상과 유일체제, 1960–1994. 서울: 역사비평사, 2011 [Lee Jong-seok, *North Korean History 2: Juche Ideology and Monolithic System, 1960–1994.* Seoul: Yukbi, 2011].

이, 한영. 김정일 로열 패밀리. 서울: 시대정신, 2004 [Yi, Han-yong. *Kim Jong-il's Royal Family.* Seoul: Zeitgeist, 2004].

임, 동원. 피스 메이커: 남북관계와 북핵문제 25년. 서울: 중앙북스, 2008 [Lim, Dong-won, *Peacemaker: 25 years of South-North relations and the North Korean nuclear problem*. Seoul: JoongAng Books, 2008].

정, 창현. 장성택 사건 숨겨진 이야기. 서울: 선인, 2014. [Chong, Chang-hyon, *The Untold Story of the Jang Song-thaek Incident*. Seoul: Sunin, 2014].

최, 은희. 최은희의 고백 영화보다 더 영화같은 삶. 서울: 랜덤하우스코리아, 2004 [Choi, Eun-hee, *Choi Eun-hee's Confession: A Life More Like Film than Film Itself*. Seoul: Random House Korea, 2004].

최, 은희. 신, 상옥. 조국은 저하늘 저멀리. Monterey: Pacific Artist Cooperation, 1988 [Choi, Eun-hee and Shin, Sang-ok. *Fatherland is Afar over that Sky*. Monterey, CA: Pacific Artist Cooperation, 1998].

하루키, 와다. 북한 현대사. 서울: 창비, 2014 [Haruki, Wada. *Modern North Korean History*. Seoul: Changbi, 2014].

황, 장엽. 난 역사의 진리를 보았다. 서울, 시대정신, 1998. [Hwang, Jang-yop. *I Saw the Truth of History*. Seoul: Zeitgeist, 1998].

Newspapers and Magazines

서, 재준. "김정은, '유일영도 10대 원칙' 간부들앞에서 직접연설." 뉴스1, 2013년, 12월, 22일 [Suh, Jae-joon. "Kim Jong-un gives speech on 'Ten Principles of Monolithic Leadership' in front of officials." *News 1*, December 22, 2013].

장, 진성. "2만 대학살! 北 피바다 만든 김정일의 숙청쇼!" *New Daily*, 2012년 6월 1일 [Jang Jin-sung, "20,000 people massacred! Kim Jong-il's show purge that turned the North into a sea of blood," *New Daily*, June 1, 2012].

정, 창현. "장성택 판결문을 어떻게 읽을 것인가?" 통일뉴스, 2013년 12월 17일 [Chong Chang-hyon, "How to interpret Jang Song-thaek's sentencing," *Tongil News*, December 17, 2013].

주, 성하. "김정은 공포통치." 동아일보, 2015년 7월 6일 [Joo, Song-ha. "Kim Jong-un's Rule of Fear." *Donga Ilbo*, July 6, 2015].

최, 진욱. "장성택 숙청 이후 한반도 정세." 외교 제108호, 2014년 1월 [Choi, Jin-wook. "The situation of the Korean peninsula after the execution of Jang Song-thaek." *Foreign Affairs* no. 108, January 2014].

Index

Angola, North Korea's Fisheries Representative in Angola, 89
Aquarium, fire, 66–67
Arduous March, famine, 3, 6, 17, 77, 93, 98, 103, 111, 114, 116
Austria, 100

Battle of Pochonbo, 54
Beijing International Airport, 104
Brezhnev, Leonid, 48

Central Party, 79
China, xi, 16; Kim Jong-il's special request, 63, 82, 84, 92, 106, 107, 137, 148, 152; delegation to, 153; DPRK-China Joint Steering Committee for the Development of Hwanggumpyong and Rason Districts, 153, 154, 157
Cho Yon-jun, 165
Choe Bong-man, 116
Choe Ryong-hae, 62, 114, 146
Choe Tae-bok, 70
Choe Yong-su, 125
Chon Byong-ho, 70
Chu Sang-song, 70
Chung Dong-young, 123
Cuba, North Korean embassy in Havana, 89

Democratic Women's Union of North Korea, 79
Democratic Youth League of North Korea, 79

East Germany, 55, 177
Eastern Europe, 82

Fujimoto, Kenji: Pleasure Troupe, 31; Kim Jong-il designates him to drink, 71; not called for two years, 73, 96, 99–100; Jang, a genuine man, 146; impression of Kim Jong-un as a child and teenager, 156–157

Geertz, Clifford, 55

Haedanggwan, 155
Ho Dam, 64, 65, 70, 108
Hwang Jang-yop: President of Kim Il-sung University, 2, 6, 10, 26, 38, 49, 96; asylum in the South, 149, 172, 175, 177, 182
Hyon Chol-hae, 70

Ice cream, 97, 104

Jang Jong-hwan, 35

Jang Kum-song, 126, 128–132;
   death of 130
Jang Kye-sun, 36
Jang Song-kil, 35
Jang Song-thaek, xi–xiv, 6; need
   for a scapegoat, 23; Kim Jong-il
   and Kim Kyong-hui, 25–29;
   Kim Il-sung University, 25, 26,
   28–29; scholastic distinctions,
   29–30; personality, 30–31;
   playfulness in later years, 31;
   inter-Korean exchanges, 31;
   reputations and changes of
   Kim Il-sung University, 32–33;
   admission of, 34; Gapsan
   faction, 35; family background
   and personal profile, 35–36;
   classification, 36–37; disapproval
   of Kim Il-sung, 38; transfer to
   Wonsan University of Economics,
   39; visits of Kim Kyong-hui,
   40; Kim Jong-il's summon to
   Pyongyang, 45–46; re-admission
   to Kim Il-sung University, 46,
   48; life in Moscow, 49–52, 54;
   officially married, 59; fast track of
   successful career, 60–62; France,
   63, 64–65; aquarium project fire
   disaster, 66–68; Choe Ryong-hae,
   troubles in marriage begin, 69;
   Pleasure Troupe parties, 69–71,
   73–75; success along with Kim
   Jong-il, conflicts in married life,
   77–78; promotions, 79; World
   Festival of Youth and Students
   (1989), 80; rescue of the Speed
   Battle Youth Chargers, 81; travel
   overseas, 100; items, nickname
   Kim Jong-il on the road
   (overseas), 82; view of the future,
   83; Chinese official, 84; (first)
   re-education (revolutionization)
   and injury, 84–86; Jang's parties,
   85, 87; Song Hye-rim's help,
   87–88; Korean Air Lines (KAL)
   858, bombing 88–90, 91; number-
   two position, 94–96; Number
   One Comrade, proposal of era-
   defining transition, immediate
   apology to Kim Jong-il, 96–97;
   Italy, ice cream, 97; Ji Jae-
   ryong, 98; Ri Ok-dol, 100–101;
   appearances overseas, red light
   districts, 102; heavy drinker, 103;
   European mullets, 100; items
   and each country's premium
   ice creams, 104–105; China-
   like progress and Chinese-style
   reforms, 106–107; special villa
   parties, 108–109; Kim Jong-un,
   his marriage becomes source for
   gossip, 109; rivals exterminated,
   111; first deputy director of the
   OGD's general administrative
   affairs, arrested on espionage
   charges, 112; Mun Song-sul, 113;
   The Yellow Wind of the Youth
   League, 113–115; executions of
   Ri Hak-chol and Pak Byong-so,
   114; (second) re-education,
   115; Kim Dong-won, Taesong
   General Department, 116;
   Pyongyang construction projects
   and overseas trade, 118; Jang
   greets President Kim Dae-jung's
   last delegation, prominent role
   in inter-Korean relations, 119;
   economic delegation to the
   South, 120; heavy drinker even
   in the South, 121; signs of
   the de-facto delegation leader,
   122; Chung Dong-young, 123;
   luxurious wedding of OGD
   deputy director Pak Chang-son's

daughter, 123–24; house arrest, 125–126; final punishment, self-criticism, loss of only child Kum-song, 126, 130–131; consumption of alcohol, 132–133; medical check-ups overseas, 133; (third) re-education, 133; care for Kim Jong-il at his bedside, 136–138; becomes member of the National Defense Commission, 138; Kim Jong-nam, 140; successor, 140–142; death of Kim Jong-il, 142; death of rivals, 143; inspection tour of regional parties, 144; the final moment, 145; his execution, 146–148; Hwang Jang-yop's memo, 149; decline of his influence, 150–151; China, head of delegation to China, report to Kim Jong-un, 152–154; expansion of special economic zones, improvement of food security, 155–156; a burden for Kim Jong-un, 157–158; U Tong-chuk, 159–160; Ri Yong-ho, 160–161; the 3rd Economy, 161, anger of Kim Jong-un, 162–163; court ruling, confessions and executions of Ri Ryong-ha and Jang Su-kil, house arrest, 164; sentence, public criticism, death penalty, 164–165; a photograph of his trial, the execution, 166, 167; more officials executed, including Jang's brother in law and nephew, 168; rumor of Jang still being alive, 169–170
Jang Song-u, 35
Jang Su-kil, 164, 166, 167
Jang Tae-ryong, 36
Jang Tae-ung, 36
Jang Yong-chol, 36

Jang Yong-hwan, 36
Japan, 140
Jo Myong-rok, 70
Juche: Juche Kingdom, 5, 17; Juche Revolution, 142, 177, 189
Kimilsungism, 55

Kang Sok-ju, 70, 165
Kilju/Myongchon Socialist farmers' movement, 35
Kim Chang-son, 73
Kim Dae-jung, 13, 14, 95
Kim Il-sung, x, xvi, 1; consult education of his son, 2; inter-Korean summit, 3; poem praising his son, 3; partisan leader, 6; on reform and opening, 8, 12–13, 16; power, 19–21; folktales of the Kim family, 21–22; disapproval of Jang Song-thaek as a future son-in-law, 25–26; Kim Il-sung statues and teachings, 28; military culture at Kim Il-sung University, 32; Gapsan faction, 33–34; mythologized activities, 33–34; reason for hesitating to accept Jang, 34; storified and memorialized; criticism of film "Sincere Devotion"; state myths, 35; Mangyongdae and Mangyongdae Revolutionary School, 36; reason for his anger upon hearing news of Jang and his daughter's relationship, 38; defiant daughter, 39; generous father, 41; strict about power, 42; drowning accident, 43; discussion with Kim Jong-il about Kim Kyong-hui's relationship, 45; DRPK-USSR summit with Brezhnev in May, 1966, 48; Special forces operations to

Kim Il-sung *(continued)*
  infiltrate the South, 52; Kim Jong-il solidifies his position; reads reports instead of father, seizes practical power, 53; 60th birthday celebration, 54; after Stalin's death; refusal to bestow power to son, 55; mother Kang Ban-sok; introduction of Pleasure Troupe, 56; loss of touch with reality; contradiction of views between father and son; enrage at brother-in-law's luxurious villa, 57; estranged from Jang and daughter, 60; power ladder, 62; expansion of the Pleasure Troupe, 65; appreciation of the Pleasure Troupe, 69; a new Pleasure Troupe era, 70; an official's wife's petition about the Pleasure Troupe, 74; co-leadership with Jang, 77; Seoul summer Olympiad, 80; Kim Il-sung medal, 82, 89, 91; 80th birthday celebration, 92; corpse embalmed, Kim Il-sung medal, 94; Constitution revised and renamed to the Kim Il-sung Constitution, 93; Eternal Leader, funeral, 94; anti-Japanese resistance, 94–95; first year commemoration, 96, 99; Song Hye-rim's former husband and in-laws, 99; Kim Jong-nam, 100; statement after visiting Shanghai, 106, 107; son tries to end father's era, 112; Kim Il-sung Socialist Workers and Youth League, 114; Kim Il-sung in North Korean history, 120; education of his children, 127; fundamental difference with his son's era, 128; Kim Il-sung Award, Rang Sun's ode to the Dear Leader, 139; chemist Ri Sung-ki on the orders of Kim Il-sung produced vinylon textile, 140; Juche Revolution, 142; former aide, An Shin kicked by grandson, 157; Kim Il-sung Kim Jong-il-ism, 163; head of the League of the Socialist Working Youth, 168; Kimilsungism, 20, 55; Kim Il-sung Higher Party School self-criticism, 121; self-criticism and re-education courses, 126

Kim Il-sung University: dating on campus, 28; Jang's titles such as class leader, 29; freedom on campus, 31; location and view of campus; military culture; Kim Il-sung Works Department, 32; entrance of Jang, 34; entrance of Kim Kyong-hui, 37; admission criteria, 37; transfer of Jang, 39; Jang's re-admission, 46, 48, 127, 128, 138, 176, 180

Kim Jong-il, ix; conflict with Jang, xiv, xvi, 1–2; becomes Supreme Commander, 3; achievements and looks, 4; collapse of the Communist regimes, food crisis in North Korea, 5–6; inheritance of a closed, limited regime, 7–8; the dictator's faith to distrust everyone, 9; the escape of abducted South Korean film director and actress couple, 9; dinner parties, 9–11; personality, 11–13; tackling of the Sunshine Policy, 13–14; Lee Myung-bak govt., 14; complex personality, 15–16; stroke at age, 70; Chinese doctors, 16; Kim Jong-il's last doctor, 17; Kim Jong-un, 17;

summon of ten most trusted men, announcement of no succession, 19–21; Jong-il Peak, 21; folktales or myths about the leaders, 21–22; consideration of a new succession system similar to the old Japanese Emperor System, 22; succession lessons for Kim Jong-un, 23; comparison of Kim Jong-il with Jang Song-thaek, 25–31; Choi Eun-hee at an outdoor party of Kim Jong-il, 29; telegram in Kim Jong-il's name, 31; former bodyguard of Kim Jong-il, 31; Gapsan faction purge, 33–35; Kim Kyong-hui, 37; strengthening his struggle for power, 41; gold watch, 41–42; stepmother and stepsiblings, 42; loss of younger brother Shura, 42–43; loss of mother, 43; Jilin Province, China, 43; Mangyongdae Revolutionary School, 44; persuades father to accept Jang Song-thaek, 45; summons of and meeting with Jang, 46–47; Kim Kyong-hui and Jang sent to Moscow State University, 48; daughter Sol-song's private tutor Pak Sung-ok, 49; opera *Sea of Blood*, 51; political situation and economy of Pyongyang and Kim Jong-il's power struggle and use of culture in the late 1960s early 1970s, 52–54; personality cult, 54; *Sea of Blood*, *The Flower Girl*, movies produced on Kim Jong-il's orders, Battle of Pochonbo, 54; Juche, Kimilsungism, transformed under Kim Jong-il, monolithic ideology, theory of the sociopolitical living body, 55; appointed organization and propaganda secretary, 55; called "Party Center," power struggle with Kim Song-ae and his step brothers, 56; conflict with Kim Il-sung regarding co-education and school grading system matters, investigation of corruption of stepmother and her aides, 57; calls Kim Kyong-hui and Jang Song-thaek back to Pyongyang, 57; Kim Jong-il's villa, 59; emerging as the new center of power, 60; Kim Kyong-hui and Jang Song-thaek become close with Kim Jong-il and earn official posts, 60–61; the penultimate year of Kim Jong-il's rule, 62; Kim Jong-il's order execution chart, 63; Jang's rise parallel, 64; Mt. Ami materials, special pavilions, the aquarium project, 65–67; fire accident claims, 130; lives of party officials and diplomats (spring, 1978), 66–68; thoughtful presents, each country's indigenous products for the Leader, 68; North Korean diplomats in illegal activities (Sweden, 1976), 68; deed for the nation and revolution, 68; the party officials' reservoir, 69; first crisis, 69; Kim Il-sung's praise of his son, 69; reason for, trainings of, parties with with the Pleasure Troupe, 69–71; Kim Kyong-hui's jealousy and complaints, 72–74; to be on the invitees list, 73; complaint and fate of an official's jealous wife, 74; waivers Jang from dinner parties, 74–75; a typical Don

Kim Il-sung *(continued)*
    Juan type, 75; co-leadership with Kim Il-sung; ambition for power, 77; World Festival of Youth and Students, 80; Hard Working Hero recommendation to Jang Song-thaek, 82; the Kim Jong-il on the road, 82; revolutionization of Jang Song-thaek, 84–85; management of his close aides, 86; dealing of Kim Kyong-hui's complaint, shrewd Song Hye-rim, 87; reinstatement of Jang, concerned by the Seoul Olympic Games, 88; comparison with US President George W. Bush, 89; upon Kim Il-sung's death, chooses continuity with the past, 93; most powerful state organization, number two, 94; work chemistry with Jang, 95; Jang's confrontation, vent in ire, 95, 96, 97; Song Hye-rim and the care of her former family, 99–100; the reach of critical political views, 101; decadent lifestyle's key player, 102; the people's fear of the State Security Department, 104; China-style progress, 106; the inter-Korean confrontation, China or Vietnam model, 107; colorful, special evening parties, 107–108; awe for, 109; full trust of, 110; order of a nationwide personal-history census, 112; firmly stabilized power, 112; Simhwajo arrests, 112–113; the "Yellow Wind" incident, 114–115; the pros and cons of knowing Jang, 115; two dozen Millennium Rings, 116; Sunshine Policy, 117; the first inter-Korean Summit, 118–119; Shanghai visit, 119; economic delegation to the South, reform, 120; Chung Dong-young, 123; ban on drunk driving, an official's daughter's luxurious wedding, 124; Taesongho guesthouse incident, 124–125; Kim's reactions upon hint of disrespect of his authority, 125–126; feelings-based governance, 126; care upon birth of his niece Kum-song, 127; educated in Pyongyang vs. overseas, 127–128; Ri Nam-ok's engagement and break off of it, 129; order to bring Kum-song back to Pyongyang and her death, 130; why those close to him defect?, 131; Kim Kyong-hui's alcohol problem, 132; the three children with Ko Yong-hui, 133; the development of nuclear arms, the first nuclear test, 134; inter-Korean relations during the Lee Myung-bak government, 135; tourist shot dead while at the Mt. Kumgang tours, 135–136; first collapse (summer, 2008), 136; efforts to keep news of Kim's illness top secret, 137; foreign doctors flown in, 137; regain of trust towards Jang, health recovery, meeting with former US President Bill Clinton, an American doctor's prophetic observation, 138; reporter Rang Sun, 139; the matter of the next successor, 139–142; February 8th Vinylon Factory, 140; bed-ridden, 142; pilot construction projects, 144; Jang's end, 145; tour of a children's hospital with

Index

Kim Jong-un, 147; last official dinner, 147–148; exhibition construction projects, 151; merge of departments, 151; comparison with Kim Jong-un, 156; his thought of China, reaction upon first success in developing nuclear arms, 157; special orders to protect the successor, 159; Ri Yong-ho's promotion, 160; transfer of slush funds, 161–162; name change of Kim Il-sung-Kim-Jong-il-ism, 163; Chinese investment, second anniversary of his death, 168

Kim Jong-nam, 87, 99–100, 128, 138–141, 179, 181

Kim Jong-suk, 56

Kim Jong-un, ix; youth, x; parallel pursuit of nuclear arms and economic development, xi, xii, xiii; encounter with his aunt xiv, 17; Villa No. 7, 59; regime, 84; help from Jang, revulsion for his father's depraved lifestyle, 109; the Yellow Wind incident, 115; Jang's execution, 126, 128; extermination up to three generations, 131; fate of Jang, 132; education overseas, 133; aggressive and strong disposition, 139; Kim Jong-un as successor, 141; successor announced, 142; pilot construction projects, 144, 145; children's hospital tour with his father, 147; relationship with Jang, 147–148; Kaesong Industrial Complex, 148; once in power, 149; onsite guidance trip with Kim Kyong-hui, 149; Jang's last official schedule, 150; Kim Jong-un's era, 150; the new Supreme Leader, 151; political stability through nuclear arms vs. risk of his power via economic development, 153; China, 153–154; order to Jang to solve food security, 155; negative views of Jang, 156; character as a young boy, 156; personality as a teenager, 157; Jang monarchy leaflet incident, 157; South Korean Ministry of National Defense's special press release, 158; Ryukyongwon machine gun incident, 158–159; U Tong-chuk, 159–160; Ri Yong-ho, 160; struggle to gain real power, 161; denial of entrance to the Sungni Trading Company, 162–163; Party Monolithic Leadership Program speech, 163; court ruling to Jang's execution, 163–164; Jang's arrest, 164; solidified authority, 166; visit to his aunt, 167, 169

Kim Ki-nam, 70

Kim Kyong-hui, xi, xiv, 25; Jang Song-thaek, 26–28; courting, 31–32; Jang's background, 34–35; birth and education, 37; standing up against her father, 38–39; drive outs to Wonsan, 40; childhood, 43–44, 45, 46; marriage, 47; Moscow, 48–51; Swan Lake ballet, 51, 52, 54; officially married, Villa No. 7, 59–60; 1st Int'l Projects Division, 60; close aide of brother, 61; earlier and last promotions, 62–63; time in France, Kim Hui-thaek, 63, 64; complaint of the Pleasure Troupe parties, 72–75; conflicts in the marriage, 78, 82; Song Hyr-rim's help, 87; Jang

Kim Il-sung *(continued)*
   returns from his reeducation, 88, 90; foster parents of Ri Ok-dol and Kim Jong-nam, 100; health problems, 104; attends Kim Jong-il' dinner parties, 108; affairs with Choe Kun, Kim Song-ho, 109, 110; Taesongho lake guesthouse incident, 124–125; loss of daughter Kum-song, 126–127, 130–133; care of Kim Jong-il at his final moments, 136
Kim Kyong-jin, 24
Kim Kyong-ok, 62
Kim Pyong-il, 1, 42, 56
Kim Sol-song, 44, 49
Kim Song-ae, 1–2, 42–44, 56–57
Kim Song-ho, violinist, 109
Kim Tong-yon, 114
Kim Yong-chun, 70
Kim Yong-il, 1, 42
Kim Yong-ju, 2
Kim Yong-nam, 146
Kim Young-sam Summit, 3
Kim Yong-sun, 70, 102, 104, 108
Ko Yong-hui, 9, 44, 59, 75, 97, 131, 133, 139, 173, 179
Ko Yong-suk, 9, 131, 173, 181
Korean Air Lines (KAL) Flight 858 Bombing, xiv, 89; terrorists Kim Sung-il and Kim Hyon-hui, 89; Kim Won-sok (Kim Hyon-hui's father), 89–90
Korean People's Army (KPA), 35, 62, 68; KPA regular attendees of the Pleasure Troupe dinner parties, 70, 152, 158, 161; Department, 54; of the KPA, 162
Koryo debit card, 155
Kye Ung-tae, 70, 112, 113

Lee Myung-bak, 14, 134–135, 183

Lim Dong-won, personality of Kim Jong-il, 11
Longevity Goods (100 Items), 82, 97, 104

Machine gun incident (Nov. 2012), 158–159
Millennium Rings, 116
Monolithic Leadership System, xii, 55, 94, 120, 124–125, 144, 145–146, 149, 153, 162, 163, 177, 185; Lee Jong-seok, 189; Suh Jae-joon, 190
Moscow, Moscow State University, apartment, 48
Mt. Ami materials, 65
Mt. Paektu lineage, 95, 146
Mullet (fish), 104
Mun Kyong-dok, 147, Kim Jong-il Medal, 168
Mun Song-sul, 112, 113

North Korean Federation of Farmers' Associations, 79
North Korean General Federation of Workers Unions, 79

O Jin-u, 70, 108
O Kuk-ryol, 70
Organization and Guidance Department, 44, 54, 56, 63, 70, 79, 94, 108, 112, 114, 119–120, 123–125, 135–137, 141–142, 150, 158–159, 162

Paektu lineage, 95, 102, 127, 130, 146, 163
Pak Byong-so, 114
Pak Chang-son, 123–124
Pak Dal memoir, 35
Pak Kum-chol, 35
Pak Pong-ju, 165

Index

Pak Sung-ok, 49; death of, 177
Park Chung-hee secret entertainment parties, 69
Party Congress, 5th, 55
Party Congress, 6th, 77
Pleasure Troupe, 56; expansion of the Pleasure Troupe, 65; Kim Il-sung, 69; name and title of regular attendees, 70, 73; Technical secretary masseuses, 74; complaint of official's wife, 74
Political prison camps, 61, 85, 90, 101, 125, 177, 185
Ponghwa Clinic, 127, 137
Potonggang Department Store, 155
Propaganda and Agitation Department, 56
Pyongyang Folk Park, 169, 170
Pyongyang Railway College soccer match, 138
Pyongyang University of Foreign Studies, 90

Rason SEZ (Special Economic Zone), 153, 155
Red Youth Guards, 137
Re-education (Revolutionization; labor camps), 86, 101, 115, 121, 126
Ri Chan, 114
Ri Il-nam (alternate name Yi Han-yong), 9, 177, 179, 181, 182
Ri Jae-il, 146
Ri Je-kang, 70
Ri Jong-hyok, 99
Ri Ki-yong, 99, 100
Ri Nam-ok, 9, 129, 130, 140
Ri Ok-dol daughter of Song Hye-rim with her first husband Ri Pyong, 99–101
Ri Pyong first husband of Song Hye-rim, 99, 100

Ri Ryong-ha, 164, 166
Ri Soe-dol, 100, 181
Ri Yong-ha, 167
Ri Yong-mu, 70
Rim Chun-chu vice president, food shortage from the early 1980s, 77
Roh Moo-hyun, 12, 14, 95
Roh Tae-woo, 171

Self-reliance, 77
Seoul, 7, 35, 80
Seven-year Plan, 77
Seoul 1988 Summer Olympic Games, 80, 83, 88–89
Simhwajo purge, 112, 113
So Kwan-hui, 113
So Yun-sok, 112
Socialist Workers Youth League, 69; North Korean Socialist Workers and Youth League, 114; Kim Il-sung Socialist Workers and Youth League, 114
Songbun classification system, 37
Song Hye-rang, 8
Song Hye-rim, 80
Soviet Union, xiv, 48–51
Stalin, Josef, 9, 10, 69, 96, 104, 175
Swan Lake, 51
Sweden North Korean diplomats: involvement in illegal activities, 68; Ri Ok-dol, 100, 128; narcotics smuggling, 168

Taedong River, 28, 32
Taedonggang Guesthouse, 108
Taedonggang Tile Factory, 84, 144; renamed Chollima Tile Factory, 185
Taesong General Department, 116
Taesong Lake, 124
Theater State, 55

United Kingdom, 66
United Nations Industrial
 Development Organization
 (UNIDO), 100
U Tong-chuk, 136, 157

Vienna, 100
Villa No. 7, 59; Kim Jong-il's villa,
 59, 70, 108, 159, 172
Vladivostok, 48

Wonsan, 31, 39, 40, 45–47, 81, 116
Women's Union of North Korea
 (the Democratic), 79

Workers and Peasant Red Guard, 137
Workers' Paradise, 7
Workers' Party of Korea, 1, 36, 54,
 55, 77, 164, 165
Workers Unions (North Korean
 General Federation of), 79
World Festival of Youth and
 Students (1989), 82

Yanbian visiting scholars, 77
Yodok political prison camp, 90
Youth League of North Korea (the
 Democratic), 79; Yellow Wind
 incident, 110, 113–115